10 BOOKS EVERY CONSERVATIVE MUST READ

10 BOOKS EVERY CONSERVATIVE MUST READ

Plus Four Not to Miss and One Impostor

BENJAMIN WIKER, Ph.D.

Since 1947
REGNERY PUBLISHING, INC.
An Eagle Publishing Company • Washington, DC

Library of Congress Cataloging-in-Publication Data
ISBN 978-1-59698-604-6
    Wiker, Benjamin, 1960-
    Ten books every conservative must read, plus four not to miss
    and one impostor / by Benjamin Wiker.
    p. cm.
    Includes bibliographical references and index.
    1. Political science--Book reviews. 2. Conservatives--Books
    and reading. 3. Conservatives--Books and reading--United States.
I.
    Title.
    JA71.W458 2010
    011.6--dc22

    2010016900

Published in the United States by

Regnery Publishing, Inc.
One Massachusetts Avenue, NW
Washington, DC 20001
www.regnery.com

Manufactured in the United States of America

10 9 8 7 6 5 4 3 2 1
Books are available in quantity for promotional or premium use.
Write to Director of Special Sales, Regnery Publishing, Inc., One
Massachusetts Avenue NW, Washington, DC 20001, for informa-
tion on discounts and terms or call (202) 216-0600.

Distributed to the trade by:
Perseus Distribution
387 Park Avenue South
New York, NY 10016

For Brian and Troy who dug us out of the snow,
and for Carter who kept us in hay—such is the stuff
of real community.

Contents

Why *These* Books and Not...

THE IDEA FOR THIS BOOK CAME FROM THE READERS OF ANOTHER of my books, *Ten Books that Screwed Up the World: And Five Others That Didn't Help*. Needless to say, that book was about bad books, books that the world would have been far better off without. Given the number of really horrible books, it was difficult to winnow it down to fifteen. Readers agreed, after they'd gotten through my analysis, that these were indeed horrible books, and their ill effects had, if anything, grown through time. In fact, one of the most important of the criteria in choosing them—from Machiavelli's *The Prince* and Thomas Hobbes' *Leviathan* to Marx's *Communist Manifesto*, Alfred Kinsey's *Sexual Behavior in the Human Male*, and Betty Friedan's *Feminine Mystique*—is that their baneful influence continues to form so many aspects of our culture.

Bad ideas and their malignant influence make for depressing news, even though it is imperative that we understand them. So, one of the most frequently asked questions from interviewers and readers was, "Why don't you write a book about *good* books?" This came as much as an inquiry as a plea. And so, here it is: *Ten Books Every Conservative Must Read: Plus Four Not to Miss and One Impostor.* Here are the good books, the books which, if taken with the utmost seriousness, could transform a rotting culture into a blossoming one.

I have no doubt that the most frequently asked question I'll have to answer about this book is "Why didn't you include _____!" Notice, it's not really a question, but as the exclamation point at the end suggests, an incredulous outcry that I didn't include a certain favorite conservative book among the *Ten Books Every Conservative Must Read: Plus Four Not to Miss and One Impostor.* When it is discovered that the impostor is Ayn Rand's *Atlas Shrugged,* I'm sure I'll hear even more howls of indignation. So a bit of explanation is due right at the get go.

Let's leave the question of Rand's status on the side for a moment, and deal with the whole business of my choice of books that every conservative must read. As with *Ten Books that Screwed Up the World,* it was extremely difficult to whittle the list down. But it's not the point of my book simply to provide a list, long or short, of books to read. This is a book about conservative ideas, key concepts, essential principles—things that, given the intellectual and moral dilapidation of much of the culture, every conservative must understand in order to make any solid rebuilding possible. As with the first *Ten Books,* the premise is that ideas have consequences. Bad ideas have bad consequences, but good ideas have good consequences.

So my focus now is on the books that every conservative *must* read. The emphasis on *must* implies that it is not *My Ten Favorite Conservative Books,* or *Ten Top-Selling Conservative Books.* Rather, the choices were made based upon what conservatives must read in light of our present condition. We live in a culture that is largely defined by liberalism, but there is a swelling conservative reaction. Unfortunately, while that reaction is welcome, it is too often simply a reaction rather than a well-thought-out and effective response deeply informed by truly conservative principles. It is my hope that this book can help to carry out a conservative renaissance, a deep revolution, so that the conservative zeal animating so many souls can have a lasting and profound effect. If the books I've chosen would form the basis of a sustained conservative conversation, the cultural battle lines would be more clearly drawn, the strategies more cogently articulated, and hope more firmly grounded.

All that having been said, there are plenty of other books that could have been included. I know this, because I had to make the painful choices. But notice, the title isn't *The Only Ten Books Conservatives Must Read.* I am not being exclusive. There are easily a hundred or more books that could be heartily recommended to conservatives.

In making this selection, you'll notice very important books that didn't make the final cut. Some are obvious, like Adam Smith's *The Wealth of Nations.* Some have been extremely important to me, but are controversial, like Leo Strauss' *Natural Right and History.* Some are theological, like St. Augustine's *City of God.* Some are exceedingly difficult, like Aristotle's *Metaphysics.* Some are works of epic poetry, like Dante's *Divine Comedy.* Some take the form of philosophic dialogues, like Plato's masterful *Gorgias.* Some are deeply conservative, but have been horribly misunderstood by conservatives, like Plato's *Republic.* Some are actually ambiguous, like John Locke's *Second Treatise of Civil Government.* Some are closely akin to the form of this book, like Russell Kirk's *The Roots of American Order* or *The Conservative Mind.* Some are extremely informative, like

George Nash's *The Conservative Intellectual in America Since 1945.*
Some are American conservative classics, like Whittaker Chambers' *Witness* or William F. Buckley's *God and Man at Yale.*
Obviously, given my quip above, Richard Weaver's *Ideas Have Consequences* would seem a must-read.

Even without entering into a discussion with anyone else, I
could get into arguments with myself over another fifty must-reads.
Let in another to the debate, and we'd never get down to actually
studying any one text. If for no other reason than space considerations, hard choices had to be made. My reasons could be given
for each.

For example, conservatism is about much more than economics—that is why I include philosophy, political philosophy, theology, and literature. Choices had to be made about which books on
economics were to be included. I chose Friedrich Hayek's *Road to
Serfdom* over Adam Smith's *Wealth of Nations.* I have always been
very wary of Smith's close intellectual and personal ties to the consummate Enlightenment skeptic, David Hume (many of whose
works would be worthy candidates for a follow-up book, *Ten More
Books that Screwed Up the World*) and worried about Smith's connections to the Parisian salon of the notorious revolutionary, Baron
d'Holbach.[1] What is of merit in Smith can be found in Hayek. That
is an arguable point, and well worth arguing. But few conservatives
would deny the great importance of Hayek's *Road to Serfdom,* and
its intellectual context—the rise of socialism in the twentieth century—is certainly more germane and instructive for conservatives
faced with a resurgence of FDR-ism in the present political administration. Hayek therefore forms a better locus of conservative discussion, debate, and action.

But I will not bore readers with a very long explanation of why
I didn't choose this or that book. That would deflect us from the

real task at hand, gathering the conservative wisdom from those I have chosen, and that is the task we must now undertake without any further delay. Readers will soon understand why I've chosen these books.

Part I
Just What Exactly Is Conservatism?

THIS BOOK ABOUT BOOKS IS DIVIDED INTO FOUR MAIN PARTS according to four important themes: the first, concerning the nature of conservatism itself; the second, focusing on the American founding; the third, dealing with economics; and the last, pressing home the importance of forming the conservative imagination.

That we should need any discussion of just exactly what conservatism really is might strike us as odd. Surely conservatives already know what it means to be conservative, otherwise they wouldn't *be* conservatives.

I think there is a kind of negative clarity among conservatives. That is, conservatives are clear about what conservatism is *not* (big government, socialism, high taxes, gay marriage), and so when they try to explain what conservatism *is* they define it negatively, as in freedom from governmental niggling and nannying. But a negative definition is a rather difficult starting point to form a positive account that conservatives can live by and defend.

Part of the problem in getting that definition is caused by the very word "conservative." The word "conservative" is, by itself, a word without much substance. To say that one is "conservative" doesn't really say much at all, because the real question is, *what* is one trying to conserve? And moreover, *why* is it really worth conserving? "We've always done it this way," is not an argument. "Because change is always bad," is a dangerous argument.

Nor can we merely reduce conservatism to the defense of what is "traditional," a point that will become obvious by illustration. The Aztec Empire spanned, roughly, the time period from the early 1300s to the early 1500s—about as long as the United States has been around. The Aztecs were culturally rich, powerful, brutal, and infamous for practicing human sacrifice. The practice of human sacrifice was much older and more widespread in the Mesoamerican region. By incorporating it into their culture as well, the Aztecs were being quite conservative. They could point to the practice as "traditional," as having been performed dutifully by their fathers' fathers' fathers leading back into the mists of time.

And it was not just a matter of tradition, of maintaining a long-standing human custom. Since the Aztecs believed that the gods sustain the universe, and that the gods themselves were placated by human sacrifice, they had profound religious reasons for defending the practice against innovators. Moreover, they didn't just believe that the gods were bloodthirsty. Human sacrifice atoned for real moral sins. We may not approve of this method of atonement, but we can have little doubt they experienced guilt for actual moral wrongs they felt needed expiation.

The point is fairly simple. Every society that has lasted for at least two or three centuries has long-standing, hallowed traditions, passed on with great solemnity from generation to generation. Whatever these traditions are or were—and whatever their moral caliber—the maintenance of them against innovators would be the task of that society's "conservatives."

If conservatism is merely the doctrine that what has been done for a long time must be preserved and defended *because* it has been done a long time, then conservatism means very little. To say the least, it would make a hash of *American* conservatism, which did away with the traditional arrangement of kings and nobles ruling the common folk.

Yet, that having been duly noted, conservatives can add some substance to the definition of conservatism by pointing to America's founding fathers. But here's the rub. Appealing to the founders no longer has much cultural weight outside conservative circles. The age of simple appeal to the founding fathers is gone. For a variety of reasons, their venerable status has been almost entirely eroded. As a consequence, it is no longer politically compelling either to state or prove that "the founding fathers said this" or "the Constitution states clearly that." For better or worse, we live in an age when the wisdom of the founders cannot be taken for granted as common coin, but must be set forth again, argued for once more, and made compelling to a new age.

But precisely here conservatives should see the problem of merely reducing conservatism to those principles of the American founders. Surely conservatism is something deeper and older, surely it rests on even more venerable and firm foundations. Or to put it another way, if the American founders were conservative, certainly they weren't just making things up on the spot, but were themselves conserving a deeper and older wisdom, a perennial wisdom that isn't peculiar to America but deeply rooted in the nature of human beings.

That is what we are trying to recover in Part One. We're trying to get to the very deepest roots of what conservatism really is. In doing so, we will find that conservatism is not merely an American thing—we'll read an ancient Greek philosopher, a late-Victorian English journalist, a twentieth century, German-born political philosopher, and a twentieth century Irish-born Christian apologist. Rather, conservatism is a fundamental way of understanding human nature and its place in the cosmos.

We'll also find out that liberalism is not some recent phenomenon, but is nearly as old as conservatism—Samuel Johnson famously quipped that the devil was the first Whig (the Whigs being British liberals). I am not out to demonize liberalism, however, but to use it to clarify what conservatism is, for the two exist in essential antagonism. Liberalism, too, at its core is a fundamental way of understanding human nature and its place in the cosmos. It is not just a surface reaction to conservatism, but a deep rebellion against the conservative account of man. The works we'll be considering in Part One will go a long way in clarifying what conservatism is through an analysis of its opposite, liberalism.

This kind of deep clarification is needed for another reason. Readers who are at all familiar with the fourteen books I've chosen for treatment as genuinely conservative will know that more than one of those fourteen authors would shudder—were they alive today—at being called "conservative." In fact, they would demand to be called "liberal." Yet, even a quick analysis of their arguments shows them aligning (for the most part) with today's conservatives.

This confusing situation is illuminated somewhat by our remembering that the American founding fathers were indeed engaging in a revolution against the mother country and her King, and that the term "republican" was, a century before our founding, a term for radicals in English politics bent on decapitating kings and putting political power into popular hands. In Europe, conservatism was associated with those who wanted to keep or restore the old regime where hereditary kings and queens, with the help of an entrenched aristocracy, ruled nations. From the European perspective, Americans looked like radicals; but Americans believed they were reinstituting the most natural and moral form of government, self-government. The habits and principles of self-government—including economic self-government—could therefore rightly be considered conservative insofar as they conserve what is most natural and moral. But by the nineteenth century, the anti-statist position, whether in Europe or America, came to be known as "liberalism" since it sought liberation from top-down governmental control.

Contemporary American conservatism is sometimes seen as having its genesis from this "classical liberalism," the old anti-statist liberalism that focused on laissez-faire economics, personal liberty, and republican institutions. But, for reasons that will soon become apparent, this isn't a satisfactory solution, because there exists a "classical conservatism," far deeper and older, that is the home, the foundation, of true conservatism, the sure fixing point of the conservative mind. Our chosen books will help us find it.

CHAPTER ONE

The Politics: Aristotle

". . . man is by nature a political animal."

Aristotle: The Father of Political Conservatism

CALLING ARISTOTLE THE FATHER OF POLITICAL CONSERVATISM should give conservatives a feeling of great relief. Conservatism is much older than America. It is not a modern invention. It goes back far earlier and far deeper, and that gives it a far firmer foundation and an even grander pedigree, stretching to ancient Greece. Conservatism is a perennial political philosophy, and its founding text is Aristotle's *Politics*.

Aristotle is the father of political conservatism in two important, related senses. First, he understood that the decisive political argument occurs between those who maintain (as he did) that political life and morality are *natural* and those who assert that political life and morality are entirely *man-made* (as did the sophists and political innovators of his day). This argument is still with us. As we'll see, it marks the crucial difference between conservatives and liberals. Conservatives tend toward political caution, because they believe man is not infinitely malleable; and they believe that morality is objective and puts limits on what human beings can and should do. Liberals tend to believe the reverse: that morality is relative, and that man is malleable and can rightfully be subject to political manipulation to advance some heady notion of the common good or expedite some grand "progressive" project.

Conservatives, like Aristotle, prefer experience to theory—in fact, conservatives cringe at utopian philosophical schemes, which liberals tend to embrace because they vivify or justify their efforts at social engineering. And like Aristotle, conservatives generally accept the world as it is; they distrust the politics of abstract reason—that is, reason divorced from experience. Liberals see no problem with reconstituting a nation's political life on the basis of some attractive but untried rational scheme used as a tempting template to draw up programs of "hope and change."

But while the conservative disposition, which we can trace to Aristotle, is suspicious of abstract reason, it is not, obviously, hostile to philosophy. Aristotle remains, after all, one of the handful of great philosophers in human history, and history has preserved only a portion of his works, which range widely, from detailed biological treatises (such as the *Parts of Animals* and the *Generation of Animals*); an examination of *The Soul*; works on *Respiration* and *Youth and Old Age*; to his seminal works on logic and language (such as the *Categories* and *On Interpretation*); more general treatises on nature like the *Physics* and *On the Heavens*; books on *Rhetoric* and *Poetics*; an exposition of the principles of *Ethics*; and the most abstract principles of *Metaphysics*. Conservatives aren't anti-intellectual. They simply and solidly demand that our reason be firmly tethered to our experience of reality as it is.

So for conservatives, like Aristotle, the practice of philosophy, the seeking of wisdom, involves the study of things as they are, not as we might like them to be, and that includes the study of human beings and political life. That is why Aristotle asserted that young men aren't good "hearers" of lectures on politics—they don't have enough actual experience of human nature and political life, and since they're passionate, they're prone to passionate and destructive schemes for overhauling society.[1] A short overview of Aristotle's life reveals that, for him, experience and philosophy went together.

Aristotle, the Man of Wisdom and Experience

Aristotle was born in Stagira in Greece in 384 BC. His father, Nicomachus, was the court physician and advisor to the Macedonian king Amyntas III. Amyntas was the father of Philip II, and Philip II was the father of Alexander III, better known as Alexander the Great. All these kings were active in the perpetual wars boiling up the Greek peninsula, and all, especially Alexander, pushed the conquering reach of Macedon beyond its borders. Alexander was born in 356 BC, and when he turned thirteen, Aristotle, almost thirty years his senior, became his tutor (and, as a reward for his efforts, got Alexander's father Philip to rebuild Stagira, one of the many towns the king had beaten to dust).

As Alexander was an heir to conquest, Aristotle was an heir to philosophy, and he had brought those riches with him, on a rather roundabout route, to the royal court of Macedon. He was the third of three great philosophers, certainly the three greatest that ever lived: Socrates, Plato, and Aristotle himself. At seventeen, Aristotle had traveled from Macedonia to Athens, from a nascent empire to one of the numerous independent city-states of the Greek peninsula—the city where Socrates, about thirty years earlier, had been sentenced to death for allegedly corrupting the young with his ideas. Aristotle enrolled in the Academy, a school started by Socrates' best pupil, Plato, and studied and taught with Plato for some twenty years, leaving Athens only after Plato's death in 347 BC.

Aristotle then emigrated to Asia Minor, where he married Pythias, the adopted daughter of Hermias, a former slave who had become the despotic ruler of the city of Atarneus. Aristotle's influence is credited with moderating and tempering Hermias' tyranny, for Hermias, too, had studied philosophy with Plato and even with Aristotle himself, and would accept much of what Aristotle had to say as the better part of wisdom. Aristotle even arranged an alliance between Hermias and Philip of Macedon. That turned to ashes, however, when Hermias was kidnapped by a Persian ally, clapped in chains, and tortured to reveal Philip's plans for the invasion of Asia Minor. He refused to betray his friends and died in 341 BC.

Before Hermias met his death, Aristotle had traveled to Lesbos, an island in the northeastern Aegean, where he had gone to study biology. His method there was typical of the man. He did not sit on a rock by the sea and dream up grand theories of the universe and the origin and destiny of life, but got down in the water and looked for himself at what living things actually did, cut them up to see what they were really made of, and looked to experienced fisherman rather than philosophers to learn about the details of sea life.

It was in 342 that Philip called Aristotle to Macedon to become a tutor to young Alexander and other important Macedonian nobles, and it seems that Aristotle's influence carried all the way into Philip's own policies, especially encouraging leniency toward Athens. After Philip was assassinated in 336, his son Alexander was proclaimed king by the Macedonian army. He was only twenty. Aristotle left for Athens, and remained there for nearly the rest of his life.

Over the next decade, while Alexander was conquering Asia Minor, Syria, Egypt, Persia, and stretching towards India, Aristotle was in Athens philosophizing, starting his own school, the Lyceum. Most of the works we have from him come from this period. When Alexander the Great died in 323 from poison, malaria, typhoid fever, pancreatitis, overeating the medicinal plant Hellebore, heavy drinking, or complications from a previous wound (you can take your pick), the immediate result was predictable. With the removal of the heavy hand of Macedonian rule, Athens rebelled, and Aristotle, the royal intimate of Macedonian kings, came under charges of impiety at Athens—the very same kind of charge that brought the Athenians to serve hemlock to Socrates three quarters of a century earlier. Aristotle fled to the Chalcis, a Macedonian stronghold on the island of Euboea, his mother's native soil, where he died in 322.

Aristotle's *Politics*, written while he was in Athens teaching at the Lyceum, is an expansive treatise, and it rests firmly upon his formidable intellect and his deep and long experience of political life. Unfortunately, we cannot possibly cover the entire argument of the *Politics* in a single summary chapter. By unearthing some of its riches, I hope I can induce readers to do further digging on their own. But it is important to remember that when Aristotle wrote about politics, he did so as someone who had been at the very center of political intrigue and jostling empires. His starting point is neither utopian, dreaming up airy schemes about the way things ought to be, nor does he take the snake's eye view of *realpolitik* later made famous by Machiavelli. Instead, Aristotle begins where political life begins, in the natural moral order of human life, and ends where it ought to end, in making us better than we were, even though we fall far short of the angels.

The Natural Foundation of Political Life

Aristotle opens the *Politics* with an argument implicitly but firmly defined against the sophists, the smart-set moral relativists— the liberals—of ancient Greece. The sophists argued that all moral standards are merely artificial, conventional, and relative to the political power structures of society. Against this claim, Aristotle (without ever mentioning sophism by name, an important strategy as it turns out[2]) makes bold to say that the starting point of society is the natural union of male and female; it is the family.[3]

From several households arise a village, and from the union of several villages, the city. The family, and by extension, the city, "belongs among the things that exist by nature," and from that we can conclude "that man is by nature a political animal."[4] We are naturally social and so we are naturally political, and politics, rightly understood, is not about power but about acting out and perfecting our human nature *insofar as it is possible*. That last proviso keeps Aristotle from being a dangerous utopian, even while it sets a moral standard that pushes us upward.

For Aristotle, size is important. The goal of perfecting our human nature means that political life has to fit our nature. A village is too small, a nation is too large. A city—not a sprawling metropolis made of concrete, but a small city surrounded by an agricultural belt—is just right.[5] Why is a city just the right size? A village can provide the necessities of life, but it isn't big enough to allow for the full flowering of our nature—which spills over into art, architecture, theater, music, literature, science, and philosophy.

But a nation is too large, too unwieldy and bloated, too filled with vices, too subject to foreign influences; citizens are too disconnected in a large nation. It is local affection that binds men together naturally; it is knowing our neighbors (and their character) that makes self-government possible. With Aristotle we find the conservative disposition that prefers the local to the national and distrusts centralism and bureaucracy.

Aristotle also denies the sophistic (and liberal) idea that society is simply an arrangement, a contract, an agreement among individuals. On the contrary, society is not a contract or agreement, but arises naturally. It rests not on atomistic individuals but on the basic building block of the family.[6] He means this quite literally: the sexual desire for reproduction defines us as naturally, fundamentally social: we desire children to create our own natural society. *Contra* Hillary Clinton, it doesn't take a village to raise a child (or a state pretending to be a village), it takes a father and mother. The children who come from this most natural of unions go on to marry and have children themselves, and help to create a village. As the family trees of the village branch out over time, the village becomes a city. Such is the natural unfolding of human society. Society doesn't rest on some kind of social contract that guarantees abstract rights, but on the natural union of husband and wife that binds the past and present to the future with children. So-called "family values" conservatism didn't begin with modern evangelicals, and it isn't just one stream of conservative thought; to Aristotle it would have been the very definition of conservatism (or of politics properly understood and practiced), because the family is the real, incontrovertible, natural origin of society.

This connects directly with another conservative concern: morality. Aristotle argues that morality is not a set of artificial and arbitrary rules, but *arises from* our natural beginning, and so it, too, is natural. The moral order is there to greet us when we are born; it is present in the natural, moral order of the family, the first society that any of us ever know. And it is in the family, says Aristotle, that we learn the natural moral law that sets the standard for civil justice.[7] The well-ordered family is a kind of miniature city, or more exactly, a well-ordered society in seed form. In Aristotle's view, legal codes and political schemes should be judged by whether they adhere to or deviate from this natural moral order.

But here we must insert a most emphatic note of caution. While the family is the natural origin of society, that does not mean that the city is just one big happy family. The family and the city are distinct, and relate as an integral part to a whole that completes it. The whole does not replace the integral part; the city does not replace the family.[8] Aristotle would rightly be horrified at the modern liberal tendency, present in both Marxism and Liberal Progressivism, to disintegrate the natural family and contrive to make the state some kind of super-family in its place.

Another note of caution. Aristotle, of course, does not say that all families are well ordered. The family is natural, but the good ordering of the family is not *automatic.* Just as a garden needs to be well cared for, so does a family. Just as plants need to be pruned, so families need to be pruned of vice, which otherwise distorts their growth. The disordered souls of a father and mother can lead to disordered families, which lead to disordered societies. Bad morality often comes from badly ordered families. The process accelerates when a disordered society reaches back into the family and twists its natural order into unnatural shapes, making the family a morbid, distorted reflection of what it should be. So just as there are good and bad families, there are good and bad governments (a point we'll get to in a minute). But first we have to deal with the most important objections to Aristotle's starting point.

The Hard Bits of Aristotle's Argument

Liberals will be quick to remind us that Aristotle also believed that slavery was natural and that the familial and political subordination of women was natural. Some liberals might say that what they support is not moral relativism but liberation from unjust traditions upheld by conservatives like Aristotle.

But this is to miss a very important point about true conservatism. It is tied to particular principles, not inextricably bound to a particular man, or book, or particular political order. Aristotle believed, as true conservatives do, that the wisdom gained from experience should be our guide, and so if we err, we can and must amend our views, just as Aristotle corrected what he thought were errors in the thought of Plato. Conservatism is not blind acceptance, but careful consideration, and that includes reconsideration. Aristotle wrongly believed that slavery is natural. He was wrong about other things as well. He believed that the law should allow, even demand, the killing by exposure of deformed children, that the state should determine the number of children parents may have, and that those children conceived beyond this number should be aborted in the first trimester.[9] We can reject all these things as wrong *if and only if* we believe that it is possible to be right, that is, only if we assume (with Aristotle and against ancient sophists and modern moral relativists) there *is* an objective moral order that we can know and follow.

We must also point out, for the record, that it was Christianity that historically allowed for the correction of Aristotle in regard to slavery, as well as abortion and infanticide.

With all that said, let's look more carefully at Aristotle's discussion of women and slaves, for even among errors here, there are insights. Aristotle says that "the female is distinguished by nature from the slave.... The barbarians, though, regard the female and slave to be of the same order."[10] In short, Aristotle marks a barbarian as barbarous precisely in his use of the female as a slave. This is not a small point, as any honest anthropologist will reveal. In a large majority of primitive cultures, precisely those that didn't own slaves, women performed a great portion of the back-breaking menial tasks that must be done for any society to survive. It follows (perhaps somewhat uncomfortably) that historically, the first emancipation of women came with the institution of slavery. Or, to put the same point in a broader context, the societies in which women had the most leisure and political power were those where upper class women depended on lower class or slave laborers of both sexes.[11]

So, Aristotle did not see women as slaves; he asserted that only barbarians did. Therefore, he did not see the relationship of husband and wife, or parents and children, in terms of master and slave. Instead, he uses overtly political terms. He compares the man's governing of a household to political rule. The just man is no despot over his family. Rather he rules his "wife and children as free persons, though it is not the same mode of rule in each case, the wife being ruled in a *political* way, and the children in *kingly* fashion."[12] In the *Nicomachean Ethics*, Aristotle remarks that the kind of friendship that unites husband to wife is *aristocratic*, and the father's friendship toward his children should be *kingly*.[13] This political language might strike us as quite odd, but it allows Aristotle to avoid being conservative in the worst, distorted sense, defending the family by defending tyrannical husbands and fathers. Here, as everywhere, Aristotle distinguishes between good and bad, just and unjust. Because Aristotle uses specifically political terms to make that distinction, we need to move beyond the family and look at Aristotle's account of political regimes.

Good and Bad Political Regimes

At the heart of Aristotle's *Politics* is the division of political regimes into different types. We are accustomed to thinking that political regimes can be divided into two kinds, democracy and everything else. Democracy is good and everything else is bad. But that is not Aristotle's way of dividing things at all. According to Aristotle, political regimes may be divided according to the *number* who rule, and what *kind* of rule, good or bad. This allows for a six-fold division of good and bad regimes. If *one* person rules for the true common good, it is *kingly* rule; if *one* person rules only for his own advantage, the regime is a *tyranny*. If a *few* rule for the true common good, it is an *aristocracy*; if the *few* rule only for their own advantage, it is an *oligarchy*. And here comes a great shock. If the *many*, the majority, rule for the sake of the true common good, the regime is called a *polity*; if the *many*, the majority, rule for their own private advantage rather than the common good, the regime is a *democracy*.[14]

A bit disconcerting, isn't it? We tend to regard democracy as the *only* good regime, and every other form of government, we brand indifferently as a tyranny. That is, we regard majority rule as sacred and good in itself, and every other form of government as a perversion. But Aristotle takes the quite sensible position that the majority can be as selfish, foolish, and tyrannical as any tyrant or oligarch. Therefore, he calls democracy a perversion.

It is a perversion of the good form of rule by the many, a *polity*, from which we get the term "political." It is of no small historical consequence that when the Romans wanted to translate Greek political thought into Roman terms, the great Roman statesman and philosopher Cicero translated the Greek word *politeia* (polity) using the Latin term *respublica*. Our Latin-based equivalent is Republic, as in "I pledge alliance to the flag of the United States of America, and to the Republic for which it stands. . . . " For our purposes, we can use either term, polity or the more familiar republic, as more or less synonymous.[15]

Before we jump to any conclusions, we had better look more carefully at Aristotle's argument, and try to understand it on its own terms. First and foremost, the difference between the good and bad regimes is, obviously, not *how many* rule, but *for what*. Kings, aristocrats, and the many rulers of the polity (or republic) govern for the sake of the true human good of their subjects, and that includes especially their moral good. For Aristotle, the perfection of our nature, the development of virtuous citizens, *is* our moral good. Tyrants, oligarchs, and democrats rule for their own private advantage—they serve only their own wants and characteristically indulge in every vice that political power can purchase.

In applying this to family life, Aristotle says that a husband and father rules his family and household "either for the sake of the ruled or for the sake of something common to both," the common good of the family.[16] The relationship of the husband to his wife is properly "aristocratic," by which Aristotle means that "the man rules. . . according to his worth, and about things which it is necessary for the man to rule, and he commits to his wife to rule as her due, those things for which she is well-fit." The perversion of this is when the husband rules his wife as an oligarch, and controls everything for his own advantage.[17] Similarly, if a man rules his children merely for his own advantage, he is a tyrant and not a "kingly" father.

Turning back to the political realm again, for Aristotle, it is better to live under a good king than in a democracy or oligarchy, or in a good republic rather than under a tyrant. In short, any good form is better than any bad form. But even here, among the good forms, there is a kind of ranking, for if there were one person, preeminent in virtue, a man of supreme goodness, it would be good for "everyone to obey such a person gladly. . . ."[18]

Aristotle does *not* say that we should abolish every bad form of government and replace it with a good one. For Aristotle, prudence is the wisdom of politics, and to be prudent means that you can't snap a bent board straight without breaking the board. That is destruction, not reform. Instead, you take what you actually find, and you work to make it better.

There is a very good reason for this cautious approach. True kingships, aristocracies, and republics are rare because true virtue is rare, either among the rulers or the ruled. Human wickedness is all too prevalent, and that means that we are far more likely to find, as political "material" to work with, tyrannies posing as kingships, oligarchies posing as aristocracies, and democracies posing as republics. The reality of wickedness, or sin, makes the creation of perfect political regimes humanly impossible, and it ensures that any imprudent attempts to create political perfection, or utopia, will end in disaster. Conservatives believe in original sin—or the simple reality of human wickedness—and understand that this limits what good politics can achieve.

Aristotle spends far more time on the bad regimes than the good, because we're far more likely to be faced with bad regimes than good ones. Therefore we will focus primarily (as he does) on oligarchy and democracy.

The Oligarch and the Democrat

According to Aristotle, neither oligarchy nor democracy is entirely unjust. Indeed, each has hold of a kind of half truth about justice. Both fasten onto "a certain sort of justice, but proceed only to a certain point."[19] The oligarchs grab onto one aspect of justice, inequality: those who work harder should receive a greater reward, those who run faster should receive the prize, those who contribute more to the political regime should have more privileges and honor, those who have more money and who therefore provide more support for the regime should have more power and prestige. The democrats seize another aspect of political justice, equality: since all are equally citizens, they believe that all should be treated equally in every way.

But two half truths about justice do not make a whole truth. Aristotle tells us that almost all men are "bad judges concerning their own things." Our biases warp our understanding. Oligarchs think that because they have far more money, they are superior in all things, and justice should focus entirely on inequality. Democrats think that because they are equally free citizens with the oligarchs, they should be equal in all things. They therefore focus on freedom and equality as if they were moral absolutes.

At the heart of this disagreement is money (or, more accurately, wealth); it is the division between the few rich and the many poor, and it represents a kind of permanent historical tension.[20] Aristotle points out that the way to blunt this tension is through the creation of something in between rich and poor. So he remarks, "In all cities there are three parts of the city, the very well off, the very poor, and third, those in the middle between these." This "middling element," the middle class, is the key. A society with a dominant middle class is where "a lasting polity is capable of existing."[21]

The stability provided by a dominant middle class is not just a matter of money, but even more, a matter of *character*. The middle class works hard. Like the rich, the middle class believes hard work should be rewarded. Since middle class people own property, they

stand ready to defend property rights and block burdensome taxation against the efforts of the property-less poor who want property and wealth redistributed equally. But like the poor, the
middle class believes in political equality; the middle class does not
believe that the rich are inherently more virtuous or better quali-
fied to hold political power than anyone else. In his attention to the
character of the middle class, Aristotle argues that farmers make
the strongest foundation for a solid middle class, and the best foundation for a polity or republic, because they are hard-working,
independent, and self-reliant.[22] And we are not surprised that,
according to Aristotle, "The best legislators are from the middling
citizens."[23] Their character makes them govern most wisely and
moderately—at least more so than the very rich or the very poor.

The American republic, obviously, has followed Aristotle's
advice—and even today our two major political parties reflect
aspects of his argument, especially in how they characterize each
other. Democrats cast the Republicans as the oligarchs, the party
of the rich who rule only for the benefit of the rich. Republicans
cast Democrats as the party of the grasping poor whose policies
entail high taxes and socialism (i.e., enforced equality in all
respects). And interestingly enough, both parties profess themselves to be the party of the middle class. (The middle class itself,
however, seems to have growing doubts about whether either
party is interested in ruling virtuously and for the common good.)

How to Destroy a Republic

If the middle class is the strength of a republic, a republic is
nevertheless easily destroyed, as Aristotle makes dolefully but prudently clear. The delicate balance between rich and poor can be
toppled; self-interest can trump the common good; the austerity
of moral virtue can be traded for soft comfort and pleasure. Such

revolutions come from small beginnings, from factions at odds with the political order.[24] Here, too, is a great conservative point: no political regime, no political order, is exempt from corruption. If the characters of the people fail, the regime will split at the seams and unravel.

For Aristotle, the "greatest factional split is perhaps that between virtue and depravity." Morality is the great cement that holds a regime together. But when war is waged on morality, when depravity comes to blows with virtue and gains the upper hand, then a good government can quickly become a bad one. On these grounds, so-called "moral issues" are the fundamental ones. Next comes the economic split "between wealth and poverty," between rich and poor, oligarch and democrat.[25]

A regime can be torn apart from the side of the poor. A democratic revolution occurs "particularly on account of the wanton behavior of the popular leaders," who, on behalf of the poor, harass "those owning property" and "egg on the multitude against them" and "slander the wealthy in order to be in a position to confiscate their goods." Even more ominous, the demagogues, "in order to make themselves popular" so they can get elected, assert that the *will* of the people is supreme over the *law* (or, in American political terms, that popular political projects can override the Constitution).[26] Democrats certainly seem to have something of the truth in defining justice in terms of political freedom and equality. But, Aristotle notes, they "define freedom badly. For there are two things by which democracy is held to be defined: the majority having authority, and freedom." But here, things start to go badly. While justice is rightly held "to be something equal," the majority come to believe that "[political] equality requires that whatever the multitude resolves is authoritative, and freedom and equality involve doing whatever one wants." The result is that "everyone lives as he wants and toward whatever end he happens to crave."[27] Liberty, the right to be a free man, then becomes license, the right to be an immoral man, and justice is defined as having an equal right to do whatever we want. The desire to "do whatever we want" and the premium on "tolerating everyone living as he wants"[28] leads to a situation not much different from tyranny, because the demagogues create something akin to tolerance police to enforce political correctness—women are encouraged to inform on men, slaves are set against their masters, and the self-flattering majority against the independent-minded. Moreover, the democrats, in order to enhance their power of numbers over the oligarchs, "add as many persons as possible" who were previously excluded as citizens, including people who were previously classified as resident aliens.[29]

If Aristotle is no friend of egalitarian democracy, he also maintains that "the aggrandizements of the wealthy are more ruinous to the polity than those of the people."[30] So he is no friend of oligarchy either. The rich can do a lot of damage precisely because they are rich, and they can buy a revolution in government. Just like the democrats, they can rule tyrannically when they rule by their will rather than according to the law.[31] This is especially a problem with elections of public officials, where monied interests more easily gain public offices.[32] Oligarchies are unstable governments because the wealthy are inevitably divided into factions, with the factions appealing to the masses against each other—but with each faction just as self-interested as the last.[33] Another kind of revolution occurs when the oligarchs "expend their private wealth in wanton living."[34] As with democrats who exchanged liberty for license, dissipated oligarchs invite a takeover by a tyrant or a rebellion of the frustrated and disgusted many who realize the oligarchs are not fit to share in rule.

Sound familiar in any way? Reading Aristotle today, he can seem like a political prophet, a conservative who foresaw many of our current political problems. But it is important to remember that Aristotle's seemingly prophetic powers were the result of his being conservative in another, all-important sense. He conserved the political lessons of history. "Looking backwards" gave him the wisdom to "look forward." Human beings are remarkably, and lamentably, all too predictable.

Political Animal or Political Beast?

We headed this chapter with Aristotle's famous statement that "man is by nature a political animal." We end it with a warning that every conservative should take to heart. The city allows for the development of the full human life that begins in the family, and so Aristotle asserts that the first person who set up the city "is responsible for the greatest of goods." But then he makes us aware of a fundamental ambiguity.

> For just as man is the best of animals when perfected, when separated from law and justice he is the worst of all. For injustice is harshest when it is furnished with arms; and man is born naturally possessing arms for [the use of] prudence and virtue which are nevertheless very susceptible to being used for their opposites. This is why, without virtue, he is the most unholy and the most savage [of the animals], and the worst in regard to sex and food.[35]

This ambiguity, that the best of animals may all too easily become the most savage, isn't addressed only to some alleged savage man against the civilized. It is addressed most of all to the civilized man as a warning. For it is precisely in civilization that we find those who, spurning virtue, will use all the developments and advantages of political life and political power for the enjoyment of the most degrading vices. Without attention to virtue, without care for a regime's moral foundation, the most savage men will soon enough rule, and we will be changed from political animals to political beasts.

CHAPTER TWO

Orthodoxy: Gilbert Keith Chesterton

*"The more transcendental is your patriotism,
the more practical are your politics."*

WE NOW LEAP FROM ARISTOTLE IN ANCIENT GREECE TO AN ENG-
lishman born in the Victorian era, a man who was a novelist, a literary critic, a Christian apologist, a political essayist, an economic
theorist, and a newspaperman nonpareil, a man much quoted but
perhaps too infrequently read, Mr. G. K. Chesterton. As we have
seen with Aristotle, true conservatism is not about political parties,
but what might be called, in high philosophic discourse, a particular "stance in relationship to being." Conservatism, wherever it
occurs, accepts nature as fundamentally good, and human nature
as the fundamental standard of human moral goodness. For Aristotle, the main political question was not whether you are ruled by
a king or by a Congress, but whether the rulers, however few or
many there be, rule for the sake of the true human good or merely
for their own advantage, for virtue or mere pleasure. The main

political question is always a moral question, but the moral question is itself rooted firmly in human nature. That is why the political and moral reasoning of Aristotle culminated in what came to be called the "natural law," and why conservatives speak of laws grounded in nature and nature's God. Whoever defends these properly, is properly called a conservative. We meet now one of the greatest conservatives who ever lived, a man so keen on defending nature and nature's God that he very rightly called himself a cosmic patriot.

The Cosmic Patriot

If I were, by some strange circumstance, compelled to offer a definitive proof of the existence of God, and do so in the least number of words, I would simply reply, "Chesterton." That so strange and marvelous a creature as G. K. Chesterton could exist makes it quite impossible, indeed unconscionable, to be an atheist. Nothing but a divine cause could explain such superabundance of intellect continually overflowing into laughter.

Chesterton could laugh because he saw the cosmos as a great and joyful gift, a gift worth defending in all its abundance. He could not abide this abundance being squeezed into some fashionable, abstract theory to fit some narrow, new-fangled view of man. We have seen, in Aristotle, the conservative insistence on beginning from particulars, from experience and fact, from how men really are. Aristotle would not allow abstract theories to take the place of concrete truths, because the theorists all too often were cut off from reality, and so cut out the parts of reality that didn't fit their theory. Chesterton takes this approach and shows us that the many abstract theories of the modern world are not expansions to a greater truth, but constrictions of it that cut off the aspects of reality deemed irrelevant or inconvenient. Chesterton will have none of that. To be a man, in Chesterton's view, means to defend the full spectrum of the truth against those who would narrow it to their own ends. So it is that Chesterton declares himself a "cosmic patriot,"[1] a lover and defender of the fullness of creation, and most especially of man.

A "cosmic patriot" might seem a contradiction. Patriotism is love for a particular place—and Chesterton did indeed love his particular place of England. But Chesterton also loved the world—indeed, the cosmos—as if it were a small and endearing shire. If he had been alive during the time of Thomas Aquinas, he would have been credited with a "love for the glory of God's creation," for that is what his cosmic patriotism meant. He defended the world against those who despised it so much that they wanted to change it into something else, a utopia of their own design. That spirit of defense defines his *Orthodoxy*. It is also what makes Chesterton a conservative in the most fundamental sense.

For those who have not read Chesterton, be forewarned. Chesterton was one of the very few human beings who actually had a "rapier wit," a mind so sharp and nimble, and footwork so quick and light, that we are left astonished at the effortless rapidity and exactitude of his strokes. Each turns out to be a stroke of genius. Chesterton can say in a short paragraph what it takes others, with much more labor, to say in entire books. Reading Chesterton is much like reading Shakespeare, except that Chesterton speaks in our own idiom, and for Chesterton, there are only comedies.

The Ever-laughing Man

Gilbert Keith Chesterton was born on May 29, 1874, in the west district of London, Kensington, the son of Edward and Marie Louise Chesterton. Edward was the British equivalent of a real estate agent, but was generally able to avoid work in his family firm through the convenient presence of delicate health. He preferred immersing himself in literature, employing himself as an amateur artist, and dispensing his imagination into puppet (or toy) theater. Marie Louise, née Grosjean, was descended from French Swiss on her father's side and Scots on her mother's (her mother's maiden name, Keith, became G. K. Chesterton's middle name). Edward and Marie's first child was Beatrice. She was born five years before Gilbert, but died when he was only three. A brother, Cecil, came in 1879.

The Chesterton boys, although of the middle class, were often dirty as chimney sweeps. Gilbert never seemed to recover from his early habit of dishevelment. All efforts at sheveling him by his mother, future wife, and friends failed wonderfully. He always looked like an unmade bed, hastily left and in need of changing.

The Chestertons were old breed liberals whose first principles were the sanctity of private property, the importance of personal initiative, and a belief in complete freedom of thought (within the confines of Victorian respectability). It also meant their religious convictions were less than those of your average Unitarian. Nevertheless, Gilbert was baptized at St. George's, an Anglican Church, and received the first name Gilbert from the last name of his godfather.

He endured being educated at St. Paul's school (founded by John Colet in 1509). He was thought to be dim and distracted, a daydreamer forever drawing strange and fantastic pictures in his notebooks rather than working on sums. In truth, he was more like "the dumb ox," St. Thomas Aquinas, who likewise had extraordinary powers of concentration that made him seem distracted to those who couldn't see the great churning of ideas within. Some glimmer of Chesterton's genius poked through when he founded a debating club at St. Paul's, and debating became a lifelong passion. Like St. Thomas, he had an amazing ability to remember every detail of his opponent's arguments (even while misplacing a comb, his watch, or the hat that was on his head), and he could answer each point in turn with the greatest charity. He also wrote poems, plays, essays, and novels, a habit he would never give up.

Gilbert then went on to the Slade School of Art. As with his prose, his illustrations expressed with a few exact strokes what it took others a whole painting (or in prose, a book) to achieve. He attended literature classes at the University College London, but as with the Slade, he was able to avoid the formality of graduating. He was too large to fit either curriculum.

That odd largeness suffused his very being. Even as a fresh-faced lad, he towered at six feet two inches. As he grew older, his horizontal aspects caught up with his vertical. Even his hair seemed to stand upright, emphasizing his size.

While he was fresh-faced, he was not innocent. During this period he lapsed into the occult and felt himself being dragged downward. "I am not proud of believing in the Devil," he would later recall. "To put it more correctly, I am not proud of knowing the Devil. I made his acquaintance by my own fault; and followed it up along lines which, had they been followed further, might have led me to devil-worship or the devil knows what."[2] He was shaken from this free fall by a real diabolist who befriended him. When Chesterton saw how his friend so casually inverted the entire moral order, embracing evil as good, he was shaken and fled from the cold, dark abyss of real evil.[3] I point this out so that the reader does not misunderstand Chesterton's sunny exuberance—he knew very well what he was against.

By the fall of 1895, Chesterton had his first job at a publishing firm and slowly worked his way from penury into prominence (if not wealth) in the literary world. He also met his future wife, Frances Blogg (whose unfortunate maiden name came from trying to anglicize the perfectly melodious, de Blogue). She was exactly one foot shorter than Chesterton.

Chesterton was a hopeless romantic—the romance being essential to his nature and the hopelessness arising from his financial situation. Though he was a prolific and increasingly famous "jolly journalist," writing on literary, artistic, social, and political topics, he had so little money that he postponed wedding Frances for several years (until 1901). During these drawn-out years of anticipation, he met one of his great, life-long friends, Hilaire Belloc, whose *Servile State* we will discuss later. Chesterton made his big professional breakthrough in 1905 with a contract for a weekly column in the *Illustrated London News*. The column brought him financial security and an even bigger public platform to address every topic that caught his fancy.

Around this same time, Chesterton wrote a successful book, *Heretics* (1905), that laid out clearly what he didn't believe. His adversaries demanded that he set out clearly what he did believe. So, in 1908, Chesterton came out with *Orthodoxy*, one of the most brilliant books of all time, written by a man not yet thirty-five years old. "I have attempted in a vague and personal way, in a set of mental pictures rather than in a series of deductions, to state the philosophy in which I have come to believe. I will not call it my philosophy; for I did not make it. God and humanity made it; and it made me." *Orthodoxy* recounts how Chesterton—like a man who sets out on a great adventure to discover unknown lands—discovered his own heritage instead. As that description might imply, it led Chesterton to a profound conservatism based on tradition, common sense, and, as he would call it, *sanity*—found most coherently in the Christianity that shaped the West. *Orthodoxy* was set against innumerable modern errors that amounted to a kind of civilizational *insanity*. The most insane of these errors was materialism.

The Madness of Materialism

For Chesterton, our experience of life—with all its ordinary strangeness, its mystery, flashing color, happy din and song, intellectual and spiritual joy, adventure, terror, and love—is real. To embrace it gratefully is sanity. But leaving sanity behind, modern men are inclined to accept reductionist explanations for life; and the most popular reductionist theory is "materialism."

Chesterton argues that materialism is too small to fit the real world, the world as we experience it, whether this materialism takes the Marxist view of reducing every facet of human experience to economics; or the Darwinist view of reducing everything to genetics and the survival of the fittest; or the modern scientific view that we do not actually feel love but a series of chemical reactions that we call love; or that we do not think but merely obey the dictates of our genetically programmed brains.

For Chesterton, a materialist of whatever stripe shrinks reality to fit into his entirely logical and simple scheme. The problem is the materialist's logic is too tight, and so the simplicity is an insane simplicity. The materialist chooses the clarity and precision of his own theory at the expense of reality—which can have calamitous consequences (some of which Chesterton lived to see). When Marxists found that actual human beings would not conform to their dialectical materialism, they took the next logical step and cut out the "class enemies" that didn't fit in—a hundred million of them. When Hitler's national socialists found groups that failed their genetic tests of fitness, they designated these people for the gas chamber. Today, our materialist laws reflect a belief that human life in the womb is merely biological "material," and if it is inconvenient, then it may be disposed of.

For Chesterton, materialism is a species of madness, albeit self-inflicted, a distortion of mind that causes its adherents to reject the healthy and obvious facts in front of them. A madman thinks he is a chicken, all evidence to the contrary. A materialist thinks that all human thought can be reduced to chemical reactions in the brain, his own thinking to the contrary, or that all human action can be reduced to deterministic physical laws, his own free actions to the contrary. Both insanity and materialism suffer a fateful contraction of reality, and so both share "the strongest and most unmistakable *mark* of madness," to wit, the "combination between a logical completeness and a spiritual contraction."[4] Materialism denies the abundant complexity of human life precisely because it denies the spiritual basis from which that abundance springs. "As an explanation of the world, materialism has a sort of insane simplicity. It has just the quality of a madman's argument; we have at once the sense of it covering everything and the sense of it leaving everything out."[5]

At the root of materialism is the laudable desire for rational certainty, but as Chesterton notes, it is carried out in pride rather than humility. A materialist wants certainty on *his* terms, or not at all. As a result, he ends up "in the clean and well-lit prison of one idea: he is sharpened to one painful point. He is without healthy hesitation and healthy complexity."[6] Tidy lucidity at the expense of the messiness of reality: that is what makes the materialist especially dangerous when he deigns to talk about human beings.

The materialist reduces man to a physical being without a soul, without any sort of divine accountability, without any inherent worth. That is why such materialist simplifiers, when they engage in politics, have all too often turned into *terrible simplifiers* (to borrow a famous phrase from historian Jacob Burckhardt). The twentieth century was the bloodiest century in human history, and it was marked by ruthless leaders full of dreadful self-confidence that their materialist idea—of which Marxism was the dominant strand—would cure all that ails humanity. As Chesterton said,

"Materialists and madmen never have doubts."[7] Had they more doubts, the twentieth century would have been far less insanely bloody.

The key to living sanely, Chesterton says, is to realize that we live in a world that is larger than our grasp, a far grander cosmos than we can ever fully understand. Our everyday lives are shot full of mystery. We act freely nearly every minute of the day, but no scientist can explain free will. We are constantly in thought, but no philosopher has come up with an adequate explanation for thought. For Chesterton, we must humbly and gratefully take things as we find them and accept the mysteries, rather than try to deny them by some entirely lucid but simplistic theory.

This fundamental stance, the stance of the cosmic patriot, has immense political implications. It means that our politics must be built upon the actual complexity of human nature, the full range of our powers and desires, our everyday needs as well as our deepest spiritual aspirations and insights. It must be built upon "healthy hesitation and healthy complexity," and the healthy hesitation is caused by the desire to *conserve* the healthy complexity. It is easy for modern liberals to come up with government programs to solve every problem because they believe that the problems are actually quite simple. Unlike liberals, conservatives have a healthy hesitation when confronted with easy answers to political questions, precisely because they have a deep appreciation for the healthy complexity of actual human life.

The Mystery of Reason and the Suicide of Thought

With all this talk of the magnitude and mystery of human life, one might conclude that Chesterton was a giddy irrationalist. On the contrary, he took up the cause of mystery in the defense of reason. Since the Enlightenment, modern liberals have insisted that they were taking up the cause of rationality by using materialist philosophy against the superstitious mystery-mongers of religion. But as Chesterton notes, the odd thing about these modern rationalists—or materialists—is that their rationalism, and their war against religious faith, ends up in an act of suicide, with reason destroying itself.

Chesterton was right. Enlightenment rationalism has ended in deep skepticism. Living at the same time as Chesterton, the philosopher Friedrich Nietzsche, who proclaimed the death of God, also declared that reason is only a mask for power, and all power is the result of the irrational strivings of the will. Other very modern moral relativists were telling us that there are no objectively discernible truths. Marxists were preaching that all thought is merely a reflection of the material modes of production. In our own time, Deconstructionists in literary theory tell us that texts have no real meaning. Neurologists go further, and inform us that our thoughts are mere chemical reactions in our brain. We have fallen into what Chesterton called the great peril—"that the human intellect is free to destroy itself."[8] That is the madness of his time and ours, "For madness may be defined as using mental activity so as to reach mental helplessness."[9]

The great mistake of all these modern rationalists is that they failed to understand that "reason is itself is a matter of faith. It is an act of faith to assert that our thoughts have any relation to reality at all."[10] This act of faith is based upon our experience of life: we sense that our minds are constructed to *know* things and that things themselves seem constructed *to be known*; that is, there is a design to the universe, and creation is full of surprises that our mind is wonderfully apt for discovering. Chesterton avers that the way to approach this design is with a humble sense of wonder, appreciating its mysteries, including the greatest mystery of all: that we can know it. Our belief in reason is, in a sense, childlike, because it is based on trust that our reason is reliable and reality knowable. Rationalism ends in skepticism because of a certain kind of pride, one that tries to ground certainty in the human mind itself, rather than in the mind's mysterious conformity to reality. In its quest for certainty, rationalism reduced reality to a mere concatenation of purely material causes that, because of their brute simplicity, the human mind could easily understand. Of course, that meant the mind itself was a merely material thing. And so, in Chesterton's time and in our own, a materialist account of the mind ends in asserting that what each person calls "truth" is merely the peculiar firing of the atoms in his brain. Truth is relative to each person's particular head. This sort of skepticism and relativism, expressed in different ways, was as characteristic of the sophists of ancient Greece as it is of liberals today.[11]

Conservatives, on the other hand, believe that we can know truth, that truth is not merely a reflection of our physiology, our historical time, our economic circumstances, our hidden lusts, or the circus of our brain circuitry. Conservatives believe that truth is discernible by men *as* men, and that in our everyday lives we can experience moral truths about human nature, what again used to be called the natural law. The natural law is not limited to experts, because it is known through natural reason and grounded in experience and common sense.

These ideas have serious consequences, for if our everyday experience and common sense are the paths to truth, then self-government makes sense because experience and common sense aren't the prerogatives of a few. But if we cannot trust our everyday experience and our common sense, then perhaps government must be steered by specially endowed "scientific experts" rather than ordinary people—which is why liberalism, the political home for skeptics and rationalists, is so comfortable with centralized bureaucratic government. And this too has implications: the conservative who believes that man is endowed with reason, common sense, and free will is apt to see man as having inviolable moral stature; the liberal, on the other hand, since he tends to be a materialist, can see man as putty to be manipulated into something different than what he is.

The Great Gift of Existence and Extraordinary Ordinariness

And so we have come to morality. For Chesterton, the fact that we are strangely and wonderfully made is a gift, a precious and precarious gift, and the proper response on our part is both gratitude and reverent caution. This reverent and cautious gratitude is the ground for morality. Thus Chesterton could say, against the sexual liberals of his day who were barking against monogamy and baying for free love, that "Keeping to one woman is a small price for so much as seeing one woman." Or against the debaucheries of the celebrated aesthete and litterateur Oscar Wilde, quipped Chesterton, "Oscar Wilde said that sunsets were not valued because we could not pay for sunsets. But Oscar Wilde was wrong; we can pay for sunsets. We can pay for them by not being Oscar Wilde."[12] For Chesterton, materialism ruins morality in two ways. By declaring that human beings are merely physical objects, it simultaneously denies that we have free will and sets us free from moral limits to pursue all physical pleasures. The materialist intelligentsia therefore declares that since our actions are determined by the iron-clad laws of nature, we can't help the way we act, and since we can't help what we do, we might as well do anything. Determinism and libertinism go hand in hand.

Chesterton would have none of the materialists' view of the cosmos that denied free will in its world clanking along with mechanical predictability.[13] For Chesterton, this was insanity. In contrast to the materialist story of an entirely determined cosmos, he had the knowing audacity to declare that our moral world is better captured by fairy tales. These at least know that existence is marvelous and that the ordinary is therefore extraordinary. Having firmly grasped this, they affirm the necessity of treating the joys that we have with reverence and humility. Fairy tales assume that human beings are free to act or not to act, and that more often than not our ultimate happiness rests on our ability to choose *not* to do something. This common sense truth, found in nearly every fairy tale, Chesterton called the "Doctrine of Conditional Joy."

> In the fairy tale an incomprehensible happiness rests upon an incomprehensible condition. A box is opened, and all evils fly out. A word is forgotten, and cities perish. A lamp is lit, and love flies away. A flower is plucked, and human lives are forfeited. An apple is eaten, and the hope of God is gone.... Such, it seemed to me, was the joy of man, either in elfland or on earth; the happiness depended on *not doing something* which you could at any moment do and which, very often, it was not obvious why you should not do [it].[14]

Chesterton has here penetrated to the heart of morality: that we have the free will to do something or *not* do it—that is the mysterious truth upon which all morality is based; and that is what makes the materialists so dangerous. Their mindset denies free will and says that we are objects governed by blind mechanical laws. That makes life no gift at all, neither gratitude nor morality are possible, and it leads inevitably to nihilism and despair.

Against this bleakness, Chesterton urged the childlike innocence of fairy tales as purgatives for morbidly sick intellects, for "Fairy-land is nothing but the sunny country of common sense."[15] If there are laws in nature that somehow govern human actions, they are like traffic laws designed to help motorists go where they like.[16] The happy, built-in regularity of nature is not some kind of prison, but what allows for all the blessed irregularity of human affairs. It accounts exactly for why history does not unfold like clockwork, as the historical materialists would have it, but instead is the unpredictable unfolding of a moral tale that depends, in every moment, on what people choose to do or not do. That is why fairy stories that assume the reality of free action are more real and moral than the fantasies of the "cosmic prison" sketched by the materialists in which we are "either unable to do things or we were destined to do them." In such a prison, morality is not possible; "one can neither have the firmness of keeping laws nor the fun of breaking them."[17]

Human life, as Chesterton sees it, is an adventure, a great unfolding drama full of romance, danger, heroism, cowardice, victory, defeat, benevolence, malice, comedy, and tragedy. It is a magnificent story largely determined, for better or worse, by our actions, a drama that takes place within the wider, deeper, unfolding story of creation. And "if there is a story" on the cosmic level, Chesterton realized, "there is a story-teller."[18]

As with most fairy stories, we enter the drama after it has been unfolding for some time, and so there is both the original magnificence and a ripple of ruin running through the unfolding plot. Someone has already opened the box, forgotten the word, lit the lamp, plucked the flower, eaten the apple. This gives us a puzzling feeling of both being at home and not at home in the world, of indignation at the ruin precisely because of the majesty that still shines through the rubble.

For Chesterton, this *feeling* of being born into magnificence and ruin was nurtured in him by fairy tales and the experience of real life; that is, he had it long before he became an orthodox Christian, and it in fact led him to become an orthodox Christian. That makes perfect sense, for the feeling is not peculiarly Christian; it is shared by human beings as human beings. But for Chesterton, it led to orthodoxy because the dogmas of Christianity precisely answered the puzzle of human existence.

"I Believe in Liberalism"

Now for some confusion: how could Chesterton declare himself a liberal ("I believe in Liberalism"[19]) and chastise "conservatism" for merely wanting to conserve the status quo, no matter how much it cried out for reform?[20] The reason lies in Chesterton's definition of liberalism, which is very different from what it means today.

> I was brought up a Liberal, and have always believed in democracy, in the elementary liberal doctrine of self-governing humanity. If any one finds the phrase vague or threadbare, I can only pause for a moment to explain that the principle of democracy, as I mean it, can be stated in two propositions. The first is this: that the things common to all men are more important than the things peculiar to any men. Ordinary things are more valuable than extraordinary things, nay, they are more extraordinary. Man is something more awful than men; something more strange. The sense of the miracle of humanity itself should be always more vivid to us than any marvels of power, intellect, art, or civilization....
>
> ...And the second principle is merely this: that the political instinct or desire is one of these things which they hold in common.... The democratic contention is that government (helping

to rule the tribe) is a thing like falling in love, ... It is not something analogous to playing the church organ, painting on vellum, discovering the North Pole ... looping the loop, being Astronomer Royal, and so on. For these are things we do not wish a man to do at all unless he does them well. It is, on the contrary, a thing analogous to writing one's own love-letters or blowing one's own nose. These things we want a man to do for himself, even if he does them badly. ... I know that some moderns are asking to have their wives chosen by scientists, and they may soon be asking, for all I know, to have their noses blown by nurses. ... [But] the democratic faith is this: that the most terribly important things must be left to ordinary men themselves—the mating of the sexes, the rearing of the young, the laws of the state. This is democracy, and in this I have always believed.[21]

We can plainly see Chesterton sketching what we would now call conservative rather than liberal principles. We are political animals, just as Aristotle said, and that means that an essential part of our perfection is *being* political. We must engage in the activity of self-government for the same reason we must engage in the activity of self-exercise. If someone else does either for us, then we are robbed of any benefit. Someone else governing for us is like having someone else do our pushups or take our walk. In the same way that the physical *exercise* makes us healthy and less in need of a doctor, the *exercise* of governing makes us self-governing and thereby less in need of some outside power to rule our unruliness.

We can see why Chesterton (guided by his friend Hilaire Belloc) rejected socialism. Chesterton would have no part of the state taking over the realm of individual moral action. He believed in individuals doing things for themselves, not in the state doing things for them. If Chesterton disliked the aristocratic tone of the conservatism of his day and what he saw as its crippling short-sightedness—"All conservatism is based upon the idea that if you leave things alone you leave them as they are. But you do not. If you leave a thing alone you leave it to a torrent of change"[22]—he knew how liberalism as he understood it could be, and was in his own day being corrupted and degraded into socialism.[23]

To be a liberal in Chesterton's sense was not to be an opponent of tradition, as some were trying to make it. "I have never been able to understand where people got the idea that democracy was in some way opposed to tradition. It is obvious that tradition is only democracy extended through time." "Tradition," he wrote, "may be defined as the extension of the franchise. Tradition means giving votes to the most obscure of all classes, our ancestors. It is the democracy of the dead. Tradition refuses to submit to the small and arrogant oligarchy of those who merely happen to be walking about. All democrats object to men being disqualified by the accident of birth; tradition objects to their being disqualified by the accident of death."[24] The deference to and veneration of tradition is, for Chesterton, merely the obvious respect we owe to the wisdom that has collected over time.

Moreover, to be a liberal in Chesterton's sense was not to be a skeptic, a "freethinker," or a materialist, though, as with socialism, such "confusion" was already apparent even in his day.

> A confusion...has arisen in connection with the word "liberal" as applied to religion and as applied to politics and society. It is often suggested that all Liberals ought to be freethinkers, because they ought to love everything that is free....The thing is a mere accident of words. In actual modern Europe a freethinker does not mean a man who thinks for himself. It means a man who,

having thought for himself, has come to one particular class of conclusions, the material origin of all phenomena, the impossibility of miracles, and the improbability of personal immortality and so on. And none of these ideas is particularly liberal.[25]

The "freedom of thought" of these so-called liberals actually means the uncritical acceptance of the "dogma of materialism."[26] Obviously, Chesterton would have none of that, either.

So, there is very little left, if anything, in Chesterton that one could identify with contemporary liberalism. At most, he was a very modified "classical liberal," but even that would bring more confusion than clarity. As we said earlier, in the European world of the time, conservatism was associated merely with conserving the old political order without asking about its caliber and whether it badly needed reforming. But reforming, for Chesterton, always meant a change in light of what is actually good for human beings as human beings. What is actually good is a moral given, the very thing that must be conserved and hence defended against degradation.

If there remains any doubt about the deep conservatism of Chesterton—deeper than the momentary historical labels in nineteenth century Britain—then his treatment of human sin and its relationship to politics should set aside any last hesitations.

Sin, Heaven, Hell, and Political Revolution

There is an important connection between the doctrines of materialism and the doctrine of original sin. Those who accept the first deny the second; the materialist denial of free will makes sin impossible. In Chesterton's day, the acceptance of materialism had led to liberal theologians who "dispute original sin, which is the only part of Christian theology which can really be proved."[27]

This theological error has terrible political implications, because it implies that it is the physical environment, something outside men, that makes them "evil" in the same way that something outside the billiard ball makes it move. On this count, the poor, for instance, cannot help being criminals because they are poor, and so the only solution is to make the poor as comfortable as the rich; and that leads to calls for socialism or revolution. But this is to get things all wrong, Chesterton argues. "The danger lies not in man's environment, but in man." The materialist view is wrong not only in that, but in failing to recognize the danger of riches, "that a man who is dependent upon the luxuries of this life is a corrupt man, spiritually corrupt, politically corrupt, financially corrupt." It is Christianity alone that "can offer any rational objection" to an oligarchy of the rich, or for that matter, to the desire to make the poor rich through socialist revolution, because it holds that a man's moral worth is in himself, in what he does, not in his possessions or his material circumstances.[28]

The acceptance of sin also has other important political implications. If sin is inherent in man, there are limits to what we can do precisely because we are *all* sinners. "In the best Utopia, I must be prepared for the moral fall of any man in any position at any moment; especially for my own fall from my position at this moment."[29] An intelligent politics needs to recognize that all human things tend to corruption and decay—a house well-built inevitably becomes a house with paint peeling, foundations cracking, and shutters blown askew. It is this very inevitability of decay that conservatives of Chesterton's day tended to ignore, not understanding the need for corrective measures. As Chesterton says, "An almost unnatural vigilance is really required of the citizen because of the horrible rapidity with which human institutions grow old."[30]

This spirit of action is part of what made Chesterton a friend of liberalism as he understood it.

Chesterton's revolutionary spirit, and hence his practical politics, led him to believe that we must "hate it [the world] enough to change it, and yet love it enough to think it worth changing."[31] That is, we hate the effects of sin, but love the world enough to want to do something about them. In short, we must be cosmic patriots whose "primary loyalty" is "to life," to God's creation, even though it is fallen. We must long for improvement, even while understanding that heaven has been placed beyond our grasp, and indeed beyond this world, so there is no bringing it down to earth.

Chesterton knew that human progress and regress are ever-present possibilities, that societies can fall faster than they can rise, and that history has no inevitable outcome. This made him happily immune to the heady utopian theories of his day that assumed human history itself was inevitably, even biologically, progressive. The idea that man achieves a sort of evolutionary perfection through history was, quipped Chesterton, a nineteenth century heresy that "taught men to think that so long as they were passing from the ape they were going to the angel. But you can pass from the ape and go to the devil."[32] And so, in the twentieth century, they did.

CHAPTER THREE

The New Science of Politics:
Eric Voegelin

"... a 'materialistic' interpreter of politics is an ignoramus who had better bone up on his elementary facts."

OUR LEAD QUOTE—A CRITICISM OF MARXISTS—IS REFRESHINGLY blunt. It catches the critical spirit of the great twentieth century political philosopher Eric Voegelin and states his central thesis in *The New Science of Politics* (and also shows us an obvious and important connection to Chesterton).

That having been said, I would be misrepresenting Voegelin's thought if I implied that working through his book is as easy as working through this snippet from *The New Science of Politics*. Voegelin's writing is exceedingly dense, but repays handsomely the effort required. (One recommendation: start with his fourth chapter, "Gnosticism—the Nature of Modernity," which focuses on Marxism, liberalism, and modern utopianism; it makes a good introduction to the whole and sets the first three chapters in context.) I will do my best to bring out his basic arguments by focusing

on certain key ideas that help define conservatism more deeply—
and explain what has nearly destroyed it.

Erich Hermann Wilhelm Vögelin was born at Cologne, Germany, in 1901, the son of Otto Stefan and Elisabeth Ruehl Vögelin.
His father, a civil engineer, moved his family from Cologne, to
Königswinter, and then to Vienna before Erich was ten. As a
young lad, the thin, blond, bespectacled Eric Voegelin (to adopt
the anglicized form of his name) was brilliant, and was especially
gifted in physics and mathematics. In his final year of high school,
he was already studying Einstein's recently released theory of rel-
ativity. He also studied Latin, English, Italian, and French, and to
these he later added Russian and Ancient Greek. He entered Austria's University of Vienna in 1919. Interestingly enough, he read
Karl Marx's *Das Kapital* and became a convinced Marxist—for five
whole months! By Christmas of 1919, however, having immersed
himself more deeply in economics, he dispatched Marxism as
grievously flawed. He received his doctorate in political science
from Vienna in 1922 (although he had very seriously considered
doing doctorates in mathematics, physics, or law instead). During
his graduate studies, Voegelin attended economics seminars with
Ludwig von Mises, and befriended one of our eminent figures to
be treated later, Friedrich von Hayek.

In 1924, Voegelin received a fellowship that allowed him to
study for two years in the United States, and then a year in Paris.
This sojourn in the United States resulted in his first published
book, *On the Form of the American Mind* (1928), in which he showed
that he did not share the stereotypical European's intellectual
snootiness concerning America and Americans. The United States
became for him a real second home.

In 1929, he accepted an offer to teach at the University of
Vienna. It was from here that he watched the National Socialists

rise to power. Later he recalled his disgust at having young students in his class wearing the black uniforms of the *Schutzstaffel* (the dreaded SS). The year that Hitler took full power as dictator, 1933, Voegelin had the wonderful audacity to publish two works critical of the Nazi race theory, *Race and the State* and *The Race Idea in Intellectual History*. Besides all his other intellectual achievements, Voegelin studied biology, and it was not difficult for him to uncover the faulty biological notions undergirding Nazi racial theories. Even more, his historical and philosophical mastery allowed him to dismantle National Socialism as politically fraudulent. Essential to his argument was the understanding that man, a creature of soul and spirit, could not be reduced to mere biological race. This reductionism of man by the National Socialists, argued Voegelin, was merely an extension of the materialism of Marxism and liberalism. Nazi anti-Semitism and Nazi theories of Aryan racial supremacy, while presented as science, were not scientific at all, but utter propaganda.

Voegelin's books suddenly "disappeared" from circulation, and Voegelin was pegged as an enemy of National Socialism. He was forced to flee with his wife Lissy in 1938, when Austria was annexed to the Third Reich. The totalitarian atrocities of Nazism seared Voegelin deeply, and he dedicated his life to understanding how the advanced culture of the twentieth century could become so barbaric and tyrannical.

After spending some time as refugees in Switzerland, he and his wife found their way to the United States (he became a United States citizen in 1944). Voegelin taught briefly at several universities, including Harvard, before taking a teaching position at Louisiana State University in 1942, where he remained until 1958. He later taught in Munich and then at Stanford where he remained until his death in 1985.[1] It was at LSU that Voegelin wrote his

New Science of Politics, as well as several volumes of his multi-volume magnum opus, *Order and History* (which was originally supposed to have been a short introduction to political theory for college students). A new science of politics was necessary, argued Voegelin, because the current "science" of politics was corrupt.

The Science of Intellectual Decapitation

Chesterton once said, "It is always easy to let the age have its head; the difficult thing is to keep one's own."[2] That is precisely Eric Voegelin's criticism of our age: we have been commanded to lose our head; we have come to a stunted view of man and of science, not to mention of the world and of politics, which, in turn, has spawned and legitimized unprecedented political violence.

The villain, again, is materialism, which tells us that we are no more than our bodies, and our bodies are no more than accidentally aggregated chemical machines cobbled together by a blind cosmos. And if we are a machine without a soul, and therefore without a head or a heart, it should be no surprise that the insane political carnage of the twentieth century resembled a tank trundling over a field of corpses.

For Voegelin, the key to understanding the political violence of the twentieth century is to recognize that the term "science" has been perverted by materialism into *positivism.* Positivism is the systematic denial of anything beyond our senses, anything that can't be measured scientifically. Chesterton faced positivism and accused it of being blind to the sunny world of common sense. You can't measure love scientifically (or at least not without reducing it to chemical reactions in the brain). You can't measure familial devotion scientifically (or at least not without reducing it to some sort of Darwinian explanation). You can't measure courage unless you reduce it to adrenalin. You can't measure the caliber of ideas unless you reduce them to the firing of synapses in the brain. But such reductionism denies our everyday experience, and makes nonsense of common sense. That is why positivism continually utters high-toned nonsense. As Voegelin says, "Disregard for elementary verities happens to be one of the characteristics of the positivistic attitude; and hence it becomes necessary to elaborate the obvious" again to a positivistic age.[3]

The proper view of science, Voegelin argues, is the Aristotelian view that "Science starts from the prescientific existence of man, from his participation in the world with his body, soul, intellect, and spirit, from his primary grip on all the realms of being that is assured to him because his own nature is their epitome."[4] In other words, the goal of science is to explain reality as we experience it, not to explain it away.

What is that experience? Before we ever become scientific, we experience our participation in the world with our bodies, souls, intellects, and spirits. We find ourselves to be a body like other bodies, something that can fall over cliffs just like any rock. But unlike rocks, we find that we grow like plants, taking in food and water and somehow turning them into ourselves. If that weren't strange enough, we discover quite quickly that we are like other animals, with much the same parts, external and internal—feet, eyes, legs, chests, hair, heads, mouths, brains, intestines, hearts, lungs. At the same time, we find ourselves vaulting above the animals—elaborately talking, singing, thinking, building; turning villages into vastly complex cities; turning clay into ornate pots, rocks into cathedrals, and the simple counting of stones into the most abstract mathematical ruminations; turning our heads to the heavens, and turning our observations of the movements of stars into astronomy; and all the while yearning in a quite extraordinary way for immortality. We experience, in all this, a deep connection to a transcendent source, a realm of spirit to which we seem both to belong and not belong. We have both worldly desires and a sense of something beyond this world. We also know that we experience ourselves as imperfect: we are a mixture of good and evil, benevolence and malice, and all the grey shading in between. All this is what Voegelin means by saying that we are the "epitome" of the "realms of being," thus defining all that is meant by the natural law, the law of our being.

To have a firm grip on reality, we need to have a firm grip on ourselves, but positivism wrenches away that firm grip on ourselves by denying that we are anything but matter that is pushed around by the laws of physics and chemistry. The great ruin of modern political science came about, argues Voegelin, when certain modern thinkers decided that political life must be understood "objectively," that is, according to the materialist grid, treating human beings and human action in the same way that chemists treat the actions and reactions of chemicals or the physicist treats the falling of rocks.[5] And so (for example) Marx argued that human life is defined by digestion (like a plant) and obeys historical laws (like a rock obeys the laws of gravity). That became the Marxist objective scientific *method*, but "method" here only means methodical materialism—the purposeful exclusion of the full reality of human nature familiar to our everyday experience. That is why Marxists are notoriously deaf to objections that arise from common sense or the obvious lessons of actual (not theoretical or dialectical) history. That is why the Marxist method of historical materialism leads to madness: because its "scientific" theory always trumps reality.

The time has come, Voegelin maintains, "to state flatly that 'historical materialism' is not a theory but a falsification of history," and further, "that a 'materialistic' interpreter of politics is an ignoramus who had better bone up on elementary facts."[6] The elementary facts of our own existence—that we are a complex union of body, soul, intellect, and spirit—must become the foundation of a New Science of Politics. This is Voegelin's great counterrevolutionary creed. Our political life must represent our full humanity and acknowledge that man "experiences himself as open toward transcendental reality," that he finds "his true nature through finding his true relation to God."[7]

This is something so fundamentally human that it is found in pagan philosophers such as Plato and Aristotle, and something so wonderfully divine that it is brought to a dramatic point in Judaism and Christianity. Openness to the divine is fundamental and definitive of human nature, and hence of human politics properly understood. The atheist himself proves this openness to be fundamental and definitive, ironically, by asserting that the most important achievement of man is the scientific demonstration that God does not exist. He realizes that the existence or non-existence of God is *the* question upon which our whole way of life should based. The difference is that he excludes the experience of God by asserting—not proving—that nothing but matter exists. He closes his soul to the divine by denying he has a soul that could be open.[8]

The Struggle between Caesar and Christ

That the great Greek philosophers Plato and Aristotle recognized this fundamental truth about the soul's openness to the divine does not mean it was either embraced, or even understood well enough to be rejected, in the politics of ancient Greece. For the Jews it was a practical, albeit precarious, achievement. Their political life was built upon God's revelation to them as a nation. With Christianity, the revelation of God-become-man (body, intellect, soul, and spirit) was extended to the world, though without political expression until the conversion of Constantine.

As Voegelin argues, Rome was characteristically blunt and practical, and Roman philosophy was Greek philosophy made to serve the state. Philosophy was okay, the Romans said, as long as it made people more obedient and dutiful, and met the political needs of the Empire. For the very same reason, the Romans declared that religion was okay as long as it didn't go too far; that is, as long as it served the state rather than upsetting the *status quo*. The highest truth was political truth, and so both religion and philosophy should be satisfied with being utilitarian handmaidens. Anything that upset political order must be ruthlessly removed. So it was that after muttering, "What is truth?" Pontius Pilate regretfully ordered the crucifixion of Christ.

Christianity remained in conflict with the empire because Christians refused to worship the emperor as divine, and refused to believe his empire was eternal. Then a strange thing happened. The Christians were proved right. The Roman emperors passed away one by one, and so did the Roman Empire. The great Christian theologian St. Augustine, bridging the fourth and fifth centuries, and hence witnessing the fall of Rome first hand, gave the enduring prognosis. Sin ensures that all things of this world are born to die, both emperors and empires. Our longing for God, our desire for lasting peace, our search for a political order that finally and permanently represents and fulfills humanity, can only be realized in the *next* world in a quite different, supernatural kingdom, the City of God. There may be better and worse political regimes in this world, better and worse Cities of Man, but human history, in and of itself, will never be anything other than the rise and fall, life and death, ebb and flow, wax and wane of one political regime after another until God creates a new heaven and a new earth, and with it a new kingdom. Profane history is going nowhere. As Voegelin explains, "Only transcendental history, including the

earthly pilgrimage of the church, has direction towards its escha-
tological fulfillment."[9] Political utopias are at once both heretical
and impossible.

St. Augustine thereby reduces any and all this-worldly political
regimes to secondary status. In Voegelin's words, "The spiritual
destiny of man in the Christian sense cannot be represented on
earth by the power organization of political society; it can be
represented only by the church."[10] We need the political state
because we live in a fallen world, but the fallen world is passing
away, and our spiritual nature must find its fulfillment in a world
to come, and that is the concern of the church. In Voegelin's view,
church and state each have their own function—they are distinct,
but they cannot be completely separate because human beings
cannot be completely separate in body, soul, intellect, and spirit.
To rebel against this truth is to rebel against ourselves.

The Modern Heresy: Gnostic Rebellion

We now come to the most difficult part of Voegelin's argument,
but it is also the most profound and instructive part. Voegelin
argues that we cannot properly understand the epically destructive
character of twentieth century utopianism unless we understand
the nature of a particular, ancient Christian heresy, Gnosticism. For
Voegelin, Gnosticism defines the nature of modernity, or more
exactly, of a particular virulent and destructive strain of modern
thought, a strain that includes liberalism, Marxism, and National
Socialism.

Here, we need a bit of a history lesson. The ancient Gnostics
twisted Christianity by claiming that there were two deities, the
God of the Old Testament who created an evil material world full
of suffering, and the good God of the New Testament who was trying to snatch pure human souls from material bondage. Human

beings were purely good spiritual beings trapped in evil bodies, and Jesus Christ was not God made man, but a pure spirit sent to rescue the elect. The chosen few had a divine spark within them. They were given special knowledge (Greek, *gnosis*) of the entire redemptive scheme by Jesus Christ. This knowledge was all the elect needed. That is, contrary to Christian orthodoxy, the passion and cross are not essential to redemption, but quite accidental, in fact illusory, because being pure spirit, Jesus Christ didn't really have a body, didn't really suffer, and didn't really die. He merely *appeared* to have done these things, but his body was a kind of phantasm. Such are the basic tenets of the Gnostic heresy.

What are the chief characteristics of the Gnostic devotee? The first is the unshakable conviction that, by virtue of his "divine spark," he is himself divine and omniscient. Whereas the uninitiated are complete fools, he is possessed of complete wisdom. For him, there are no longer any mysteries, because his wisdom and God's wisdom are identical. The second follows from the first. He is completely redeemed. He is not a man balanced precariously between two possible destinies, virtue and vice, heaven and hell. He's got the divine spark, the divine *gnosis*. He cannot go wrong; he cannot help but fly heavenward no matter what he does. So it was that some of the Gnostic elite engaged in all manner of licentious behavior—since they were already purely spiritual, it was a matter of indifference how they acted in the body. The final characteristic, and one especially important to Voegelin's analysis, is that the Gnostic was a simplifier (and as it turns out, a terrible simplifier). He substituted his very own cut-and-dried scheme for the complexly balanced and ultimately mysterious dogmas of orthodox Christianity.

According to Voegelin, we find a parallel in modern Gnosticism. Modern Gnostics give their own reductionist political theories the status of divine (scientific) revelation. They claim omniscience—

they've figured out everything from the laws of physics to the laws of human history and the human mind. Like the ancient Gnostics, they think their wisdom is identical to God's, except without the God part (for modern Gnosticism ends in atheism). Like the ancient Gnostics, they believe their theoretical *gnosis* puts them beyond sin, so they can do *anything* for the sake of their theory. Those who disagree with them are not only wrong but irredeemably wrong, and can therefore be eliminated.

But there is a difference between ancient and modern Gnosticism. Ancient Gnostics were pure spiritualists who condemned matter as evil. Modern Gnostics (at least in their more important and enduring secular form) are materialists and quite this-worldly. Underlying this difference, however, are even deeper similarities.

Ancient Gnostics believed that matter was evil. Modern Gnostics believe that matter is the *source* of all evil. For the ancient Gnostic we must escape from matter into the spiritual world. For the modern Gnostic, we must recreate the material world to eliminate evil. For the ancients Gnostics, the material world was created by the terrible God of the Old Testament. For the modern Gnostics, the material world as we find it was created by the fickle god "chance," and it therefore contains endless defects in nature and human nature that can only be remedied by technological and political recreation. The modern Gnostic throws the same religious zeal into the recreation of the material world that the ancient Gnostic spent on his escape from it. Here we have, then, Voegelin's argument that the modern secular passion to create a heaven on earth is actually a reformulation of an ancient Christian heresy. It's not an accident that Marxism envisions a glorious kingdom (communism) ushered in by an apocalypse (revolution).

The modern Gnostic attempt to invest *this* world with all the elements that orthodox Christianity held to be achievable only in the

next world is what Voegelin calls the "re-divinization" of the political realm,[11] which means treating the state as a replacement divin-
ity. This idea comes down to us from the philosophers of secular
liberalism. It started with calls for the subordination of religion to
the aims of the secular state (in Hobbes and Spinoza among others), and led to calls for the elimination of religion and the diviniza-
tion of man (with Comte and Marx). In the place of religion, the
secularists offered a new science—secular science—that would
deliver now what Christianity promised for the hereafter. The secularists rejected religion but redivinized mere politics, which justified the creation of an all-encompassing, omnipotent, secular state
Leviathan, the alleged giver of all that is good and the professed
eliminator of every evil.[12] Such is the dread spirit of modern totalitarianism and liberalism (and why liberalism tends naturally to
totalitarianism).

For Voegelin, then, liberalism is part of this Gnostic rebellion
against Christianity, or more accurately, an heretical simplification
of it. It offers a fundamentally materialistic view of humanity,
where man can be led to a technological utopia administered by
an ever more powerful and centralized government.

Conservatives are often take aback by the dogmatic self-assurance of modern liberals, but that is, as Voegelin points out, the
self-assurance of the Gnostic elite who believe they have seen the
whole truth. During the Cold War (and before) conservatives were
astounded at how easily liberals were duped into thinking that
Communist countries like the Soviet Union were achieving
heaven on earth. The reason is that communism and liberalism
share the same modern Gnostic heritage; they "see" with the same
eyes. Conservatives are often aghast at the ease with which liberals embrace the endless medical and technical manipulation of
humanity (whether through *in vitro* fertilization, embryonic stem

cell research, selective abortion, and so on), but that is fully con-
cordant with the Gnostic notion that matter is the source of evil
and must be reformed to suit human needs. Conservatives are
often shocked at how casually liberals treat the moral order, but
they do not realize that the Gnostic elite, by virtue of having the
right ideas, have risen above that order and may therefore treat it
with indifference. Conservatives are often curious as to why liberals seem to have a particular animosity toward Christianity, and
the reason, ironically, is that Christianity, since it is what they
have fallen from, offers the most powerful and telling critique of
liberalism.

With Voegelin's analysis as background, we are ready for
Lewis's astounding *Abolition of Man*, the book that rounds off our
attempt to understand the deepest differences between conservatism and liberalism.

CHAPTER FOUR

The Abolition of Man: C. S. Lewis

"Man's conquest of Nature, if the dreams of some scientific planners are realized, means the rule of a few hundreds of men over billions upon billions of men.... Each new power won by man is a power over man as well."

The End of Conservatism and Liberalism

C. S. LEWIS'S EXTRAORDINARY BOOK, *THE ABOLITION OF MAN*, IS primarily concerned with the modern attempt to completely master nature, an attempt, Lewis warns, that will end in the subjection of human nature itself to complete technological control and manipulation, a tyranny of a very few people over the mass of mankind. It thereby spells the end of conservatism. Since conservatism regards human nature itself as inviolable, as the very foundation of all morality, the attempt to reconstruct human nature by technological art spells the end, the elimination, of conservatism. Human nature will be erased and redrawn by the scientific planners of the age. There will be no human nature left to conserve. Man will have been abolished.

It is also the end of liberalism—but in the sense of this being liberalism's ultimate goal, which is liberating man from any natural limits on his desires, allowing everyone to live "as he wants and toward whatever end he happens to crave"—the very words Aristotle uses to describe extreme democracy. That is why the inherent drive of liberalism to remove all limits to the human will inevitably brings it to transform, stage by stage, a good form of government into its evil opposite, a republic into a mild democracy, a mild democracy into extreme democracy, and extreme democracy into tyranny.

While it might, in the abstract, sound delightfully libertarian to allow everyone to "live as he wants and toward whatever end he happens to crave," the reality is that it leads not to a society of sturdy, self-reliant citizens (Aristotle would have been all in favor of that), but to a selfish, pleasure-addicted populace pulling government in manifold and contradictory directions to satisfy a multitude of incompatible desires. The natural trend in a democracy where everyone aims to live as he wants is for politicians to promise more and more to fulfill the multitude of incompatible desires of the populace. To meet these promises, they print reams of money and borrow in epic proportions. As the system becomes unstable and begins to collapse, the people call for a leader to "bring them out of this crisis." The result is concentrating ever more power in government, which is how extreme democracy leads to tyranny. And, as Lewis warns, at the center of this tyrannical regime will be the small cadre who have the greatest technological power over nature and human nature, the liberal social engineers who want to remake man as they think he should be made. This all too familiar situation is the very one Lewis warned us about over a half-century ago in *The Abolition of Man*.

C. S. Lewis, the Man

Clive Staples Lewis, one of the most beloved Christian apologists of the twentieth century, was an Irishman. His grandfather Richard Lewis had come from Wales and built up an industrial firm from scratch, the successful partnership of MacIlwaine and Lewis: Boiler Makers, Engineers and Iron Ship Builders. Lewis's father, Albert, didn't join the family firm, but became a lawyer (or more accurately, a solicitor as opposed to a courtroom lawyer, a barrister). His mother, Flora, was the daughter of a priest of the (Anglican) Church of Ireland. They were married in 1894, after a lengthy courtship.

Albert and Flora had two children: Warren, who was born less than a year after they were married, and Clive Staples, born in 1898. Not quite ten years after Clive was born, his mother died of cancer. Of this dark childhood experience, Lewis wrote, "With my mother's death all settled happiness, all that was tranquil and reliable, disappeared from my life. There was to be much fun, many pleasures, many stabs of Joy; but no more of the old security."[1] Unfortunately, Clive's father seemed baffled about how to raise his two sons, and Clive and Warren ("Warnie") relied very much on themselves; they remained extremely close and indeed shared a home for the last thirty years of Lewis's life.

Lewis surrendered the name "Clive," which is the Old English equivalent of calling someone "Cliff" (its literal meaning), at age four, after his dog Jacksie was killed, run over by a car. Lewis vowed to take the dog's name as his own, and would answer to nothing else. To his friends, Lewis was ever after known as Jack.

Lewis was not always a man of faith. In fact, as a 15-year-old at Malvern College, he became a professed atheist. He was eventually converted through literature and his expansive imagination, which found its fulfillment in the Christian vision of life. His imagination was fed early on by Beatrix Potter and his own elaborate "Animal-Land" that he developed with his brother Warnie (a literary training-ground for his later Narnian tales).[2] Later it was Greek mythology, the great Icelandic sagas, and the fairy tales and fantasy novels of the Scotsman George MacDonald. And later still it was his scholarly study of literature and the Gospels.

And there was something else: several times in his early life Lewis felt "stabs of joy," which he came to recognize later as visionary flashes of a transcendent reality.[3] These "stabs of joy" all occurred when Lewis was young, that is, before his falling into atheism as a teenager at Malvern College. By this time, he had traded any vestigial Christianity for a fascination with pagan Norse mythology. But the transcendent would not let him alone, and in fact used his pagan fascinations. One day Lewis's eyes fell upon a picture from Arthur Rackham's illustration of *Siegfried and the Twilight of the Gods*. "Pure 'Northerness' engulfed me; a vision of huge, clear spaces hanging above the Atlantic in the endless twilight of Northern summer...." Lewis recognized it was the same feeling that had engulfed him years ago, one of those "stabs of joy."

> And with that plunge back into my own past there arose at once, almost like heartbreak, the memory of Joy itself, the knowledge that I had once had what I had now lacked for years, that I was returning from exile and desert lands to my own country; and the distance of the Twilight of the Gods and the distance of my own past Joy, both unattainable, flowed together into a single, unendurable sense of desire and loss.... And at once I knew... that to "have it again" was the supreme and only important object of desire.[4]

Lewis was again open to the transcendent, but he was not yet open to its implications. While not as bad as his previous nightmarish boarding school (Wynyard), Malvern was a bad fit for Lewis, something even his father recognized. He hired Lewis a private tutor to complete his studies. From there, it was on to Oxford in 1917, interrupted by a brief stint in the Great War, in which he was wounded and invalided home (his brother Warnie also served in the Great War and was a career Army officer). As a student at Oxford, Lewis still regarded himself as a happy pagan—one who had decided that Christianity was all mythology, and not even the best mythology. He was an excellent scholar, and upon graduation was able (after some effort) to land a fellowship at Oxford's Magdalen College in 1925.

Lewis made many deep and lasting friendships at Oxford, including one with the creator of *The Lord of the Rings,* J. R. R. Tolkien, who was enormously influential in helping Lewis appreciate Christianity as something real and tangible. Lewis became first a theist and then, by the end of 1931, a Christian. "And what, in conclusion of Joy?" Lewis later asked. "It was valuable only as a pointer to something other and outer"[5]—the most important something one could ever know.

Lewis's experience of transcendence, an experience that most people feel they have at one time or another, in various ways exemplifies Voegelin's assertion that man "experiences himself as open toward transcendental reality," and that he finds "his true nature through finding his true relation to God." However subjective they may seem to others, these experiences are profoundly real, just as real as our having bodies, and they clarify what we really are, what the world is really like, and what is ultimately worth desiring. Any view of man that systematically denies the reality of these experiences, and that to which they point, and any views of politics built upon this denial, are, in the view of Voegelin and Lewis, distorted and destructive of man as man.

With this all too brief summary of Lewis's background, we can turn to *The Abolition of Man*, an argument in three parts, each representing a chapter: "Men without Chests," "The Way," and "The Abolition of Man." Lewis's subtitle to the book was *How Education Develops Man's Sense of Morality*, but it could just as easily have been subtitled *An Inquiry into the Heart of Modern Liberalism*.

Men without Chests

Lewis begins by focusing on a little book of grammar meant for high school students. "I doubt whether we are sufficiently attentive to the importance of elementary schools textbooks," in this case one "on English intended for 'boys and girls in the upper forms of schools'"[6] (i.e, high school). Out of politeness, he never tells us its actual title, preferring to call it *The Green Book* by Gaius and Titius. (It is in fact *The Control of Language: A Critical Approach to Reading and Writing* by schoolmasters Alec King and Martin Ketley, published in 1939.)

Lewis uses this book to expose a dangerous way of thinking, in fact (as Chesterton rightly argued), the most dangerous way of thinking. It is unlikely that Gaius and Titius had any idea of the harm they were inflicting. It was all done with the best of intentions (as much harm is). Their chief crime is to teach young impressionable minds that we cannot speak the truth, or more exactly, that when we think we are saying something true about reality, we are only describing our own subjective feelings. Gaius and Titius preach the suicide of thought. In this, they simply pass on the poison of skepticism that Chesterton warned against in *Orthodoxy*. They use it to kill the childlike faith in reason, and in doing so, slay what is essentially human, our rationality.

How do they go about it? The authors argue that (for example) when a man says of a waterfall, "That is sublime," he is not actually "making a remark about the waterfall, but a remark about his own feelings. What he was saying was really *I have feelings associated in my mind with the word 'Sublime,' or shortly, I have sublime feelings.*" They add, "This confusion is continually present in language as we use it. We appear to be saying something very important about something: and actually we are only saying something about our own feelings."[7]

Obviously, after Lewis's experiences of "stabs of Joy" far more sublime than any waterfall, he could not let such nonsense go unchallenged. Unfortunately, such nonsense is even more widespread now than in Lewis's day. Gaius and Titius and their kind have done their work well. But the work they have done, Lewis points out, is to make us less than fully human, declaring null and void the human experience of transcendence, but even more, destroying our everyday experience of ourselves as creatures who can know and speak about real things (and not be merely saying something about our own feelings).

As our previous authors have argued, what makes humanity distinct—what defines us *as* human—is our ability and our desire to know. The ability and the desire go together, and we find them together from the time we are very small children. We find that unlike other animals we *can* know things and we *want* to know them. "What's that bug?" "Why do cats have whiskers?" "Where does snow come from?" The merest human child asks such questions all the time. Bugs do not inquire after their own kind. Cats do not ask after their own whiskers. And neither bugs nor cats care about the origin of snow.

That is our common experience. It forms our common sense notion of the difference between animals and human beings. It also instills a common-sense rejection of Gaius and Titius. When a child asks innocently, "What's that bug?" he is not saying something about his feelings (e.g., "I am having curious feelings"). He wants to know what *that* bug is called, and anything interesting about it. When a mother answers, "It's a grasshopper. See its big hind legs. And look at the wings!" she is saying something very important about something, and not just saying something about her feelings (and what would they be?—"I am having answering feelings"?).

Books like that of Gaius and Titius undermine common sense by a kind of cheerful but insidious indoctrination posing as education, introducing sophisticated (or better, sophistic) skepticism where there should be childlike innocence and wonder. There are obvious moral ramifications. If a child says, "That's not fair!" or an adult cries, "That is unjust!" neither thinks that he is merely describing his own subjective feelings. They are speaking about violations of a real moral order.

In both cases, intellectual and moral, we believe that we are saying something about something. We experience a natural connection, then, between our feelings and the real world. Our feeling of curiosity, our desire to know, is directed outward to things outside us, to reality. Our feelings of outrage at unfairness are directed to real actions and real injustices. The so-clever intellectual skepticism and moral relativism of Gaius and Titius aim at the destruction of this natural connection. They aim at the destruction of truth.

There are other varieties of this relativist poison. One kind argues that there is no objective truth, but that all our opinions and feelings are inevitably those of our own sex, class, color, society, or historical era. In this view, the statement "I am disgusted by that senator's adulterous affair" actually means "I live in a particular society historically indebted to the Christian admonition of monogamy and prohibition of adultery, and that society trains the feelings of its members accordingly." Another kind argues that "I am disgusted by the senator's adulterous affair" actually means, "I have an evolved sense of disgust that arose in connection with the desire to ensure that my offspring actually carry my own genetic material rather than the DNA of my mate and another man."

Lewis counters such relativism by saying that the question is not what feelings anyone *happens* to have, or *where* he might have gotten them, but what feelings he *should* have. Education inevitably entails a moral lesson, and, as Lewis notes, it used to be that teachers understood that there was an objective moral reality to which students should be trained to adhere, a reality that was expressed in human nature itself and written into the very cosmos, a reality that we had fallen from but still must try to conform to. One of the great tasks of education was to train our thoughts and feelings to reflect the actual moral order, rather than the disorders of sin. Selfish feelings needed to be replaced by generous feelings, feelings of indifference toward the suffering of others needed to give way to feelings of compassion, feelings of overweening pride must recede and feelings of humility take their place, feelings of greed must concede to feelings of charity, feelings of cowardice must be overcome by feelings of courage. In short, we must *fight* against the wrong feelings with the right feelings, and this fight is real—it is about real things, fighting against real injustice and on behalf of real justice, against real malicious deceit and for the truth, against slavery and tyranny and for real liberty.

It is precisely this *fighting spirit* that Gaius and Titius destroy. In cutting us off at feelings, they attack the very heart of our fighting spirit. Why fight for justice if feelings of injustice are just that— mere feelings? To the degree that these two schoolmasters succeed in convincing students of this, they create "men without chests," men whose reason and passions have been deprived of the middle element, the heart, that yokes reason and passion to moral ends, that gives men their fighting spirit, that makes us firm in the conviction that there are things in this world worth fighting for and defending.

Why would anyone want chestless men? Well, perhaps because men without chests are, it would seem, entirely peaceful men. And here we have stumbled upon another aspect of modern liberalism that explains why it combines moral relativism with a general intellectual skepticism (even while it remains dogmatic about its own views). Liberals think that this is the path to peace.

As Lewis points out, the irony of the Gaius and Titius approach (or the modern liberal approach) is that, contrary to the self-avowed doctrine that words are merely subjective descriptions of feelings, it attempts to train unsuspecting pupils in the "right" connection between words, feelings, and reality, in what is really a 1939 liberal version of "political correctness."

We see the connection quite clearly, claims Lewis, in what Gaius and Titius praise and blame. As for blame, they assert that a mother's appeal to her child to be brave is "nonsense," that the word "gentleman" is "extremely vague," that to call a man a coward "tells us really nothing about what he does," and that patriotic feelings are "about nothing in particular." Yet they heartily approve of those who prefer the arts of peace to the arts of war, and they assert that we "may want to call them wise men." They expect readers "to believe in democratic community life," and they assume that "contact with the ideas of other people is, as we know, healthy."[8]

Lewis underlines one of the ironies of Gaius's and Titius's hidden "value system." While they uphold that "comfort and security, as known to a suburban street in peace-time, are the ultimate values: those things which can alone produce or spiritualize comfort and security are mocked.... [P]eace matters more than honour and can be preserved by jeering at colonels and reading newspapers."[9] They desire an end, but are dismissive of those traits in human nature (what we might shorthand as "traditional morality") that support the end. Part of this is liberal snobbery and faux sophistication against tradition. But it goes far deeper than that. It is no accident that *The Green Book* was written between the First and Second World Wars.

Modern liberalism is based on a fear of war. Liberals would prefer that men be without chests and live in peace, than have chests and be shredded, gassed, mowed down, and blown to unrecognizable bits by the millions. They would prefer that men not be patriots, if patriotism leads to annihilation. They would accept a complete moral and intellectual skepticism, if they could avoid an apocalypse brought on by rival certainties.

But modern liberalism did not begin in the twentieth century; it has a longer pedigree. The kind of liberalism embraced uncritically by Gaius and Titius was born in the midst of the bloody English Civil Wars of the mid-seventeenth century, and just after the even bloodier Thirty Years' War that devastated Europe between 1618 and 1648. These religious-political wars left a permanent scar on the European mind. One of the most scarred was the Englishman Thomas Hobbes, who is the father of modern liberalism (at least, of this type). It was he who first gave us men without chests, and did so out of a desperate desire for peace. Gaius and Titius are his disciples.

With Hobbes, we can see some very important historical connections that give us insight into characteristic aspects of modern liberalism. Hobbes was the first modern thinker to systematically attack the notion that there is any natural, moral order. He argued that the words "good" and "evil" are merely descriptions of our own individual likes and dislikes. He was thus the father of modern relativism. For Hobbes, it was the conviction that there *were* moral truths, and that we must fight for them, that was the cause of all war. He was, we should add, the first to understand that the maintenance of peace in such a relativistic world required the acceptance of political tyranny—and that makes him the father of modern absolutism (and the statism of modern liberalism) as well. If that weren't enough of a patrimony, in his attempts to bend Scripture to the uses of the state (in order to cut short the religious squabbles that led to civil war), he developed an approach to Scripture that makes him the father of modern liberal scriptural scholarship.

An impressive patrimony to say the least,[10] but for our purposes, it is enough to note that the liberal believes men without chests are at least peaceful men. They are peaceful because they are stunted men. They have no desires above the belly and the groin, and if these are amply and indiscriminately satisfied, then the fires of spiritedness will die down and the chest atrophy and become harmless. The liberal believes that if men will just live by bread alone, rather than tearing each other to shreds over the Word of God, a definite historical gain will be made for humanity. If they will give up arguing about ultimate truth, so the liberal opines, they might at last enjoy permanent peace with tolerant relativism. In this vision, the state must be given absolute power to educate and direct men along the lines laid down by Gaius and Titius. Public education must become indoctrination.

We must end "Men without Chests" by making some obvious but important connections to our previous thinkers. Clearly, Gaius and Titius stand in a long line of sophists, running all the way back to Aristotle's time. Although they do not express it explicitly, they share in the blunted, materialist vision of man—they cut off the top of man, the part of him that rises above his animal nature, and leave only his animal feelings. In doing so, they obviously hack out the fullness of human nature as Voegelin outlined it, body, soul, intellect, spirit, leaving only the feelings of the body as the highest reality. As materialists, they are not cosmic patriots with Chesterton, but cosmic traitors turning against the full reality that should define human nature. In pressing for skepticism, they implicitly deny that human beings naturally experience themselves as open to transcendent reality and that we find our true nature in our relationship to God. They close off that reality and relationship as too dangerous and too disruptive of earthly peace. (Or, to take another tack used by liberalism, they allow for transcendence *as long as no one can be either right or wrong about God*; hence they allow for a vague "spiritualism" as having the status of one more subjective feeling—when someone is saying something about God, he is only saying something about his feelings.) Moreover, in accepting moral relativism, they are undermining the conservative assertion, found in Aristotle, that an essential part of politics is the perfection of our moral nature. As Lewis's argument unfolds, we will find more connections.

The Way

Against the liberal vision of Gaius and Titius, Lewis sets another, which he calls *The Way*, but which we might also call "natural law," or "traditional morality," or as the Chinese refer to it (and Lewis follows), the *Tao*.[11] It undergirds "the traditional moralities of East and West, the Christian, the Pagan, and the Jew," all of which recognize that moral standards are ultimately *natural* standards to which we need to submit ourselves for our own good. We may argue about *what* the precise moral standards are, but it is the acceptance of the *reality* of a larger moral order that makes such arguments possible and fruitful. As we have seen with Aristotle's account of slavery, it allows us even to be critical of conservatives.

Lewis's goal in this chapter of *The Abolition of Man* is not to provide a detailed analysis of the Way, but to demonstrate that there is no escape from it (even for the likes of Gaius and Titius). Every-one depends on it, even those who attempt to do away with it. It is, claims Lewis, "not one among a series of possible systems of value. It is the sole source of all value judgements. If it is rejected, all value is rejected. If any value is retained, it is retained."[12]

Liberalism wants to deny this, but it can't. Despite the profession of complete moral skepticism, there are certain, definite moral truths that liberals themselves take as absolute, for example, that peace is good, or that chattel slavery is bad, or that starving your wife if she doesn't meet your sexual demands is an outrage (though approved of by law in Afghanistan).[13] So liberalism is confused—and it is a very good thing that it is, because it is this reluctant occasional concession that there is an objective right and wrong that gives us an agreed upon starting point for moral discussions.

But that common ground is at best precarious. As Lewis shows, liberals are uncomfortable not only with the idea of natural law, but most especially with the idea that it might presuppose a Lawgiver. Liberals flee from God—at least from a definable God, a God of "religion," say, rather than "spirituality"—because they fear him as a God of war and division, a God who sets restrictions on human liberty (especially sexual liberty, as they see it). They will not allow religion as a definite feeling of awe and obligation directed to God as a definite person, even while they are often quite comfortable with an indefinite spiritual feeling directed to anywhere else.

Since they cannot allow a Lawgiver, they seek an alternative source of moral order—and that is, indeed, another defining characteristic of modern liberalism, the attempt to ground morality in anything but God. Modern liberalism has tried one scheme after another of not-God morality: morality as arbitrarily defined by a totalitarian sovereign (Thomas Hobbes); morality defined by an agreement ("social contract") not to harm others if they don't harm us, or not to steal their property if they don't steal ours (Hobbes, John Locke, and Jean-Jacques Rousseau); morality understood as providing the greatest amount of physical pleasure for the greatest number of people (Jeremy Bentham and John Stuart Mill); morality defined by the stronger (Friedrich Nietzsche); morality defined as those instincts that allow us to live together so that the most fit can breed successfully (Charles Darwin); morality defined as tolerating everyone else's entirely subjective view of morality (contemporary liberalism).[14] The one common element in this liberal moral menagerie is the rejection of the essential element defining conservatism: that morality is defined by the Way, the natural law; that is, by the conformity of our minds, hearts, passions, and actions to a moral order created and defined by God.

Here we must be very careful. It might seem that at least some liberals do try to root their views of morality in the natural order. They often seek to find "natural" explanations for human morality, not in traditional natural law, but in Darwin's law. Since this attempt is so pervasive, Lewis took especial care to refute it.

For Lewis, this meant simply showing that Darwinists contradict themselves. They argue, for instance, that "an instinctive urge to preserve our own species"[15] explains and justifies the moral idea of charity or altruism. But this seems to set the argument backwards. They have merely accepted a moral idea common to most religions and then tried to prove that it is actually an instinct. But an "instinct" cannot find or explain or justify some already established, particular moral "trait" that we agree is good and worthy. And the reason is simple: the instinct could just as well support an opposite trait. An instinct to preserve the species, after all, might just as well be expressed by killing off the sickly as attempting to cure them. Moreover, if our presumed instinct to preserve the species really is an instinct—like the spider's instinct to build a web—then we would *already* be obeying it. Like geese flying south for the winter or bears hibernating, we would happily and automatically be fulfilling whatever moral obligations the Darwinist saw entailed in "preserving the species." But if that's true, then why bother pointing that out, any more than a particular fact about our digestive systems? The answer is clear: the Darwinist recognizes that we aren't instinctively trying to be charitable or altruistic. That's what he hopes we will do.

The problem, of course, is that the Darwinist liberal is really sneaking a moral argument about what we *should* do into a particular scientific explanation that is only supposed to describe (as with other animals) what we *actually* do. What we actually do, as the liberal should well know from his fear of war, is indulge in violence and carnage at an alarming rate throughout history. Not only that, but it is quite open to doubt that any such instinct to preserve the species exists. As Lewis notes drily, "I do not discover it in myself. . . . Much less do I find it easy to believe that the majority of people who have sat opposite me in buses or stood with me in queues feel an unreflective impulse to do anything at all about the species, or posterity. Only people educated in a particular way have ever had the idea 'posterity' before their minds at all."[16]

In short, the notion that there is some universal instinct that both binds our actions and orders our other instincts hierarchically is *not empirical* (the very thing a Darwinist claims to be). Some people might have a highly evolved sense of charity or altruism. It might be desirable that everyone should have them. But our experience of the horrors of the twentieth century would seem to be ample empirical counter-evidence to the notion that they are either universal or that humanity is somehow inevitably evolving toward them. By contrast, the natural law explains this doleful situation quite reasonably. Morality is about choosing between good and evil, it requires free will, and so neither charity nor altruism are instinctive. The horrors of the twentieth century make sense if we are creatures that can choose not to be charitable, or twist the meaning of charity toward epic destruction.

The error of liberalism here is at least instructive, and actually supports Lewis. Ironically, even while liberals deny the natural law, at least if they are humane, they borrow from it those parts that they like. According to Darwin's theory, nature is red in tooth and claw, and human evolution is the result of a struggle for existence between tribe and tribe; but the liberal Darwinist, rightly recoiling, borrows a virtue from the natural law, charity, and tries to bend evolution to its support. This is what Lewis means when he says that The Way, the *Tao,* the natural law, "is the sole source of all value judgements. If it is rejected, all value is rejected. If any value is retained, it is retained." To admit that charity *is* good, and that Darwinism does not support it, is to realize that morality is only possible if moral truths are written into the cosmos in another, deeper way.

Yet, we need to remind ourselves, these two "ifs" constitute real choices. It is possible to reject all value, all moral standards, all notions of a real natural law. But it ends in the abolition of man, the subject of Lewis's last chapter.

The Abolition of Man

Our short foray into Darwinism allows for an essential insight into the main point of Lewis's book. Once we regard man as having come about accidentally, that is, by evolution in a godless universe, then human nature itself is taken to be impermanent and hence infinitely malleable. Our nature is putty in our hands, to be reworked into whatever image strikes the fancy of those who have the power to do it. In short, Darwinism gives rise to an urge to take evolution into our own hands.

But, recalling Voegelin, this urge has deeper roots in Gnosticism. Ancient Gnostics argued that matter was evil, created by an evil god. Modern Gnostics assert that matter is evil because it was accidentally contrived. As noted previously, on this view, the "evil god" of the Old Testament is replaced by the equally fickle god, Chance; the spiritual power to escape from the material world is replaced by the technical power to reshape the material world. That is why, in modernity, we measure progress by how far we have nature in our power. But, ironically, "what we call Man's power over Nature turns out to be a power exercised by some men over other men with Nature as its instrument."[17] A fundamental ambiguity arises, one that every conservative must think about long and deeply. Any technological power that can be used *for* men (e.g., television, to inform them), can also be used *against* men (e.g., television as a tool of state or ideological propaganda).

Lewis isn't talking about power in the abstract, but real political power, since the funding of such Promethean power will come from a restricted number of sources, and is therefore most likely ultimately to be funded by governments or those financial powers that control governments. We might wish that we could count on their universally benevolent motives, but more likely, power will be used by those with a very particular agenda, one that sees such power as a means to transform the world and human nature with it. In Lewis's chilling words, "The final stage is come when Man by eugenics, by pre-natal conditioning, and by an education and propaganda based on a perfect applied psychology, has obtained full control over himself. *Human* nature will be the last part of Nature to surrender to Man.... The battle will indeed be won." These victors will be "the man-moulders of the new age ... armed with the powers of an omnicompetent state and an irresistible scientific technique: we shall get at last a race of conditioners who really can cut out all posterity in what shape they please."[18] Behold, the abolition of man, and the creation of something else.

This is not a kind of silly alarmism. We must understand, Lewis warns us, what is unique about our current situation. There have been tyrants in all ages, and there have also been moral relativists who reject the existence of a natural moral order. In ancient Greece there were both—the moral relativists, the "sophists," were all too often advisors to tyrants. But our time is unprecedented because there has arisen a new kind of sophistry that rejects the natural moral order and asserts relativism in a new way with a new kind of argument, and hence forms a new relationship to tyranny. This new kind of sophistry is what we call modern liberalism, and a comparison to its ancient form will reveal the new danger.

The old sophistry of ancient Greece was a philosophical argument; its rejection of the natural moral order was *theoretical.* Since it was theoretical, the battle against sophism by Socrates, Plato, and Aristotle could be waged by finding better, more powerful arguments. But when the rejection is *practical,* that is, when it is *technological,* we face a whole new problem.

The new sophistry works through a union of moral relativism and technical power. "Should we do this?" (which assumes that there is a moral order) is replaced by "How can we do this?" Questions of morality are considered obsolete in the face of practical demonstrations of the technical power to transgress all natural and hence moral boundaries. To take an obvious example, we now have the power to perform a wide variety of experiments on human embryos, including robbing them of their stem cells and killing them. The question today is, for the most part—and certainly for most secular audiences—not *should* we should go about this, but *how*, and *what* can we use these bits of a living human being for? Moral questions are replaced by technical questions.

Or take an example closer to home (literally). Marriage between a man and a woman was once considered natural by society because in the natural order it took the union of a man and a woman to create a child and a family. But the advance of reproductive technology and cloning technology will make this no longer true. Through genetic manipulation and abortion, it will become technically possible for a state to entirely bypass natural human procreation and design its own population, to create the posterity its rulers or managers want it to have. On the day I write this sentence, scientists announced the creation of *one* offspring from *three* parents: sperm from a male monkey, an egg from a female monkey, and additional DNA material from a third monkey. Such experimentation is justified not only because we can do it, but because it is said to open up the possibility of eliminating genetic diseases. It will certainly not end there, any more than the technique of *in vitro* fertilization that allowed it to happen was a scientific end in itself.[19] The moral boundaries are being erased so quickly, one has trouble keeping up. Recently, in the summer of 2009, another interesting "development" took place, one that would make males themselves obsolete: scientists created sperm cells from embryonic stem cells.[20]

The effect of such scientific "advances" on how we regard human sexuality is profound. If the sexual union of a man and a woman becomes just *one* way to make a human being, then it is not *the* way to make a human being, and heterosexuality thereby loses its privileged status in defining what *way* we are to be sexual. The natural gives way to the entirely artificial, and what was once a natural standard defining sexuality—not just heterosexuality as a norm, but traditional marriage, and the already crumbling proscriptions against sexual activity before or outside marriage—becomes a quaint option for sexual antiquarians.

We have discovered what would appear to be a fundamental difference between true conservatism and the new liberalism. A true conservative regards moral limits as natural, somehow written into our nature, something that must be conserved to protect human nature from tyrannical manipulation, degradation, and destruction. By contrast, the new liberalism regards these natural limits as artificial, mere accidents of history or evolution that are not to be revered but tested and surpassed. And we may call this techno-sophistry by the name "the new liberalism" precisely because it seeks the greatest possible liberation of the human will, the liberation from all natural limits. Older forms of liberalism undoubtedly paved the way for the new, but at least some liberals of two centuries ago, like Thomas Jefferson, could invoke deistic natural law as the basis for human rights. That is the case no longer.

And this brings us to a deeper division between conservatism and liberalism. A conservative considers such moral limits to be inviolable because they are natural *and* sacred; that is, what is natural and hence good has been defined by a greater, wiser power. A true conservative will not violate these limits *even if he can*, and in fact, considers his moral caliber to show forth most clearly when he *can* violate them but he *will* not. By contrast, the new liberal as techno-sophist believes we can demonstrate that the limits are not natural or sacred simply by violating them.

The defining difference between true conservatism and the new liberalism is, then, ultimately theological (and it was in no small part through the rejection of religion by the older form of liberalism that it unwittingly paved the way for the new). It was for this reason, among others, that Russell Kirk in *The Conservative Mind* put as his first canon of the "six canons of conservative thought" that the true conservative has a "belief in a transcendent order, or body of natural law, which rules society as well as conscience. Political problems, at bottom, are religious and moral problems."[21] It was for this reason that Eric Voegelin warned that the materialist denial of our openness to God led directly to the horrors of Nazism and is still taking us deeper into sophisticated barbarism today. And indeed, the political problem we face today from the new liberalism is the moral problem of its seeking to go beyond what is human, to go beyond good and evil, to use to the power of the state to create a new creature of its own design.

Part II
Democracy and the Founding
of the American Regime

IN PART ONE, WE NOT ONLY SHOWED WHAT CONSERVATISM IS, BUT also that it isn't a peculiarly American phenomenon. The same is true for contemporary liberalism: it's not distinctively an American thorn in the side of conservatism. And it is not new, but goes all the way back to the ancient Greek sophists.

Now we go to four books that can help us understand the American situation more clearly—specifically, the relationship of conservatism to modern democracy, the American founding, and the American character: Edmund Burke's *Reflections on the Revolution in France* (to contrast that disastrous radical revolution with America's reclamation of lost liberty), Alexis de Tocqueville's *Democracy in America*, Alexander Hamilton's, James Madison's, and John Jay's *Federalist Papers*, and *The Anti-Federalists*.

CHAPTER FIVE

Reflections on the Revolution in France: Edmund Burke

"In history a great volume is unrolled for our instruction, drawing materials of future wisdom from the past errors and infirmities of mankind."

Burke: The Great Conservative Prophet of a New Dark Age

EDMUND BURKE WAS THE MOST INSIGHTFUL POLITICIAN OF HIS time. Had his counsels been heeded, the British government would have understood that taxing the American colonists could lead only to disastrous rebellion. If he had had the ear of the French monarchy and nobility, he would have been the advocate of reform to stave off the looming revolution.

Even in his own time Burke seemed a paradoxical figure: an adamant defender of monarchy who was also a passionate critic of absolute or arbitrary power, including when it came from a king; a staunch British patriot who excoriated British corruption and misgovernment in India; a devout Anglican who defended the rights of Irish Catholics; a self-declared Whig who was one of the greatest critics of liberalism and is today seen as one of the founders of modern conservatism; a reformer whose purpose was always to defend tradition.

Burke was born in Dublin on January 12, 1729, the son of a lawyer, one Richard Burke. Richard was a member of the Anglican Church of Ireland while his wife, Mary, was a Roman Catholic. The three Burke sons were brought up as Anglicans, and the daughter as Catholic.

Burke enrolled at Trinity College when he was fifteen (1744), and read widely in the classics, math, logic, history, and poetry. He was also politically minded. Even as a young man, he smelled the distant smoke of coming catastrophe in Europe. "We are on the verge of Darkness," he wrote to his friend Richard Shackleton in 1746, "and one push drives us in."[1] Precocious as well as prophetic, he wrote a philosophical treatise on *Our Ideas of the Sublime and Beautiful* when he was only nineteen.

After graduation in 1748, Burke went to London, hoping to make a go of it as a writer. His father wanted him to study law, which Burke to some extent did, but the world of letters was his chief love—except for Jane Nugent, the daughter of a physician, and a Catholic, whom he married in the spring of 1757. They had a son, Richard, in 1758.

Burke published a satire, *A Vindication of Natural Society*, in 1756, and his youthful treatise on the *Sublime and Beautiful* a year later. He was also working in these early years on several historical projects. A common theme in his work was the importance of not simplifying reality to fit an abstract and rigid theoretical scheme (such as Enlightenment thinkers liked to do), but to understand reality in its full complexity and detail. Rather than theories of history, Burke preferred the details of histories, and warned that theorists were bad judges of current affairs and likely outcomes. Burke himself was a practical politician, eventually becoming a Whig member of Parliament, but he brought to the task a greater depth and breadth of learning than we are used to seeing in our politicians. Burke signed a contract with *The Annual Register*, begun in 1758, agreeing to serve as its editor and major contributor. In the course of that work, he wrote on history, philosophy, politics, and literature— indeed, it is said by some that he was possibly the *Register's* sole contributor until his election to Parliament in 1765. As such, Burke stands as a great counter-example to politicians who know only politics, or were trained solely and narrowly in the law. That is why Burke remains profound and prophetic, while most politicians are readily (and rightly) forgotten.

His writings quickly brought him prominence in the world of letters, accompanied by the genteel poverty that so regularly afflicts the writer. But his talent and aspirations did qualify him to be a member of the great Samuel Johnson's literary club, which was a circle of the leading intellects of the day. To pay his bills, he became the private secretary of William Gerard Hamilton, a well-off member of Parliament who was also Chief Secretary of Ireland, which meant for Burke a return to his homeland where he became an advocate for Irish Catholics who were oppressed under British law. His criticisms were so powerful that his political enemies frequently accused him of being a secret Catholic. But what motivated Burke—what always motivated him—was a hatred of oppression and of laws that ignored the traditions of the people, in this case the Catholic Irish. After three years in Ireland, he returned to England as secretary to Lord Rockingham. That same year, 1765, Burke was elected to the House of Commons where he became the intellectual spokesman of the Rockingham Whigs, a faction notable not only for blue blood and wealth, but for its support of reconciliation with America and guarding against corrupt monarchical influence in Parliament.

The Whigs, as a whole, represented the merchant class that was keen on limiting monarchical authority. The Tories stood for the crown. In one sense, it was the familiar political struggle between old wealth (Tory) and new (Whig), between the landed wealth of the nobility and the new wealth of commerce. But in a deeper sense, the Whigs stood in a kind of half-way position between the Cavaliers and Roundheads, the monarchists and parliamentarians, the Anglican Church and Protestant Dissenters, the divine-right monarchists and advocates of extreme democracy, who had torn England apart during its Civil War of 1641 to 1651. The Glorious (and bloodless) Revolution of 1688, which ushered out the Catholic James II (who had once been supported by the Tories), and ushered in the Protestant William of Orange, was a glorious or at least competent compromise made by the Whigs: a monarchy limited by Parliament.

It was this compromise that Burke sought to defend, to *conserve*, as a Whig. He thus battled against King George III because he thought the king had ambitions to be an absolute monarch. At the same time, Burke was most certainly a conservative Whig. He was a vehement opponent of self-serving Whig oligarchs, and a blistering critic of Whig radicals whose Enlightenment ideas he saw illustrated in blood and tyranny in France.

Being a man who stood on principle, he often had to stand outside of political power, and was most often in opposition in Parliament. Yet, when he took up the unpopular causes of the American colonists, the native population of India, and the Catholics of Ireland, his opponents recognized Burke's greatness of mind and speech. That greatness found its biggest target in the French Revolution.

Burke's *Reflections on the Revolution in France* (1790) is considered by many to be the first great modern conservative masterpiece, a book written in the spirit of Aristotle with the rhetorical power of Cicero. It was a warning to the world that the radicalism underlying the revolution of 1789 was only a foretaste of the destruction to come. Many called Burke a prophet even in his own time, since he prophesied that the foolish policies of England toward the American colonists would lead to rebellion, and even more vividly, that the French Revolution, however glorious its beginning seemed, would soon drench its own citizens in an orgy of blood. But we who have lived to see the apocalyptic devastations of the twentieth century can understand all too clearly the dread future glimpsed by Burke, that spread from France to the world. In his prescience, Burke was like Winston Churchill who saw, before many others did, that Bolshevism (communism) was a menace to the world (and not, as many liberals believed, a progressive, rational, "humanitarian" form of government), and that the Nazis were aggressive barbarians who had to be stopped and could not be appeased or ignored. What allows such prophetic powers, wherever they occur, is seeing things from the right vantage point.

The Conservative Vantage

It has often been asserted that Burke was a defender of tradition for tradition's sake, a conservative only in the sense that he detested change and defended settled habits merely because they were his and they were settled. But that is to misunderstand Burke entirely. He defended tradition against innovation because tradition is the repository of prudence, the commonsense wisdom rooted in the long experience of human nature.

With Aristotle, Burke believed that society is natural to man; it is not, as liberals and radicals would have it, some kind of artificial social contract—a view championed in Burke's time by

Jean-Jacques Rousseau and picked up by the radicals of the French Revolution. Against such views, Burke thundered, "Society is indeed a contract," but not a mere "partnership agreement in trade" or an agreement of abstract rights. Rather,

> It is a partnership in all science; a partnership in all art; a partnership in every virtue and in all perfection. As the ends of such a partnership cannot be obtained in many generations it becomes a partnership not only between those who are living, but between those who are living, those who are dead, and those who are to be born. Each contract of each particular state is but a clause in the great primeval contract of eternal society, linking the lower with the higher natures, connecting the visible and invisible world, according to a fixed compact sanctioned by the inviolable oath which holds all physical and moral natures, each in their appointed place.[2]

We have here the essentially Aristotelian notion, repeated by Chesterton and Voegelin, that politics must be rooted in the whole human being, body and soul, and that the proper order of human affairs somehow represents the full reality of the cosmos, from the merest material elements to the most exalted spiritual elements. Our given nature is the sure standard of morality, and to acknowledge the Giver of the gift is entirely natural. Thus, all reasonable societies, says Burke, "perform their national homage to the institutor and author and protector of civil society," recognizing God as the one who gave them both human nature and the means of its perfection, "the state."[3] As Aristotle argued, we are political animals, for society is the proper context of our perfection and happiness.

And this brings us to the importance of particular traditions. For Burke, a "nation," a "state," or a "people" are particular things, with their own particular conditions, history, laws, traditions, customs, manners, and prejudices, and if these have endured for any length of time, they must have some grounding in human nature. The worst error—which the French revolutionaries made—is to damn all ancient institutions, manners, and customs because of their flaws, and to uproot and destroy a society and try to build an entirely new and perfect one from scratch.

The Secular Revolution of the Philosophes

Burke calls the French Revolution a "philosophic revolution,"[4] a satirical tag referring to the *philosophes*, the radical Enlightenment secularists like Voltaire and Diderot, who sought to replace traditional society—and most especially the Catholic Church—with a society based entirely on reason.[5]

The hostility to traditional Christianity so evident among the French revolutionaries came from their secular self-assurance—(*they* had seen the light, hence the term "Enlightenment")—that Christianity was the chief superstitious obstacle to be overcome. The Enlightenment Gnostic spirit, as Voegelin later described it, animated the revolutionaries. They believed that they alone had a complete vision of the truth. As Burke said, the "leaders of the legislative clubs and coffeehouses are intoxicated with admiration at their own wisdom and ability. They speak with the most sovereign contempt of the rest of the world."[6]

One essential lesson that such secularist revolutionaries ignore, a lesson taught both by pagans such as Aristotle and Christians such as St. Augustine, is that *the* greatest problem is wickedness or sin—not social classes, not private property, not the lack of powerful technology, not the ignorance or inattention to mathematics, astronomy, chemistry, or physics. That is a lesson that history itself teaches. In Burke's words, "In history a great volume is unrolled for our instruction, drawing the materials of future wisdom from the past errors and infirmities of mankind. . . . History consists for the great part of the miseries brought upon the world by pride, ambition, avarice, revenge, lust, sedition, hypocrisy, ungoverned zeal, and all the train of disorderly appetites."[7]

These vices are found spread throughout humanity, in both male and female, in every time, every race, every social class, and every situation. Sin is the problem. The effects of these vices can be understood and in some way ameliorated, but they cannot be erased by man without destroying him, so deeply does the stain of sin go. Against this wisdom, the French revolutionaries declared presumptuously that *they* were founding a Republic of Virtue, and then proceeded to act with a viciousness that shocked the world.

The ultimate source of that viciousness was their rejection of Christianity, for in rejecting Christianity, they rejected sin. In rejecting sin, they believed that the causes of human misery in history could be cured entirely by human effort. The source of the corruption in political life, so the Enlightened thought, was not in the soul but in bad social institutions, in unjust social orders, and especially in a religion that held the doctrine of original sin. Destroy the social institutions, obliterate the social orders, annihilate Christianity, and construct by force an entirely "rational" secular order, and all problems that had plagued previous ages would magically disappear.

Yet the rejection of sin by itself could not explain the revolution's furious destructive bent. What came with it was a spirit of profanation. For those who reject the sacred, nothing is sacred— not the desecrated churches; not the guillotined priests and nuns;

not the massacred women and children; not property, tradition, customs, manners, or laws. Nothing is holy; anything may be destroyed for the sake of the revolutionary utopia. This spirit of profanation filled the populace with a "black and savage atrocity of mind," which superseded "in them the common feelings of nature as well as all sentiments of morality and religion."[8] This bold spirit of profanation, they believed, would usher in a new, just social order.

Instead, the people got Robespierre and the Reign of Terror (1793 to 1794), ever more degrading social chaos, and then, to bring order out of mayhem, the dictator Napoleon (1799)—all of which were prophesied by Burke in his *Reflections* in 1790.[9]

Burke's visionary powers were not the result of some inner magical gift. They came from his respect for the lessons of history and the reality of human nature; they come in short from Burke's conservatism. The French Revolution is not something dead and gone; the same spirit ran through the devastations of Marxism; it is running now through secular liberalism. All of this keeps Burke's prophecies fresh, his analysis still painfully accurate—only the characters and countries have changed.

The Preparation for Revolution by the Intelligentsia

One of the most fascinating aspects of Burke's analysis, one too often overlooked, is the kind of intellectual-cultural preparation for revolution perpetrated by the Enlightenment intelligentsia in the decades leading up to the French Revolution. "The literary cabal had some years ago formed something like a regular plan for the destruction of the Christian religion. This object they pursued with a degree of zeal which hitherto had been discovered only in the propagators of some system of piety. They were possessed with a spirit of proselytism in the most fanatical degree." The radical Enlightenment intelligentsia realized that to gain power they must first gain control of the most important "medium of opinion. To command that opinion, the first step is to establish a dominion over those who direct it. They contrived to possess themselves, with great method and perseverance, of all the avenues to literary fame.... To this literary monopoly was joined an unremitting industry to blacken and discredit in every way, and by every means, all those who did not hold to their faction."[10] A great part of their efforts were spent in *retelling history* in such a way that the Christian religion was the single source of all misery and oppression, priests were all crafty hypocrites preying on a superstitious population, and religion was the source of all wars and the great superstitious obstacle to human social and scientific progress.[11]

The parallels between the *philosophes* who ushered in the French Revolution and secular liberals today should be obvious—the domination of the media, the politically correct retelling of history, especially the desire to "blacken and discredit" traditional Christianity. All of this brings them "to rake into the histories of former ages (which they have ransacked with a malignant and profligate industry) for every instance of oppression and persecution which has been made by that body [the clergy] or in its favor in order to justify, upon very iniquitous, because very illogical, principles of retaliation, their own persecutions and their own cruelties."[12]

Again we face the revolutionary's terrible simplifications. He looks for evil only in one class of men (not in himself or his own kind); his zealous but myopic search for that class's faults gives him the deep impression that he has found *the* source of evil; he is then easily convinced that the elimination of this class would bring the elimination of all evil, and any means that would bring about the elimination of all evil is justified in his mind. Now that *the* enemy has been identified, all that is needed to exterminate evil, so he thinks, is a concentration of power in the right hands and the determination to eliminate the irredeemable classes—in the case of the French Revolution, the clergy and the nobility.

The Collapse and Concentration of Power into Extreme Democracy

The Reign of Terror, like the terrible atrocities committed by Hitler, Lenin, Stalin, Mao, and Pol Pot, is still largely misunderstood as an aberration of the high principles of the revolution, rather than (as Burke would argue) a fulfillment of them. How could *liberté, égalité, fraternité* turn so quickly into the bloodlust tyranny of the Jacobins? We have seen one cause: Enlightenment propaganda that all evil was located in the nobility and the Church, and its implication that all virtue and goodness resided in the secular rationalists and the common people. It is no accident, then, that the terror was carried out by Maximilien de Robespierre, a disciple of Rousseau, and the poor working-class radicals, the *sans-culottes*, who had been primed by propaganda to destroy the nobles and the clergy.

This Reign of Terror would still not have come about if power had not been radically centralized by the revolutionaries. The revolution not only dispensed with the monarchy, but it collapsed the Three Estates of the French government—the First Estate (the clergy), the Second Estate (the nobility), and the Third Estate (the commoners, which ran from wealthy bourgeoisie to the workers)—into one. The Third Estate, drawing all power and representation into itself, was renamed the National Constituent Assembly on July 9, 1789. The result was what Aristotle called "extreme democracy" (or what Burke calls a "pure democracy"). "If I recollect rightly," Burke notes with dry wit, "Aristotle observes that a democracy has many striking points of resemblance with a tyranny." Burke warned that "in a democracy the majority of the citizens is capable of exercising the most cruel oppressions upon the minority whenever strong divisions prevail in that kind of polity, as they often must; and that oppression of the minority will extend to far greater numbers and will be carried on with much greater fury than can almost ever be apprehended from the dominion of a single scepter."[13] In short, an angry massive mob can do much more damage than a king. The danger of an extreme democracy is that nothing obstructs its will, nothing stands in the way of its destroying anything, including itself.

But the mob does not lead itself; it is headed by the handful of revolutionaries. It is the radicals that form and direct the passions and direction of the many. Let us follow them as they assume power.

Full of pent-up zeal from years of coffee-house discussions of what *they* would do if only they had power, suddenly the power is theirs, and all things seem possible if only they can centralize power and apply enough force. As they are theorists rather than realists, they have little understanding of practical politics, or human nature, or even basic economic principles. They are impatient with arguments from history, because the only history they know is the propaganda drilled into them by their own clique of historians, which has dismissed the past as something to be gotten over. They are supremely confident that they have all the answers, and in their haste to apply them they have a "fondness for tricking shortcuts," where the "defects in wisdom are to be supplied by the plenitude of force."[14] Because of their lack of real political wisdom, they are easy prey for charlatans. "By their violent haste and their defiance of the process of nature, they are delivered over blindly to every projector and adventurer, to every alchemist and empiric."[15] And so, the predictable happens: having discounted the voices of experience and prudence, the radicals are perplexed at the chaos that ensues when their cherished plans, with all their obvious (but unexamined) difficulties and defects, are put into effect.

"The great machine, or paper-mill, of their fictitious wealth"

Having been all too successful in their attack on the order and wealth that created and supported the power they have now seized, the revolutionaries face a serious problem. The revolution—and the inevitable chaos and mismanagement that have followed—causes industry to collapse and men with money to be eager to hide it. But the revolutionaries need money to fund their grand visions of a new social order. "They panted for a currency of any kind which might revive their perishing industry."[16] Their answer: printing paper money.

Why resort to printing money? There are three sources of income open to governments: taxation, confiscation, and the printing of worthless paper currency. Newly established revolutionaries seldom use taxation because they cannot afford to create immediate hostility in the populace. The wealthy are still too powerful, and could more easily raise antagonistic armies if taxed. In the French Revolution, the middle class and the poor—the main constituents represented in the Third Estate—were the very ones that the revolutionaries claimed to represent, and they obviously weren't too keen to foot the revolutionary bill. In France, there was an "easy" answer—confiscate all Church lands.

The answer was "easy," not only because the Church itself couldn't fight back, but also because the radical Enlightenment propaganda had already blackened the Church and therefore made it ripe for pillage. The brilliant plan of the revolutionaries was to take the land and print paper currency (called *assignats*) that represented the stolen property (or more exactly, what it would be worth upon its sale). Thus, the secular revolutionaries had complete control of the Church (which they would soon abolish, desecrating churches and murdering clergy), and its wealth could be used to fund their costly political vision. Behold, the first Bolsheviks!

Such a glorious plan would need a little brute force for implementation. The revolutionaries "rendered their paper currency compulsory in all payments."[17] But the more frightened the honest and industrious became, the more they hoarded real wealth—not only gold, but the fruits of their industry. Revolutionaries are rarely industrious; that is, they know how to spend wealth, but not how to produce it. The result is that they try to spend their way out of the political crisis they have caused by printing even more paper currency to fill the gaps between the cost of their promises and their dwindling revenue.

The obvious problem, obvious at least to anyone with a real grasp of economic and political history, is that such "paper circulation" is "not founded on any real money deposited or engaged in,"[18] it does not represent gold or silver, but is merely *fiat* currency, a piece of paper *declared* to have value as a legal tender for trade even though it represents nothing but the mere command of the government that it must be accepted. The effect of madly printing *faux* money, Burke warns, must be "to put the whole of what power, authority, and influence is left" in the crumbling regime "into the hands of the managers and conductors of this [paper] circulation." That is, power passes (1) into those who speculate on land, rather than use it to produce goods, and (2) into those who speculate on money itself—two entirely unproductive and predatory groups, who come to control the government. These two groups, which Burke calls the "new dealers, being all habitually adventurers and without any fixed habits of local predilections, will purchase to job out again, as the market of paper or of money or of land shall present an advantage."[19] The speculators have no love of the regime itself, no healthy patriotism, no rootedness in the soil; they care only for quick profits. Since the source of their wealth is not real substantive wealth, but the production of wealth based upon speculation on the ephemeral and baseless paper currency, the basically sound pre-revolutionary economy is quickly turned into a post-revolutionary gambling casino enabled by the government. Burke trumpets,

> Your legislators . . . are the very first who have founded a commonwealth upon gaming, and infused this spirit into it as its vital breath. The great object in these politics is to metamorphose France from a great kingdom into one great playtable; to turn its inhabitants into a nation of gamesters; to make speculation as extensive as life; to mix all its concerns and to divert the whole of the hopes and fears of the people from their usual channels into the impulses, passions, and superstitions of those who live on chances.[20]

Of course, the runaway inflation caused by printing ever more money produces even more speculation, turning people away from productive labor that makes long-term wealth and forcing them by fear into becoming short-term speculators madly bent on keeping their present assets from disappearing overnight. If we might use a handy analogy, they watch the daily perturbations of the speculative stock market rather than watching over the livestock in the fields. Who benefits from this situation? "The truly melancholy part of the policy of systematically making a nation of gamesters is this, that though all are forced to play, few can understand the game; and fewer still are in a condition to avail themselves of the knowledge. The many must be the dupes of the few who conduct the machine of speculations."[21]

The mass of people, who were promised so much, end up living in fear, not knowing the worth even of their own labor, as the printed paper is worth less in the evening than it was that morning. Burke chides the revolutionaries:

> With you a man can neither earn nor buy his dinner without a speculation. What he receives in the morning will not have the same value at night. What he is compelled to take as pay for an old debt will not be received as the same when he comes to pay a debt contracted by himself, nor will it be the same when by prompt payment he would avoid contracting any debt at all. Industry must wither away. Economy must be driven from your country. Careful provision will have no existence. Who will labor without knowing the amount of his pay? Who will study to increase what none can estimate? Who will accumulate, when he does not know the value of what he saves? If you abstract it from its uses in gaming, to accumulate your paper wealth would be not the providence of a man, but the distempered instinct of a jackdaw.

Even in 1790, less than a year after the Assembly voted to snatch the Church's lands and issue the paper *assignat*, Burke could easily predict the effects, especially on the common rural man.

> What effect it must have on the country people is visible. The townsman can calculate from day to day, not so the inhabitant of the country. When the peasant first brings his corn to market,

the magistrate in the town obliges him to take the assignat at par; when he goes to the shop with his money, he finds it seven per cent the worse for crossing the way. This market he will not readily resort to again. The townspeople [who need the food of the farmer] will be inflamed; they will force the country people to bring corn. Resistance will begin, and the murders of Paris and St. Denis may be renewed through all France.[22]

Those who control the money, but do not produce any of the basic goods related directly to the provision of food, clothing, heat, and shelter, will end up forcing those who do work to provide them with necessities. They must use force because the real producers realize that there is no selling their goods for a profit when they are paid in inflationary currency. The power that was promised to the people by the revolutionaries is soon used against them, as the ruling clique becomes ever more concentrated on the preservation of its own power and new-found privileges. And so, warned Burke,

France will be wholly governed by the agitators in corporations, by societies in the towns formed of directors of assignats, and trustees for the sale of church lands, attorneys, agents, money jobbers, speculators, and adventurers, composing an ignoble oligarchy founded on the destruction of the crown, the church, the nobility, and the people.[23]

The Republic of Paris

The economic crisis brought on by the revolutionaries had the natural effect of concentrating power in a very few hands in "the city of Paris; and this I admit is strongly connected with the . . . principle of paper circulation and confiscation. . . . The power of the city of Paris is evidently one great spring of all their policies. It is through the power of Paris, now become the center and focus of jobbing, that the leaders of this faction direct, or rather command, the whole legislative and the whole executive government."[24] Under the old regime, there were still feudal divisions of power throughout France, but now power was concentrated at the capital.

The revolutionaries abolished the old regional, local, feudal repositories of power and divided France "into eighty-three pieces, regularly square, of eighteen leagues by eighteen [a bit over 50 miles by 50 miles]." These were called *Departments*. They were further squared into geometrically perfect subunits, *Communes*, and then *Cantons*. They were wonderfully, mathematically precise, but ignored the historical boundaries that had evolved naturally over the centuries.[25] This didn't bother the revolutionaries, because the dusty past was to be discarded in favor of what was *scientific* and *efficient*. The revolutionaries believed that politics could be a science based on mathematics and physics, and this freed them to treat men as numbers, or as pieces on a squared political game board to be moved by the technocrats in Paris.[26] This, of course, is utterly at odds with a conservative's proper understanding of human nature and of natural law and that political regimes are built upon local loyalties. As Burke wrote:

> No man ever was attached by a sense of pride, partiality, or real affection to a description of square measurement. He never will glory in belonging to the Chequer No. 71, or to any other badgeticket. We begin our public affection in our families. No cold relation is a zealous citizen. We pass on to our neighborhoods and our habitual provincial connections. These are our inns and resting places. Such divisions of our country as have been formed by habit, and not by a sudden jerk of authority,

were so many little images of the great country in which the heart found something which it could fill. The love to the whole is not extinguished by this subordinate partiality.[27]

Those local enclaves of affection—intermediate institutions, we might call them—are precisely what the revolution destroys. Centralized power advances as local attachments are dissolved, as families are broken apart, as neighborhoods and counties become ever more dependent on the distant government, either through fear or funding. An antipathy to regional loyalties, local government, the authority of the church, and the authority, integrity, and rights and responsibilities of families, in short, to any thing that stands between the individual and the state, runs through the French Revolution, every Marxist revolution, and the liberalism of our own time.

France had been a great kingdom; it had turned itself into a charnel house. Burke concluded: "No common folly, no vulgar incapacity, no ordinary official negligence, even no official crime, no corruption, no peculation, hardly any direct hostility which we have seen in the modern world could in so short a time have made so complete an overthrow of the finances and, with them, of the strength of a great kingdom." He then quotes Cicero: "*Cedo qui vestram rempublicam tantam amisistis tam cito?*" "Tell me, how did you lose a republic as great as yours so quickly?"[28] It's a question our children might someday ask us.

CHAPTER SIX

Democracy in America:
Alexis de Tocqueville

"Materialism is a dangerous malady of the human mind in all nations; but one must dread it particularly in a democratic people...."

Tocqueville: The Aristocratic Prophet for American Democracy

IT IS A MATTER OF SOME INTEREST, TO SAY THE LEAST, THAT A 25-year-old French aristocrat could visit America for only nine months at the beginning of the 1830s and produce what is surely (in Harvey Mansfield's words) "the best book ever written on democracy and the best book ever written on America."[1] The two volumes of Alexis de Tocqueville's *Democracy in America* (published in 1835 and 1840) remain the classic texts describing the strengths and weaknesses of the American character, and what we have most to hope for and to fear. Turning the pages of *Democracy in America* can be a shocking, and salutary, experience.

Alexis de Tocqueville came from an ancient Norman family that took its name from the village of Tocqueville, which it owned as a fief. Born in 1805, Alexis was a true child of the French Revolution—a revolution that almost prevented his being born at all. His father, Hervé de Tocqueville, and mother, Louise, were snatched up on December 17, 1793, as enemies of the state during the Reign of Terror, and kept in prison in Paris awaiting the guillotine. The guillotine claimed the lives of Louise's grandfather, Chrétien-Guillaume de Lamoignon de Malesherbes, and Malesherbes' sister, daughter, son-in-law, as well as a granddaughter and her husband. Malesherbes, a lawyer, made the mistake of defending King Louis XVI before the revolutionary National Convention, which had already decided that both the king and all nobles were criminals. Hervé de Tocqueville and his wife Louise were saved only because the architect of the Reign of Terror, Robespierre, was himself guillotined on July 28, 1794.

Alexis was born a year after Napoleon Bonaparte crowned himself emperor of France. He was ten when Napoleon was defeated at the Battle of Waterloo in 1815, and came to manhood under the restored monarchy of the Bourbon kings, Louis XVII (1815 to 1824) and Charles X (1824 to 1830). As his father had endured the first French Revolution, Alexis was a witness to the second, in July 1830, when King Louis-Philippe, a supporter of the original French Revolution, ousted Charles X who was trying to reestablish an absolute monarchy. And Alexis was later a witness to a third revolution, in 1848, when Napoleon's nephew, Charles-Louis-Napoleon Bonaparte, deposed King Louis-Philippe and became president of the Second French Republic. The Republic soon became the Second French Empire (1852), and Louis-Napoleon Bonaparte was crowned Emperor Napoleon III (1852 to 1870). Alexis died during his reign, in 1859.

Alexis de Tocqueville certainly saw the destructive side of popular government, but he believed that democracy was an irresistible albeit ambiguous force—the rule of the many could, as Aristotle had noted, take positive or negative forms. In 1831 the young Alexis sailed to America with his friend Gustave de Beaumont. Their ostensible goal was to investigate the American penal system, but the real goal was to understand the pure, orderly democracy of the United States. "I confess that in America I saw more than America," Tocqueville wrote in the first volume of *Democracy in America.* "I sought there the image of democracy itself, with its penchants, its character, its prejudices, its passions; I wanted to become acquainted with it if only to know at least what we ought to hope or fear from it."[2]

We might say, as an Aristotelian clarification of Tocqueville, that what we find in the pages of *Democracy in America* is the republican and democratic aspects of popular government wrestling to see which shall determine the American regime. Obviously, from his title, Tocqueville did not make use of Aristotle's distinction between the good and bad forms of popular rule. He simply called the popular form by one name, "democracy." Yet, as we'll soon see, he was much like Aristotle in looking for distinct beliefs and characteristics of popular government, and dividing its good propensities from its bad. He therefore ends up giving us something very like Aristotle, a way to judge our national character, and the caliber and direction of our political regime.

The American Character
(and the American Constitution)

It might seem out of place, at least historically, to read Tocqueville before reading the Federalist and Anti-Federalist works written over forty years earlier, during the debates surrounding the ratification of the Constitution. We discuss Tocqueville before discussing the Constitutional debates on grounds that Tocqueville himself set out: if you want to understand a nation, you must first understand the "prejudices, habits, dominant passions, of all that finally composes what is called national character," all of which are found in a people's earliest experiences.[3] We must understand out of what material the nation was *constituted* before we can understand its written *Constitution*—the duplication is intentional and instructive.

The Americans were a *particular* people, as all nations are. From the beginning, they were defined by social equality and by strong religious beliefs. The religious refugees who first settled these shores arrived with "no idea of any superiority whatsoever of some over others."[4] They came to a land with no titled nobility and no political order at all; and the order they created was an order of self-governing farmers. In Europe, the land was cut into hereditary aristocratic estates. By contrast, "the American soil absolutely repelled territorial aristocracy." It was clear to everyone that with all the raw, available land, "nothing less than the constant and interested efforts of the property owner himself were necessary" to be an independent farmer, and so the "territory was therefore naturally cut up into small estates that the property owner alone cultivated."[5] This laid the foundations for the strong property-holding middle class, rooted in agriculture, which has always defined America.

But even more important was the religious foundation, particularly the strong Puritan influence in New England. If the French Revolution with all its excesses was the result of Enlightenment skepticism, the American Revolution and its successes can be ascribed to the particular Christian principles of the American colonists. "The emigrants or, as they so well called themselves, the *pilgrims*, belonged to that sect in England whose austere principles had brought the name Puritan to be given to it. Puritanism was not only a religious doctrine; it also blended at several points with the most absolute democratic and republican theories."[6] The Puritans' political egalitarianism was matched by a theological egalitarianism that all men were equal before God. In fact, it was their understanding that sin affected all men that made them distrust monarchical or aristocratic government, for this gave individual sinful men too much power. Undergirding the Puritan vision was the absolute moral authority of God as known through Scripture.[7]

We can see Tocqueville's conservative bent in picking out these starting points as defining the solid and good foundation of the American regime. While Tocqueville thought of himself as a kind of liberal—an aristocrat suspicious of privilege who saw the promise as well as the perils of popular rule—he was certainly not a liberal in our contemporary sense. Like Burke and Chesterton, he was a liberal who was actually a conservative, as we use the terms now. He saw in the American character what had made the American experiment a success, and he pinpointed the American people's Christianity, their self-reliance, and their long traditions of self-government. He knew that it was this character that had shaped the Constitution, not the Constitution that had shaped that character. But it was a character with both strengths and weaknesses. That is a very important point for conservatives to remember, especially today. The meaning and effectiveness of our Constitution depend upon the strengths of our character. If the strengths fail, the weaknesses will render the Constitution a meaningless and ineffective piece of parchment.

Self-Government from the Ground Up

In America, government was not something that was imposed from above, but something that grew up from seeds planted on local ground. It was not a theoretical beginning point, but a very practical one. Self-government, we might say, was a necessity before it was a theory, arising from the practical needs of a people starting

from scratch, who from the very beginning were responsible for ruling themselves. What in Europe was a matter of theoretical discussion among proponents of popular government was in America a
matter of practical urgency. Americans were on the cutting edge of
modern political theory because they were on the practical edge
of cutting down forests and planting crops. As Tocqueville noted,
this gave Americans a decided advantage over Europeans.

> The general principles on which modern constitutions rest, the
> principles that most Europeans of the seventeenth century hardly
> understood and whose triumph in Great Britain was then incom-
> plete, were all recognized and fixed by the laws of New England:
> intervention of the people in public affairs, free voting of taxes,
> responsibility of the agents of power, individual freedom and
> judgment by jury were all established there without discussion
> and in fact.
>
> These generative principles were applied and developed as
> no nation in Europe has yet dared to do.[8]

They were "applied and developed" in America *because* of our
particular situation, a situation that helped form our political
character. With no already established national government
above us, we had to be political animals, developing and perfecting our political nature as individuals through self-government. We had to establish our own government on local ground,
and these solid foundations were happily still quite visible when
Tocqueville arrived. In the America of the early 1830s, Tocqueville recognized that the localism, the strong family ties, township, county, and state governments were natural buttresses
against tyranny from above. In his words, "It is . . . in the township that the force of free peoples resides." A township is the

most natural governing unit—something akin to the village for Aristotle, a community of families—a unit so natural that it "appears to issue directly from the hands of God."[9] Here, people know each other intimately, and govern themselves directly in the affairs that most touch their daily lives and hence, are most near and dear to them. Here is true sovereignty of the people; here is the school of ordered liberty that provides the most solid foundation for the larger society.

> The inhabitant... is attached to his township because it is strong and independent; he is interested in it because he cooperates in directing it; he loves it because he has nothing to complain of in his lot; he places his ambition and his future in it; he mingles in each of the incidents of township life: in this restricted sphere that is within his reach he tries to govern society; he habituates himself to the forms without which freedom proceeds only through revolutions, permeates himself with their spirit, gets a taste for order, understands the harmony of powers, and finally assembles clear and practical ideas on the nature of his duties as well as the extent of his rights.[10]

The organic growth of political life in America, Tocqueville emphasizes, marks the key difference between the way in which political power and freedom manifest themselves in Europe and America. "In most European nations, political existence began in the higher regions of society and was communicated little by little and always in an incomplete manner to the various parts of the social body." But in "America, on the contrary, one can say that the township had been organized before the county, the county before the state, the state before the Union."[11] That essential difference gives us the key to understanding why, in the twentieth and now twenty-first centuries, Europeans are much more easily led into top-down socialism, while Americans bristle at it.

Well-ordered Liberty

Since Americans built their social order from the ground up, their understanding of liberty is quite the opposite of extreme democracy's view of liberty as the freedom to do whatever one wants. Rather, for Americans, liberty is an achievement, the result of individuals learning to rule themselves; that is, true liberty rests on a solid moral foundation. Liberty is not license, let alone, as modern liberalism would have it, licentiousness. Tocqueville quotes an excerpt of a speech by one John Winthrop approvingly:

> [N]or would I have you to mistake in the point of your own *liberty*. There is a *liberty* of corrupt nature, which is affected both by *men* and *beasts*, to do what they list; and this *liberty* is inconsistent with *authority*, impatient of all restraint; by this *liberty*, *Sumus Omnes Deteriores* [we are all inferior]; 'tis the grand enemy of *truth* and *peace*, and all the *ordinances* of God are bent against it. But there is a civil, a moral, a federal *liberty*, which is the proper end and object of *authority*; it is a *liberty* for that only which is *just* and *good*; for this *liberty* you are to stand with the hazard of your very *lives*.[12]

We note, with Tocqueville, that in this conservative account of liberty, it is our nature as rational animals that is being conserved, our better nature that lifts us above the beasts and distinguishes us as moral animals. The religious foundation for the moral order is not imposed arbitrarily, as some would claim today. Rather, the "ordinances of God" are bent against a liberty that is mere license to act as beasts—or, as Aristotle said, worse than beasts, for "without virtue," man "is the most unholy and the most savage" of all animals.

That is why, Tocqueville points out, for Americans "the *spirit of religion* and the *spirit of freedom*" go hand in hand.[13] "Freedom sees in religion the companion of its struggles and its triumphs, the cradle of its infancy, the divine source of its rights. It considers religion as the safeguard of mores"—from the Latin word *mos,* meaning habit or custom—"and the mores as the guarantee of laws and the pledge of its own duration."[14] Self-government begins with the moral government of the self. Without it, ordered liberty slips into chaotic license, and sturdy republicanism slides into extreme democracy. About this Tocqueville issues a strong warning to Americans: watch that your love of true liberty rooted in virtue is not destroyed by other, lesser loves, including the love of equality itself.

The Love of Liberty and the Passion for Equality

While a friend of American democracy, Tocqueville was well aware of the dangers inherent in the American passion for equality, a passion that leads all too quickly to extreme democracy and the destruction of liberty.

> There is in fact a manly and legitimate passion for equality that
> incites men to want all to be strong and esteemed. This passion
> tends to elevate the small to the rank of the great; but one also
> encounters a depraved taste for equality in the human heart that
> brings the weak to want to draw the strong to their level and that
> reduces men to preferring equality in servitude to inequality in
> freedom. It is not that peoples whose social state is democratic
> naturally scorn freedom; on the contrary, they have an instinctive
> taste for it. But freedom is not the principal and continuous object

of their desire; what they love with an eternal love is equality; they dash toward freedom with a rapid impulse and sudden efforts, and if they miss the goal they resign themselves; but nothing can satisfy them without equality, and they would sooner consent to perish than to lose it.[15]

Tocqueville agrees with Aristotle that extreme democracy leads to a tyranny, although in America it is likely to take the form of a tyranny of the majority.[16] The tyranny is not imposed from without, but arises from an inordinate love of equality, what we might call "egalitarianism." "I think that democratic peoples have a natural taste for freedom," remarks Tocqueville. "But for equality they have an ardent, insatiable, eternal, invincible passion; they want equality in freedom, and, if they cannot get it, they still want it in slavery."[17]

Such egalitarianism can lead to the tyranny of relativism—a belief that no way of life, no religion, no morality can be judged to be better than any other. To make choices better and worse means to decide between right and wrong, and that would set up an evaluative hierarchy. Since extreme democracy is defined by everyone doing whatever he wants, such evaluation is itself considered evil (or, as we would say, "intolerant"). Each person decides for himself what is good and evil, and that is why in extreme democracy, the egalitarian impulse leads man to make a god of himself. As Tocqueville warns, pantheism is the natural religion of egalitarian democracy. The extreme egalitarian satisfies his desire for ultimate equality by "enclosing God and the universe within a single whole."[18] Needless to say, self-divinization strives to remove all limits on government, because there is nothing that such a man can deny himself. But the release from objective moral order also means social chaos, and the only remedy is the ushering in of tyranny. Thus, a too great passion for equality leads to the madness of tyranny, but it is not the only kind of madness about which Tocqueville warns Americans.

The Mad Pursuit of Material Happiness

Another risk to democracy in America is materialism, even in regard to religion. In the 1830s Tocqueville ran into evangelists who preached the gospel of prosperity: instead of focusing on heaven, the "American preachers constantly come back to earth and only with great trouble can they take their eyes off it. To touch their listeners better, they make them see daily how religious beliefs favor freedom and public order," that is, they inadvertently try to "sell" the Gospel as *useful.* As a result, "it is often difficult to know when listening to them if the principal object of religion is to procure eternal felicity in the other world or well-being in this one."[19]

Americans have always had a strong streak of materialism: they came to an undeveloped land, and they had to provide for themselves, focusing first of all on their physical wellbeing. In addition, from early on, America was the land of opportunity: a place where a poor man could come and make his fortune. Certainly much of this familiar story is a positive one, but a problem arises when a man becomes so *bent* on practical matters, on the production of wealth, on the acquisition of material goods, that his soul becomes defined entirely by the pursuit of material things. That makes him a blunted man. "Materialism," Tocqueville writes, "is a dangerous malady of the human mind in all nations; but one must dread it particularly in a democratic people.... Democracy favors the taste for material enjoyments. This taste, if it becomes excessive, soon disposes men to believe that all is nothing but matter; and materialism in its turn serves to carry them toward these enjoyments with an insane ardor."[20]

Is the merely material man a happy man? He is certainly a restless, agitated man. As Tocqueville famously said of Americans, "One cannot work more laboriously at being happy."[21] The problem is that, in America, anyone may rise *and* anyone may fall. There are no set social classes into which one is born. Social fluidity means that every poor man has the possibility of becoming rich, and every rich man the possibility of becoming poor. Poor men are filled with envy, rich men are filled with fear, and everyone is filled with anxiety. "In America I saw the freest and most enlightened men placed in the happiest condition that exists in the world; it seemed to me that a sort of cloud habitually covered their features; they appeared to me grave and almost sad even in their pleasures."[22]

Everyone is focused on satisfying "the least needs of the body" and providing "the smallest comforts of life,"[23] because the satisfaction of these material gratifications is also a sign of success. The problem for Americans is not (as in aristocracy) that they will indulge in exotic and forbidden pleasures, but rather that they will lose their souls in the mad pursuit of non-forbidden pleasures: a bigger house, a more comfortable chair, a more expansive wardrobe. "Among material goods there are some whose possession is criminal," and these, Tocqueville asserts, Americans generally avoid. "There are others the use of which is permitted by religion and morality; to these one's heart, one's imagination, one's life are delivered without reserve; and in striving to seize them, one loses sight of the more precious goods that make the glory and the greatness of the human species."[24] Democratic men can become mere consumers who toil all week in order to consume trivial entertainments on the weekend.

The soul shrivels in such circumstances, but it also rebels. Materialism can't satisfy the soul of man; the constant pursuit of material gratifications produces "the singular melancholy that the inhabitants of democratic lands often display amid their abundance, and the disgust with life that sometimes seizes them in the midst of an easy and tranquil existence." This is a deadly serious condition. In France, says Tocqueville, the characteristic despair brought on by materialism is responsible for increasing rates of suicide. In America, however, "suicide is rare, but one is sure that madness is more common than everywhere else." Tocqueville explains that "Americans do not kill themselves, however agitated they may be, because religion forbids them from doing so, and because materialism [as a philosophical dogma]...does not exist among them, although the passion for material well-being is general." That is, the passion for material well-being has in America not yet become the full-blown materialism against which Tocqueville warns; religion has, thus far, kept Americans from the natural end of materialism, which is suicide, the despair of a man who knows that his pursuit of material gratification has no ultimate end and no final satisfaction. Yet Americans often hang on to their lives by a thread. "Their will resists, but often their reason gives way," and their melancholy drives them to insanity.[25]

Even if the pursuit of material gratification does not drive one to madness, it certainly tends to make Americans agitated and this-worldly. As Tocqueville notes, Americans are restless and "dream constantly of the goods they do not have." Indeed, the "inhabitant of the United States attaches himself to the goods of this world as if he were assured of not dying, and he rushes so precipitately to grasp those that pass within his reach that one would say he fears at each instant he will cease to live before he has enjoyed them. He grasps them all but without clutching them, and he soon allows them to escape from his hands so as to run after new enjoyments."[26] To point out the obvious, such this-worldliness is in direct conflict with the religious foundation of self-government—not by making men atheists, but by gradually, persistently washing away their connection to a transcendent source of moral order.

Sounds like an uncomfortably familiar situation. Tocqueville is nothing if not prophetic. During the Cold War he was often quoted for having predicted that the United States and Russia would be the great nations of the future. But today, other prophecies hit us harder. How about this one? Our characteristic agitation and social-climbing means that "In the United States, a man carefully builds a dwelling in which to pass his declining years, and he sells it while the roof is being laid; . . . He settles in a place from which he departs soon after so as to take his changing desires elsewhere."[27] Part of this is caused by house envy. As Tocqueville, remarked, "One must not conceal from oneself that democratic institutions develop the sentiment of envy in the human heart to a very high degree,"[28] and envy drives us ever upward in the housing market. The credit gap—the yawning chasm between what we could buy according to our actual income and what we in fact bought through mortgages and credit cards—is entirely understandable in terms of our character as described by Tocqueville in the 1830s.

Any more prophecies waiting to be fulfilled? As we know from Aristotle, or from simple observation, one danger of democracy is that the many poor are driven by envy of the few rich, and when the masses come to power, they either seize the property of the rich directly or indirectly through taxation. America, however, has been different because of our large property-owning middle class. "The profuse spending of democracy," Tocqueville notes, "is. . . less to be feared as the people become property owners, because then, on the one hand, the people have less need of the money of the rich, and on the other, they encounter more difficulties in not striking themselves with the tax they establish."[29]

But a great danger that Tocqueville warned about is coming to pass. Our characteristic passions (egalitarian envy, restless impatience, intense desire for immediate gratification of material wants) are in danger of overcoming our characteristic middle-class prudence. Many Americans, including many in the middle class, have been complicit in living far beyond their means—not only in mortgages and credit card debt, but in the astronomical federal government debt. If they begin to see the federal government as the source of every satisfaction that would otherwise extend beyond their reach, they might just give up their liberties to a government that, through ever-increasing taxes, tries to provide their every want.

Conserving the American Constitution

We can now see what it should mean to conserve the American constitution—with a small "c." Our constitution is, first of all, those original traits and institutions that provided the firm foundation for self-government: social order built from the family up; political order built from the town and township up; and moral responsibility built up from the individual before God. That is what must at all costs be conserved; that is what true conservatism strives to maintain and, if it should fall into decay, restore. So, oddly enough, when conservatives say that we need to get back to the Constitution, they are not going back far enough. The Constitution is, by itself, a mere parchment with a set of assertions. But if the Constitution is understood as presupposing and protecting the original traits and institutions that preceded it, then it is a work of political genius that guides and fosters self-government. And now that we have a better understanding of our character, we may turn with a more discerning eye to the debates surrounding the adoption of our Constitution.

CHAPTER SEVEN

The Federalist Papers: Alexander Hamilton, James Madison, and John Jay

"The moment we launch into conjectures, about the usurpations of the federal government, we get into an unfathomable abyss, and fairly put ourselves out of the reach of all reasoning.... [We should] confine our attention wholly to the nature and extent of the powers [of the federal and state governments], as they are delineated in the constitution. Everything beyond this, must be left to the prudence and firmness of the people; who, as they will hold the scales in their own hands, it is to be hoped, will always take care to preserve the constitutional equilibrium between the general and the state governments."

Recovering the Great Debate

IN THIS AND THE FOLLOWING CHAPTER WE ARE DEALING WITH THE arguments concerning the ratification of the U.S. Constitution. Roughly speaking, the Federalists argued for ratification, and the Anti-Federalists argued against. But while that rough distinction is accurate, it is also not very illuminating. It would be an improvement to say that the Federalists wanted a strong national government and the Anti-Federalists feared it, putting their trust, instead, in state and local governments. Yet, it would be confusing to leave it there, because it would lead us to believe that the two sides were caught in a wholly incompatible either-or argument: either one national government or thirteen state governments. What makes the debate about the Constitution so complex and enduring is that it was a both-and, not an either-or debate. Both Federalists and anti-Federalists wanted a federal system of government; that is, a government consisting of two distinct but interrelated aspects, *both* a governing power that represented the union of the states *and* the separate governing powers of each state in that union. The disagreement, in great part, was how to set it up.

The Federalists feared dissolution of the union, anarchy, and national weakness, and the remedy for them was to put enough power in the national government to avoid these ills. It also cannot be denied that the Federalists were in addition animated by the prospect of America becoming a great and powerful nation, a vision that demanded a strong and ambitious national government.

The Anti-Federalists feared the tyranny and loss of local liberty and independence that goes with a powerful centralized government, and the remedy, for them, was to ensure that the national government, however necessary, was not made too strong. They, too, had their fears. They were unwilling to have fought so bloody a war against the British crown, only to lose their local liberty and independence to an all-dominating and ambitious national government. The Anti-Federalists had their vision as well, but it was not one of national glory; it was one of freedom and independence of local communities and states.

I think it is fairly accurate to say that our Constitution (along with the Bill of Rights) represents this tension between the Federalists and Anti-Federalists, rather than a victory for either side. To be more accurate, it *is* largely a Federalist creation, and hence leans toward making the national government stronger than the states, but with safeguards. Unfortunately those safeguards have in some respects been knocked over, and many things have occurred over the last two centuries, especially over the last century, that have strengthened the federal government to a point that would scare even the most devout Federalist. Many conservatives today find themselves making the very same kind of arguments made over two hundred years ago by the Anti-Federalists. What a prudent conservative statesman needs to do is help us find our way back to the balance the Framers of the Constitution thought they had achieved.

In reconsidering our founding, we must not forget the obvious historical context of the debate. Here, etymology is instructive. The Latin word *constituere* means "to set up." The Constitution is quite literally the "set-up" of the government, or more specifically, the federal government; the state governments were well-established long before the idea of a union.

The great press for a union of the states came with the Revolutionary War (1775–1783), arising from the need for a united effort against a common enemy. The notion of a *national* legislative body arose with the First Continental Congress (1774) that set out the common grievances against the British king. It grew with the Second Continental Congress (1775), called specifically to carry out a united and effective war effort, and with the issuance of the Declaration of Independence (1776) that confirmed the American nation as an independent national entity of "free and independent states." This point cannot be overstressed: the need for a national government was born amidst the exigencies of war.

The national governing body received its first official "set-up" with The Articles of Confederation and Perpetual Union, ratified in 1781, the year that brought the effective end to the war with the defeat and surrender of Lord Cornwallis at Yorktown. The official end came with the Treaty of Paris (1783). It took only half a dozen years for many, including the national congress (the Congress of the Confederation), to conclude that the Articles of Confederation were sadly inadequate and needed to be reformed. Instead of carrying out a mere reform of the Articles, the famous Philadelphia Convention of 1787 (driven by Federalists Alexander Hamilton and James Madison) turned the call for revision into an opportunity to draft a new Constitution. This new Constitution was then sent to the thirteen states for ratification. The *Federalist Papers*, written on behalf of ratification by Hamilton, Madison, and John Jay (using the pseudonym Publius), began appearing in late October 1787. The last of them, Number 85, is dated August 15, 1788. The Constitution was officially ratified with the affirmation of the ninth state, New Hampshire, in late June 1788. (The last state to ratify the Constitution was Vermont on January 10, 1791.) Largely to assuage the fears of the Anti-Federalists, the Bill of Rights, or first ten amendments, introduced in 1789, was ratified by the states into the Constitution by the end of 1791. Such is the end of the story. Now let's return to the time when ratification was yet a matter of debate.

The Need for a Strong Federal Government (and Money to Support It)

Perhaps the most succinct statement of the Federalist position is uttered by Alexander Hamilton in Federalist 33. Hamilton asserts that the framers of the Constitution in the convention "foresaw, what it has been a principal aim of these papers to inculcate, that the danger which most threatens our political welfare, is, that the state governments will finally sap the foundations of the union...."
As hard as it is to believe today, the Federalists during the time of

the Constitutional debates feared that strong state governments would simply overwhelm the new and feeble federal power representing the union. Something had to be done to give some substance and strength to the union or it would unravel, and the states would go their separate ways. The context of Hamilton's statement is a discussion of the federal "power of taxation," the "most important of the authorities proposed to be conferred upon the union."[1]

Hamilton's position is quite simple. Everyone agrees a union is necessary, even the Anti-Federalists. That means that certain definite powers must be placed in the national government. But it is a "fundamental maxim of good sense and sound policy... that every POWER ought to be proportionate to its OBJECT...."[2] If the national government has certain defined tasks, then it must have the appropriate *means* to carry them out, and the most important means is money. Money is "the vital principle of the body politic; as that which sustains its life and motion, and enables it to perform its most essential functions."[3] For this reason, "the power of taxation... is the most important of the authorities proposed to be conferred upon the union."[4]

It is difficult to fault Hamilton in his desperate plea for sufficient funds for the union. During the Revolutionary War, the Continental Congress had to beg the individual states for money, and the national treasury was often embarrassingly and dangerously depleted. The Articles of Confederation did little to remedy the situation. This "experience of the insufficiency of the existing Federal Government"[5] as defined by the Articles of Confederation seared into Hamilton and the Federalists the conviction that they would never again "leave the general government in a kind of tutelage to the state governments," a situation that (as they learned all too painfully during war) was "inconsistent with every idea of vigour or efficiency" in the national government.[6]

The powers of the new Federal Government must be sufficient to carry out its duties, and mandated power without adequate money is a body without life-blood. The national government cannot be in a position of having to beg from the states, a fact all too clearly understood in 1787 at the rag-end of the war. "We...have reached almost the last stage of national humiliation," lamented Hamilton at the first of December of that year. As a result of the war, the national government owes "debts to foreigners, and to our own citizens," and there is no "proper or satisfactory" way to pay them off. "Are we in a condition to resent, or to repel the aggression" of foreign powers? No, "We have neither troops, nor treasury, nor government." Public credit in these dangerous times?

> We seem to have abandoned its cause as desperate and irretrievable. Is commerce of importance to wealth? Ours is at the lowest point of declension. Is respectability in the eyes of foreign powers, a safeguard against foreign encroachments? The imbecility of our government even forbids them to treat with us: Our ambassadors abroad are the mere pageants of mimic sovereignty....to shorten an enumeration of particulars which can afford neither pleasure nor instruction, it may in general be demanded, what indication is there of national disorder, poverty, and insignificance, that could befal [sic] a community so peculiarly blessed with natural advantages as we are, which does not form a part of the dark catalogue of our public misfortunes?[7]

There can only be one remedy for providing a sufficient flow of funds to restore the health and vigor of the union, "that of permitting the national government to raise its own revenues by the ordinary methods of taxation,"[8] rather than depending on the states to supply it voluntarily. That is, the national government must be able to tax individuals *directly*. No merely theoretical argument about the structure of government will have any effect without providing life-giving funds to the national governing body.

How Much Blood Is Enough?

At this point, Hamilton steps into dangerous territory, at least from the point of the Anti-Federalists. Granting that a national government is necessary and that you cannot have a national government continually begging states for a penny here and a penny there, what limit should be placed on the federal power of taxation? Hamilton argues, quite bluntly, that "the federal government must of necessity be invested with an *unqualified power of taxation* in the ordinary modes."[9] This he takes to be the logical result of following the maxim that "the means ought to be proportioned to the end," so that in regard to taxation, "there ought to be no limitation of a power destined to effect a purpose, which is itself incapable of limitation."[10]

Unlimited power of the Federal Government manifested in the unqualified power of taxation? The wildness of this claim is somewhat subdued if we look at the immediate context, where the concern is "national defence" and "securing the public peace against foreign or domestic violence...."[11] It is certainly quite impossible to predict when national military threats will arise, and what will be necessary, in terms of funds, to address them.

The difficulty is that Hamilton actually draws a much larger scope for the ends of the Federal Government, and hence the necessary funds to support it. The Federal Government needs the unlimited power of taxation because our wants as a nation are unlimited. If we listen to the Anti-Federalists, who want to put a quite definite limit on the Federal power of taxation, Hamilton tells the reader,

> [O]ne would be led to conclude, that there was some known point
> in the economy of national affairs, at which it would be safe to
> stop, and to say: Thus far, the ends of public happiness will be pro-
> moted by supplying the wants of government, and all beyond this
> is unworthy of our care or anxiety. How is it possible that a gov-
> ernment, half supplied and always necessitous, can fulfill the pur-
> poses of its institution; can provide for the security, advance the
> prosperity, or support the reputation of the commonwealth? How
> can it ever possess either energy or stability, dignity or credit, con-
> fidence at home, or respectability abroad?... How can it under-
> take or execute any liberal or enlarged plans of public good?[12]

Certainly, the Federalists' main concern is with the national
defense.[13] But, to say the very least, Hamilton has in mind a rather
larger shopping list of "wants." With Hamilton, we have a vision
of the power and scope of national government that seems suspi-
ciously "liberal," one that foresees the need for ever "enlarged
plans of public good." This vision is moderated, as liberalism tends
not to be, by his understanding that the Constitution supplies a
rightful balance of power between the states and a limited federal
government.

Indeed, Hamilton dismisses the charge that he is setting the
country up for an overweening federal government. "The moment
we launch into conjectures, about the usurpation of the federal government, we get into an unfathomable abyss, and fairly put ourselves out of the reach of all reasoning." There is no need to worry
because, "the state governments, by their original constitutions, are
invested with complete sovereignty." For that very reason, the real
worry is actually the continuing power of the state governments,
because they "commonly possess most influence" over the people,
so that "there is greater probability of encroachments by the mem-

bers [i.e., the states] upon the federal head, than by the federal head upon the members." Look at the actual Constitution, instructs Hamilton, where the "nature and extent of the powers" of state and federal governments are clearly delineated. Madison concurs: "The powers delegated by the proposed constitution to the federal government, are few and defined. Those which are to remain in the state governments, are numerous and indefinite." And so, concludes Hamilton, "Every thing beyond this, must be left to the prudence and firmness of the people, who, as they will hold the scales in their own hands, it is to be hoped, will always take care to preserve the constitutional equilibrium between the general and the state governments."[14] They must keep balanced the "stability and energy" of the national government with the "liberty" of local rule.[15]

The Constitution provides the limits, argue the Federalists. It is the burden of the people to ensure that the federal government does not transgress them. "If the federal government should overpass the just bounds of its authority, and make a tyrannical use of its powers; the people, whose creature it is, must appeal to the standard they have formed," warns Hamilton, "and take such measures to redress the injury done to the constitution, as the exigency may suggest and prudence justify."[16] Federal encroachments would surely result in a swift and determined reaction. "The ambitious encroachments of the federal government, on the authority of the state governments" would cause a "general alarm," and "Plans of resistance would be concerted" by the states, adds Madison.[17]

From what we have just learned, resistance to the ambitious encroachments of the federal government should not be difficult—at least it wasn't at that time. The original national government was weak because it lacked money. Thus it would seem that to weaken a too-strong federal government, simply reduce the flow of tax money, and the "ambitious encroachments" must recede for lack of blood to nourish them. Or, to be more conservative, ensure that the blood flow is minimal all along, and the federal government will be forced to limit its ambitions. If it's that simple, how, then, has the federal "creature" become so big? Perhaps we need a short history lesson.

A Short History of Taxation: Wars, Rumors of Wars, and Endless Crises

It was the Revolutionary War that taught the Federalists the need for a strong, well-funded federal government. Wars always strengthen national power. Such national emergencies make the case for centralized authority easy and compelling; and of course taxes are needed to meet the crisis. What we have learned, however, is that once the emergency has been met, the taxes often remain in place; government expands to imbibe them.

Before the twentieth century, the United States seemed to avoid this trap. Up until the Civil War, every attempt at significant direct federal taxation was quickly rebuffed or soon repealed, and excise taxes (e.g., on tobacco, sugar, distilled spirits) and import taxes were the main sources of federal revenue. The first federal income tax was passed with the Revenue Act of 1861 to pay for the extremely costly Civil War, but happily, it was abolished in 1872, and the federal government had to live on excise taxes again, supplemented by tariffs. In 1913, however, with the passage of the Sixteenth Amendment, Congress was empowered "to lay and collect taxes on income, from whatever sources derived," and World War I caused this power to be put to immediate use. Federal income taxes started their long and continual expansion. Taxes were lowered during the boom years of the 1920s, but were raised again during the economic crisis of the Great Depression. The Social Security Act of 1935 contrived a new method of taxation, and the welfare state was born with it. This set in stone a fundamental *dependence* of the people directly on the federal government, and people who depend on federal power are exceedingly unlikely to resist or rebel against its "ambitious encroachments" for "enlarged plans of public good."

World War II expanded national power even further, and a method of "painless" taxation was devised—income tax withholding. In the name of efficiency, it helped make the people less vigilant about the government's confiscatory tax power. Even more ominous, the people began seeing themselves not as jealous guardians of their own liberty, but as beneficiaries of government programs: not just Social Security, but Medicare, Medicaid, and other programs, all of which required more taxation. The Reagan era Economic Recovery Tax Act of 1981 and Tax Reform Act of 1986 tried to reverse the ever-increasing bloat of direct federal taxation. The Clinton administration tried to make a reverse of the reverse, raising the taxes on upper income levels. The Bush administration tried to constrict the tax flow once again, but Bush's domestic fiscal policies and two wars drove America into extreme debt, which exploded into an "economic crisis" that the Obama administration has used to justify a massive expansion of government spending and a doubling of the money supply in less than a year.

The lesson seems fairly obvious: it is the government's increased powers of taxation that have allowed it to grow—expansions that Alexander Hamilton justified in theory, though he might not have justified the particulars in practice.

The Federalist Plan for Inflating the National Government: Soft Despotism?

The fact is, the blueprint for expanding federal power was given in the *Federalist* itself. Again, the context is important. At the time

of the Revolution the state governments were indeed well-established and more powerful than the feeble, fledgling federal
government. The problem, as the Federalists saw it, was how the
federal government could gain any power at all. To be more
exact—and profound—the Federalists believed that their bid for a
stronger central government was working *against* human nature.

Local politics come first because our affection, our love, is first
of all local—our family, our town, our city. *That* is why, argue both
Hamilton and Madison, we don't have to worry about the development of a strong national government. In Hamilton's words,

> It is a known fact in human nature, that its affections are com-
> monly weak in proportion to the distance or diffusiveness of the
> object. Upon the same principle that a man is more attached to
> his family than to his neighbourhood [sic], to his neighbourhood
> than to the community at large, the people of each state would
> be apt to feel a stronger bias towards their local governments,
> than towards the government of the union, *unless the force of that
> principle should be destroyed by a much better administration of the lat-
> ter* [emphasis added].[18]

That is a big "unless," a key to what could reverse the natural
conservative emphasis on the local over the national. Hamilton
even outlined a strategy for attaching people to the national government: "The government of the union, like that of each state,
must be able to address itself immediately to the hopes and fears
of individuals; and to attract to its support, those passions, which
have the strongest influence upon the human heart."[19] This meant
that federal laws should not just be directed to the states; rather,
"we must extend the laws of the federal government to the individual citizens of America...."[20] Extending the laws of the federal

government directly and deeply into the intimate lives of individual citizens fostered affection for and dependence on the national government—even at the expense of state and local governments. Hamilton continues,

> [T]he more the operations of the national authority are intermingled in the ordinary exercise of government, the more the citizens are accustomed to meet with it in the common occurrences of their political life; the more it is familiarized to their sight, and to their feelings; the further it enters into those objects, which touch the most sensible cords, and put in motion the most active springs of the human heart; the greater will be the probability, that it will conciliate the respect and attachment of the community.... A government continually at a distance and out of sight, can hardly be expected to interest the sensations of the people. The inference is, that the authority of the union, and the affections of the citizens toward it, will be strengthened, rather than weakened, by its extension to what are called matters of internal concern; and that it will have less occasion to recur to force, in proportion to the familiarity and comprehensiveness of its agency. The more it circulates through those channels and currents, in which the passions of mankind naturally flow, the less it will require the aid of the violent and perilous expedients of compulsion.[21]

It is important that this insight is offered to placate Anti-Federalist fears that the national government shall constantly need to use military force to compel citizens, against their nature, to obey a distant national government over their state and local governments. Hamilton ingeniously suggests that greater dependence of individuals on the national government will make the need for force all but unnecessary! And he was right. That is the "genius" of the welfare state. It literally supplants all local affections, all natural ties, and replaces them with a national "big brother" or nanny state. The duties of a husband and father are taken over by the welfare state which provides child support. The duties of a wife and mother are taken over through state-supported daycare. The individual depends directly on the national government, rather than on the family and neighborhood.

About a half-century later, Tocqueville described this relationship as "soft despotism," a despotism "more extensive and milder" than occurred in ancient tyrannies, one that "would degrade men without tormenting them."[22] Tocqueville saw the possibility of soft despotism as a result of our character, more than our Constitution—more the result of our passion for equality and our envy, our passion for immediate material gratification, our devotion to self-interest at the expense of virtue, and our impatience at getting what we desire. All these things, warned Tocqueville, could lead us, step-by-willing-step, into the gentle hands of a soft but despotic federal government. Tocqueville's powers of prophecy in trying to "imagine" the "new features" of this despotism are chillingly accurate. Tocqueville envisioned that

> an immense tutelary power is elevated [above the people], which alone takes charge of assuring their enjoyments and watching over their fate. It is absolute, detailed, regular, far-seeing, and mild. It would resemble paternal power if, like that, it had for its object to prepare men for manhood; but on the contrary, it seeks only to keep them fixed irrevocably in childhood; it likes citizens to enjoy themselves provided that they think only of enjoying themselves. It willingly works for their happiness; but it wants to be the unique agent and sole arbiter of that; it provides for their

security, foresees and secures their needs, facilitates their pleasures, conducts their principal affairs, directs their industry, regulates their estates, divides their inheritances; can it not take away from them entirely the trouble of thinking and the pain of living?

So it is that every day it renders the employment of free will less useful and more rare; it confines the action of the will in a smaller space and little by little steals the very use of free will from each citizen. Equality has prepared men for all these things: it has disposed them to tolerate them and often even to regard them as a benefit.

Thus, after taking each individual by turns in its powerful hands and kneading him as it likes, the sovereign extends its arms over society as a whole; it covers its surface with a network of small, complicated, painstaking, uniform rules through which the most original minds and the most vigorous souls cannot clear a way to surpass the crowd; it does not break wills, but it softens them, bends them, and directs them; it rarely forces one to act, but it constantly opposes itself to one's acting; it does not destroy, it prevents things from being born; it does not tyrannize, it hinders, compromises, enervates, extinguishes, dazes, and finally reduces each nation to being nothing more than a herd of timid and industrious animals of which the government is the shepherd.[23]

Timid and industrious animals, the ultimate "men without chests." Hamilton would no doubt have cringed at this outcome, but he lacked Tocqueville's prophetic powers to see its likelihood. With the other Federalists, Hamilton thought the Constitution had sufficient safeguards against an excessive concentration of power in the federal government; and he also warned the people that, ultimately, *they* must be vigilant. Again, we must remember the context: the Federalists were trying to strengthen a very weak, very new federal government against well-established state governments. And even in strengthening the federal government, the Federalists were careful to insert additional checks on federal power.

"Ambition must be made to counteract ambition."

The Federalists attempted to ward off the danger of centralized power by pitting the national government against itself. Our celebrated division of powers—the separation of the federal government into three branches, the executive, legislative, and judicial— was designed to act as a constant check on the aspirations of any person or group that attempted to take tyrannical control of the national government. Rather than setting up a Constitution that allows all power to flow into one pool, the genius of the Federalists (working upon the arguments of Montesquieu[24]) was to set the separate powers in a kind of perpetual antagonism. It is a "great security against a gradual concentration of the several powers in the same department," if each such department—the president, Congress, and the judiciary—have both the "necessary constitutional means, and personal motives, to resist encroachments of the others.... Ambition must be made to counteract ambition."

It may be a reflection on human nature, that such devices should be necessary to control the abuses of government. But what is government itself, but the greatest of all reflections on human nature? If men were angels, no government would be necessary. If angels were to govern men, neither external nor internal controls on government would be necessary. In framing a government, which is to be administered by men over men, the great difficulty lies in this: You must first enable the government to control the governed; and in the next place, oblige it to control itself. The dependence on the people is, no doubt, the primary control of government; but experience has taught mankind the necessity of auxiliary precautions.[25]

The Federalists considered the legislative branch to be the most likely place for power to concentrate. So, in regard to Congress itself, the ambitions to power were further checked by dividing "the legislature into different branches," the House and the Senate, and rendering "them by different modes of election, and different principles of action, as little concerned with each other" as possible.[26] Thus, rather than having an efficient, vigorous, wholly united federal government, one that *could* use its great energy in a united effort for good, the Federalists envisioned the three branches as three giants tied together at odd angles by tight ropes, a step forward by one causing a painful pinch and a reaction by the other two.

The Federalists were willing to sacrifice significant energy and efficiency because they realized an important conservative principle. Among mere human beings, power is ambiguous. The power to do great good is also the power to do great evil. Since human beings are inclined toward wickedness, and absolute power corrupts absolutely, we would be safer hamstringing federal power.

One of the key differences between conservatism and liberalism emerges precisely here. Despite what some conservatives might think, liberals want to do great good and they realize that great power is necessary to do it. As secularists, they have largely discarded any notion of human sin as a pervasive toxin in every human heart. Certain classes of people may be corrupt, but there is no fundamental corruption plaguing man. All that is needed to fix our problems is power, which they assume they can wield with unambiguous goodness. For this reason, liberals chafe at the federal checks and balances and incline to methods of political change that disregard them, such as using the judiciary as a legislative power to make laws, or allowing the president to have special czars and make endless use of executive agencies not accountable through elections to the people, or bypassing protective legislative procedures to ram through favored programs. If the president and the Judiciary both take upon themselves the power to make laws, then we no longer have a division of power, but all three branches expressing the same power.

Happily, the "dependence on the people" is still "the primary control of government," and conservatives, at least, can see the wisdom of the further check against tyranny of the federal government in the Constitution, the election of a third of the Senators and of all the Representatives every two years.

Yet, it seems that mere procedural checks and balances are not enough. If our character is bad, then no formal institutions, no formal mechanisms, can save us from contriving our own self-destruction as a nation. Without virtue, no clever balancing of powers can thwart the passions that have so regularly led to the inner collapse of great nations. The importance of virtue, of character, brings us to our last topic, the nature of the American Republic as understood by the Federalists.

The American Republic?

We recall, from Aristotle, the important distinction between good and bad political regimes, and hence the important distinction between a republic and a democracy, where a republic was rule of the many directed toward the true good as defined by virtue, and democracy was rule of the many directed toward their own satisfactions. Both the Federalists and Anti-Federalists agreed that Americans should be a republic, but they had important disagreements about what that meant. The Federalists argued for a new, expanded definition of a republic—one big enough to fit a large nation consisting of distinct, sovereign states. The Anti-Federalists held to the older notion of republic—that a true republic, defined by virtue and familial and local affection, could only exist on a smaller scale. The Anti-Federalists believed that the state defined the largest possible limit of a republic, and that the union should be considered a union of sovereign republics. (Hence the importance in the Constitution of Article IV, Section 4: "The United States shall guarantee to every State in the Union a Republican Form of Government..."). For the Anti-Federalists, once a government reaches beyond a particular size, it must necessarily be despotic in order to rule effectively over so large a territory.

The Federalists understood the Anti-Federalist position well, and attempted to answer it. For better or worse, they answered it by redefining what "republic" meant. Madison argued that the union was "a confederacy founded on republican principles, and composed of republican members...." For this reason, a "superintending government" was necessary, one that possessed both authority and power "to defend the system against aristocratic or monarchical innovations."[27] To shore up against the congealing of an American aristocracy, the Constitution demanded that "No Title of Nobility shall be granted by the United States" (Article I, Section 9). Here, a republic is contrasted with kingship and aristocracy, the latter two undesirable because of their tendency to degrade, into their respective bad forms, tyranny and oligarchy. By contrast with the rule of the one or few, republican government "requires that the sense of the majority should prevail."[28] But "sense of the majority" does not mean democratic rule. The Federalists did not want majority rule to degrade the government from a republic into a kind of majority dictatorship. Virtue and the true common good still had to define the government.

What the Federalists proposed was a kind of national republic over the several state republics, each with its own proper domain. The "general government is not to be charged with the whole power of making and administering laws," Madison noted. "Its jurisdiction is limited to certain enumerated objects, which concern all the members of the republic, but which cannot be attained by the separate provisions of any."[29] Simply put, the national republican government is charged with the task of doing those things, *and only those things*, that state governments cannot (such as regulating commerce between states; maintaining and directing a national military defense; minting a common coin to be used by all states). The state republics do not have the power *left over* from the national government; the state republics remain the *primary* political sphere. True to conservative principles, politics is built from the ground up—family, village, county, state—and then when the state republic has reached its limit, the federal republic does what the individual states cannot. In this way, republican government as it has been understood—a *small* regime based in virtue and ordered to the true common good—was retained. Each state was a republic, and the national government both respected and protected their republican nature and sovereignty.

Yet, how could the national government be considered a republic? By a rather adroit expansion, even redefinition, of what "republic" meant, creating a so-called "extended republic." Madison contrasts a republic with a democracy, not in the sense in which Aristotle did, but in regard to the question of *representation*: "in a democracy, the people meet and exercise the government in person: in a republic, they assemble and administer it by their representatives and agents. A democracy, consequently, must be confined to a small spot. A republic may be extended over a large region."[30]

A system of representation allows us to get around a problem with democracy where individuals *directly* participate in government, voting on laws and deciding matters of policy themselves. That may work on a small scale of a village or county, but is entirely impractical either on the state or national scale. Having the people vote for representatives, who in turn vote directly on laws and decide matters of policy, gets around this difficulty. That allows for self-government by the people, although mediated through elected representatives. Thus, the national representative republic satisfies the definition of a republic: it is not rule of the one, either a monarch or a tyrant; it is not rule of the few, be they aristocrats or oligarchs; it is rule of the many through representation. Of course, none of the states were democracies, and all had some system of representation, and so fit, more or less, the new definition of a republic as well.

But the original distinction between a republic and a democracy is made in regard to what each rules *for*, the true good or mere private interest. Madison addresses this as well, calling the rule of the many for their own interest not democratic rule but rule by *faction*. A faction, explains Madison, is "a number of citizens . . . united and actuated by some common impulse of passion, or of interest, adverse to the rights of the other citizens, or to the permanent and aggregate interests of the community." The number can even be a minority, rather than a majority, because in gaining political power, they can act with the force of the majority. The way to control such factions arising and gaining power is not to "abolish liberty" simply because "it nourishes faction," but to control its effects. The federal system of republican representation controls its effects by passing majority rule "through the medium of a chosen body of citizens, whose wisdom may best discern the true interest of their country, and whose patriotism and love of justice, will be least likely to sacrifice it to temporary or partial considerations." Since, on the national level, this is done with the good of the entire union in mind, local or even state-wide factions will be unable to form against the interests of all states. Indeed, the national government will be more likely than the state republics to attract representatives with "enlightened views and virtuous sentiments" that "render them superior to local prejudices, and to schemes of injustice."[31]

The Federalist vision of a government imbued with virtue was contested, as we'll see, by the Anti-Federalists. They were extremely skeptical that national representative bodies were more likely to contain men of greater virtue, and they thought that the temptations to national power in the Constitution were insufficiently checked. To their side of the debate, we now turn.

CHAPTER EIGHT

The Anti-Federalists

*"For what did you throw off the yoke of Britain and call yourselves
independent?—Was it from a disposition fond of change, or to procure
new masters?—if those were your motives, you have your reward before
you—go,—retire into silent obscurity, and kiss the rod that scourges you—
bury the prospects you had in store, that you and your posterity would
participate in the blessings of freedom..."*

The Anti-Federalists and
Fear of Federal Despotism

THE *ANTI-FEDERALISTS* IS REALLY A COLLECTION OF PUBLIC ESSAYS
written by a variety of different opponents of the proposed Constitution. As with the Federalists, the Anti-Federalists generally
wrote under a number of pseudonyms (e.g., Cato, Centinel, Federal Farmer, Brutus, Old Whig), but scholars have been able to fer-
ret out the real identities of almost all of them. To these writings,
we add the fiery speeches of Patrick Henry, who boldly held forth
in his own name. Anti-Federalist opinions and arguments also have
greater diversity than we find in *The Federalists*, given that the Federalists Hamilton, Madison, and Jay formed a small circle aiming

at the ratification of a single written document, and the Anti-Federalists were responding from many places, situations in life, and angles as critics. Yet, within all this variety, we can find common and powerful arguments against Federalist aspirations, the chief of which is that the proposed Constitution yielded too much power to the federal government, and would ultimately result in the loss of liberty to national despotic power.

No conservative today can read the Anti-Federalists without feeling a deep sense of kinship, and there are lively conservative groups forming nearly every day that espouse much the same concerns as the Anti-Federalists. In this, we are experiencing a revival of the original debate surrounding the Constitution, but with an important difference: all that the Anti-Federalists feared, indeed far more than they feared, has come to pass. The Anti-Federalists' warnings have turned into prophecies. Happily, the new Anti-Federalists are not calling for a dismantling of the Constitution itself, but a return to the original balance between federal and state government as defined by the Constitution. More accurately, they stress (as did the original Anti-Federalists) the Bill of Rights as a surety against powers delegated to the federal government in the Constitution, most emphatically the Tenth Amendment, which guarantees that "The powers not delegated to the United States by the Constitution, nor prohibited by it to the States, are reserved to the States respectively, or to the people."

The Importance of Intermediate Institutions as a Bulwark against Despotism

We must understand this stress on the Tenth Amendment in its most profound form, and why Anti-Federalists were upset that the proposed Constitution lacked an explicit guarantee of states' rights. Tyrannies, whether in their hard or soft form, are always the result of a centralized power *directly* ruling individuals. Such a power becomes centralized by eliminating any intermediate institutions— the family, local civic organizations, churches, clubs, independent local governing authorities in municipalities and townships—that could stand in the way of its direct control of the people. Totalitarians want total control, and realize that yielding control to lesser, intermediate organizations lessens their grip on the people accordingly. As Aristotle noted long ago, tyrants preserve their iron rule by "not permitting common messes, clubs, education, or anything else of this sort, but guarding against anything that customarily gives rise to two things, high thoughts and trust." Despots do not want people who have high thoughts, thoughts that are uppity, thoughts that question the despots' power in light of a higher, grander understanding of what a human being is. They certainly don't want citizens trusting each other, for trust builds friendship, and friendship fuels the courage to throw off tyranny. Rebellion always begins on the local level among people talking together about the most important things. For this reason, tyrants make sure that "leisured discussions are not allowed, or other meetings connected with leisure, but everything is done to make all as ignorant of one another as possible, since knowledge tends to create trust of one another." Instead, citizens must be atomized, broken apart from one another, put in direct dependence on the tyrant, so that they may "become habituated to having small thoughts through always acting like slaves."[1]

There is both hard tyranny and, as we have seen in Tocqueville, soft tyranny. It is a matter of record that the hard tyrannies, such as those perpetrated by the Soviets and Nazis, came about through top-down violent destruction of what has been called the "intermediate institutions"—any autonomous organizations existing below the level of the national power.[2] But Tocqueville warned us that if we became so concerned with personal physical comfort and ease, we would trade our hard-earned liberty for dependence on the soft but all-pervasive despotism of a nanny state.

We recall that when Tocqueville came to America in the early 1830s, he also saw that we had a built-in guard against despotism: the family, the self-governing structures of towns and their environs (townships), county, and then state governments. As we have noted, America was historically built from the ground up, and this provided an enormous bulwark against encroachments by power from above. We repeat Tocqueville's words, "It is...in the township that the force of free peoples resides."[3]

American social order proceeds from the township to the county, and then state, with each higher level *supplementing*, not supplanting the "lower" orders (a principle which has a technical name, *subsidiarity*). Counties do what townships cannot, states take over where the reach of counties fails. As we've already noted, that was how even the Federalists viewed the federal government: not supplanting state and local authority, but supplementing it. The citizens should have guns, but the township and county would have trouble raising an effective militia. A state can raise an effective militia, but in regard to the defense of the union of all the states, a national militia is essential. A state can regulate commerce within its own borders, but unlike a national government, it cannot regulate commerce between itself and other states. Despotism creeps in where larger, more artificial authorities take control of areas that smaller, more natural authorities should oversee. The greatest tyranny occurs when the largest power, the national government, usurps the self-governing activities of the local government, extending its reach even into the inner recesses of the family. The Tenth Amendment was written to guarantee subsidiarity; that is, the primary governing power of the states against the secondary and supplemental power of the federal government. Again, the principle is quite simple: *no more general, more complex, more remote power should do what a more particular, simpler, and local power can do.* That is the only way liberty could be preserved against despotic encroachments of the federal government, and that is why the Anti-Federalists were unhappy that the proposed Constitution did not explicitly state a guarantee of state sovereignty.[4]

The liberty that the Anti-Federalists championed was not democratic liberty, the freedom to do "whatever I want," but the freedom of citizens of a republic to engage in the activities of self-government on the most natural levels. It is this activity of self-government that trains citizens, from the ground up, in the practices that produce ordered liberty, and which create the virtues of the intellect and passions that constitute true self-rule. When the Anti-Federalists defended the states as republics, *that* is what they had in mind. That is what they feared would be destroyed by allowing for the development of a strong national government.

And so the Anti-Federalists resisted ratification of the Constitution. As Cato (New York governor George Clinton) put it, the members of the Philadelphia Constitutional Convention "have exceeded the authority given to them, and have transmitted to Congress a new political fabric...in which the different states do not retain separately their sovereignty and independency, united by a confederated league" as it had been under the Articles of Confederation, but instead are offered "one entire sovereignty—a consolidation of them into one government."[5] They believed the greatly empowered national government would destroy the state republics and supplant all the layers of ordered liberty they nourished and protected.

A union on so large a scale can only be despotic and unnatural,[6] working directly against the real, natural, original sources of social union. "The strongest principle of union resides within our domestic walls. The ties of the parent exceed that of any other; as we depart from home, the next general principle of union is amongst citizens of the same state, where acquaintance, habits, and fortunes, nourish affection, and attachment."[7] But the state is the natural limit of a republic, large enough to supply everything needed and properly desired, but small enough to be knowledge-able about and directly concerned with the particular conditions of its citizens.[8] Indeed, the Anti-Federalist writer Federal Farmer (Melancton Smith), suggests that those who oppose the Constitu-tion would best be described as "republicans," and the Federalists would more properly be called "anti-republicans."[9]

The Constitution strengthens the federal government consider-ably, but for the Anti-Federalists, it did not provide adequate safe-guards against federal despotism. In the words of Centinel (whom scholars think was Samuel Bryan, a Pennsylvanian Anti-Federal-ist), "The general government would necessarily annihilate the par-ticular governments"—especially through its power of taxation— "and . . . the security of the personal rights of the people by the state constitutions is superseded and destroyed; hence results the neces-sity of such security being provided for by a bill of rights to be inserted in the new plan of federal government."[10]

The Dread Power of Taxation, and the Invasion of Federal Bureaucracy

We have seen in the previous chapter that even the Federalists admitted that the enhanced power of federal taxation was the most necessary means of giving it the energy they thought it needed. We are not surprised to find the Anti-Federalists in agreement, and hence unhappy about granting it. The main error in the Federalist argument, asserts Centinel, is that (to put it in terms that have become familiar to us) the Federalists are using a "crisis" to grab power; that is, they are taking advantage of the country's "temporary and extraordinary difficulties," brought on by a protracted war, as a means to cement into place permanent extra powers.[11] The power to tax for the "common defence" is one thing; but the asserted constitutional power of the federal government to raise taxes to promote the "general welfare" is quite another. "Now, what can be more comprehensive than these words? Every species of taxation, whether *external* or *internal* are included." The "general welfare" is so broad that there would be no boundaries to the federal government's powers of taxation. The "unbounded power of taxation does alone include all others, as whoever has the purse strings will have full dominion."[12]

If you are in doubt about the Anti-Federalists' prophetic worry about granting the new federal government *internal* taxing powers, consider this: IRS stands for the *Internal* Revenue Service (and it was founded under the name "Bureau of *Internal* Revenue" by Abraham Lincoln in 1862 to oversee the collection of our country's first Income Tax). If you are in doubt about the effect of giving the federal government the power to promote the general *welfare*, then do a little research about the growth of government taxation and spending since FDR inaugurated the Social Security program. This, and other entitlement programs such as Medicare and Medicaid, take up about half the staggering federal budget.

As Anti-Federalist Luther Martin colorfully asserted, the unlimited power of taxation will allow the federal government "to sluice them [the people] at every vein as long as they have a drop of blood, without controul, limitation or restraint."[13] The main power of taxation, internal taxation, should remain with the states, for the states are "much better judges of the circumstances of their citizens, and what sum of money could be collected from them by direct taxation, and of the manner in which it could be raised, with the greatest case and convenience to their citizens, than the general government could be."[14]

Anti-Federalist Brutus (Robert Yates) paints the most amusing and accurate picture of the endless reach of unlimited taxation into every nook of individuals' lives. "This power [of taxation], without limitation," warns Brutus,

> will introduce itself into every corner of the city, and country—It will wait upon the ladies at their toilett [sic], and will not leave them in any of the their domestic concerns; it will accompany them to the ball, the play, and the assembly; it will go with them when they visit, and will, on all occasions, sit beside them in their carriages, nor will it defect them even at church; it will enter the house of every gentleman, watch over his cellar, wait upon his cook in the kitchen, follow the servants into the parlour, preside over the table, and note down all he eats or drinks; it will attend him to his bedchamber, and watch him while he sleeps; it will take cognizance of the professional mail in his office, or his study; it will watch the merchant in his counting-house, or in his store; it will follow the mechanic to his shop, and in his work, and will haunt him in his family, and in his bed; it will be a constant companion of the industrious farmer in all his labour, it will be with him in the house, and in the field, observe the toil of his hands, and the sweat of his brow; it will penetrate into the most obscure cottage; and finally, it will light upon the head of every person in the United States. To all these different classes of people, and in all these circumstances, in which it will attend them, the language in which it will address them, will be GIVE! GIVE![15]

The problem is not just more taxes, but more government. Allowing the federal government unlimited taxing powers will yield unlimited federal government. The Anti-Federalist Federal Farmer points out presciently that mere external taxes (such as import duties) will be insufficient for the more comprehensive national government desired by the Federalists. The larger and more inclusive it gets, the more it will "take every occasion to multiply laws, and officers to execute them, considering these as so many necessary props for its own support." The support of its own bureaucracy will call for ever greater funding. "The internal sources of taxation then must be called into operation, and internal tax laws and federal assessors and collectors spread over this immense country."[16] We will end up with "a permanent and continued system of tax laws of the union, executed in the bowels of the states by many thousand officers, dependent as to the assessing and collecting [of] federal taxes, solely upon the union."[17]

The federal government will grow, if even merely to feed itself. Soon enough, a vast and invasive federal bureaucracy will arise. The tyranny from above will become ever more oppressive because the federal government will soon become an entity bent on its own self-preservation and expansion, rather than on the public good. A large standing army is a great danger, the Federal Farmer noted, and provisions must be made that the national army does not use its powers to "depress and inslave the people." But "it is equally true that a large body of selfish, unfeeling, unprincipled civil officers has a like, or a more pernicious tendency to the same point." Given the size of the country, and hence the extent of the federal reach, a "vast number of officers [is] necessary to execute a national system in this extensive country."[18] Since these bureaucracies will be the creation of the national Congress, and the legislators will be responsible for the appointment of the bureaucrats who fill them, then enormous numbers of federal civil servants become direct dependents on Congress. The welfare of the bureaucratic dependent class then becomes a prime goal of the national legislature.

Security against this limitless growth must be placed in a "federal republic," that is, a "confederation" of state republics, which is "a league of friendship among the states or sovereignties for the common defence and mutual welfare," where "each state expressly retains its sovereignty, and all powers not expressly given to congress...." In this federal republic, the "several state or district legislatures" must retain "the means of opposing heavy internal taxes and oppressive measures in the proper stages."[19] The state governments must act as "barriers between congress and the pockets of the people."[20] Endless federal bureaucracies cannot grow without feeding on tax dollars.

But the proposed Constitution, without a Bill of Rights, does not provide such protection, so that if the national Congress, which is given the "power to lay taxes at pleasure for the general welfare," does indeed "lay unnecessary oppressive taxes, the constitution will provide...no remedy for the people or the states—the people must bear them, or have recourse, not to any constitutional checks or remedies, but to that resistence which is the last resort, and founded in self-defence."[21]

But again, Tocqueville reminds us of a sadly neglected means of resistance and defense: self-control. If *we* look to the federal government to provide for our complete cradle-to-grave welfare, to bail out our foolish personal and business decisions, to subsidize our every whim and comfort, to underwrite our immorality, to write out endless pork barrel checks to local projects we don't want to pay for ourselves, then who is to blame when we embrace the soft despotism the federal government so solicitously offers? If we do not have the virtue to control *ourselves*, then why should the federal government control *itself*?

Other Dread Powers of Congress and the Supreme Court

The Anti-Federalists had more worries than the proposed federal taxing power. As we have seen, they were alarmed at the implications of the federal government assuming the undefined task of promoting the "general welfare." Their fear was only multiplied by the Constitution's asserting that (1) Congress had the power "To make all Laws which shall be *necessary and proper* for carrying into Execution the foregoing Powers, and all other Powers vested by this Constitution in the Government of the United States, or in any Department thereof,"[22] and (2) that "the Constitution ... shall be the *supreme Law of the Land*; and the Judges in every State shall be bound thereby, any Thing in the constitution or Laws of any State to the Contrary notwithstanding."[23] The first gives unlimited power to Congress; the second gives unlimited power to the federal judiciary, most prominently, the Supreme Court. Combined with the power of direct, internal taxation, these two provisions would ensure a complete consolidation of power on the federal level,[24] and, in the words of Brutus, "there is [then] nothing valuable to human nature, nothing dear to freemen, but what is within its power."[25] Patrick Henry warned, "This Constitution can counteract and suspend any of our [state] laws, that contravene its oppressive operation; for they have the power of direct taxation; which suspends our Bill of Rights; and it is expressly provided, that they can make all laws necessary for carrying their powers into execution; and it [the proposed Constitution] is declared paramount to the laws and constitutions of the States."[26]

In regard to the "necessary and proper" clause, the danger resides both in the vagueness of the Constitution itself and in human nature. As to the vagueness, Brutus drives home the central problem with giving Congress enormous powers to promote the general welfare: it is, to repeat, a concept so entirely vague that nearly anyone can use it for anything.

> It will then be [a] matter of opinion, what tends to the general welfare; and the Congress will be the only judges in the matter. To provide for the general welfare, is an abstract proposition, which mankind differ in the explanation of, as much as they do on any political or moral proposition that can be proposed; the most opposite measures may be pursued by different parties, and both may profess, that they have in view the general welfare; and both sides may be honest in their professions, or both may have sinister views.[27]

If Congress *can* use it for anything, they *will.* These proposed federal powers will only be intensified by a natural tendency in "every man, and every body of men" who, when "invested with power, are ever disposed to increase it, and to acquire a superiority over every thing that stands in their way."[28]

And the Supreme Court? The Constitution declares itself to be the supreme law of the land, notes Brutus. It's Preamble asserts that the supreme law is ordained to "form a more perfect Union, establish Justice, insure domestic Tranquility, provide for the common defence, promote the general Welfare, and secure the Blessings of Liberty to ourselves and our Posterity." And as we've seen, it claims the power for Congress to make "all Laws ... necessary and proper" for carrying out these goals. But the very vagueness of these goals will mean that the federal judiciary must "explain the constitution, not only according to its letter, but according to its spirit and intention," and no one doubts that they "would strongly incline to give it such a construction as to extend the powers of the general government."[29] Indeed, it is precisely because the Supreme

Court is "authorised to decide upon the meaning of the constitution...according to the spirit and intention of it" that it "will not
be subordinate to, but above the legislature."[30] It will not make laws
directly, but establish judicial "principles" of interpretation, "which
being received by the legislature, will enlarge the sphere of their
power beyond all bounds."[31] The power of the Supreme Court and
the power of Congress grow together, and "in proportion as the
general government acquires power and jurisdiction, by the *liberal*
construction which the judges may give the constitution, will those
of the states lose its rights, until they become so trifling and unim-
portant, as not to be worth having."[32]

I have added emphasis to "liberal" in this last quote. Obviously
Brutus was not speaking about "liberal" in our sense of the term
relating to the far Left. He means that the Supreme Court will
inevitably tend to expand federal power by expansive interpreta-
tions of the Constitution. But there is a serious and important
connection between his warning and the advance of the causes of
liberalism through judicial activism.

Liberalism seeks centralized power, especially through the judiciary, because it is a revolutionary force trying to change, from the
top-down, the habits, beliefs, customs, and institutions on the local
level. To be more exact, liberalism is a top-down secular revolution trying to change a conservative culture built by Judeo-Christian beliefs from the bottom up. For them, promoting the general
welfare *means* changing the conservative views on marriage, the
family, sexuality, abortion, euthanasia that still largely define the
"locals" clinging (as Obama contemptuously said) to their "guns
and religion."

Since the "locals" still vote, staging a cultural revolution through
Congress is not easy. But staging a revolution through the Supreme
Court and the federal court system is. You only have to win one

case, like *Roe v. Wade*, and suddenly all state laws and all moral convictions and arguments to the contrary must bow and crumble before the will of five Supreme Court judges. Abortion is made legal, and Congress is free to enact law after law that extends abortion even to the infanticide of partial-birth abortion. The destruction of marriage by the gay rights movement will undoubtedly follow the same course: win a Supreme Court case, establish a precedent, state and local laws to the contrary are all struck down, and Congress advances the agenda with more extensive laws based upon the original judicial victory. That was exactly the fear of Brutus: such court cases establish principles and precedents that strike down state and local laws, and moreover, give Congress the power to enact legislation that advances the revolution.

Having the unlimited ability to define the Constitution *and* strike down any laws made even by Congress as unconstitutional meant, for Brutus, that there "is no power above them [i.e., the Supreme Court], to controul...their decisions...they cannot be controuled by the laws of the legislature. In short, they are independent of the people, of the legislature, and of every power under heaven. Men placed in this situation will generally soon feel themselves independent of heaven itself."[33] That, perhaps, is why they feel entirely free to interpret the First Amendment, that "Congress shall make no law respecting the establishment of religion," to mean that religion must be expunged from the public square.

The Ultimate Choice: Federal Republic or Consolidated Government

We recall that the Federalists argued for a new definition of republic. A republic was not a monarchy or aristocracy, asserted Madison, but a government that (in contrast to direct-rule democracy) allowed the people to rule indirectly through representation.

Representation allowed for an "extended republic," so that the union would be considered "a confederacy founded on republican principles, and composed of republican members."

Against this, the Anti-Federalists repeatedly stressed two points: a proper republic had to be small (the state was the natural limit of its size, *even with representation*[34]), and the power given to the national government by the Constitution would eventually swallow up the state republics into one despotic national government. Opponents of the Constitution therefore argued that we faced a choice between a "federal republic," where the states remained sovereign republics, and a "consolidated government," where the national government swallows up state and local government. Despite the argumentative efforts of the Federalists, some Anti-Federalists considered the consolidated government not to be a republic at all. As Anti-Federalist Old Whig, whose identity remains unknown, starkly put it, we will either have a "confederacy of Republics [i.e., a federal republic], or we must cease altogether to retain the Republican form of government."[35]

What, exactly, is the difference? "To erect a federal republic, we must first make a number of states on republican principles," instructed the Anti-Federalist Federal Farmer, where each state has "a government organized for internal management of its affairs." The Anti-Federalists agreed that there needed to be a national, supplemental government, for the "states...must unite under a federal head, and delegate to it powers to make and execute laws in certain enumerated cases, under certain restrictions." But in a federal republic, each state manages its own internal affairs, and the states delegate to "the union power to manage general concerns."[36] The states are primary. *They* are the republics. The national government is not a super-republic,[37] but a federal head that acts for the good of the sovereign states as a whole, a "head...dependant on, and kept within limited bounds by, the local governments."[38] Whatever defects there are in such a federal republic, they are "as a feather in the balance against a mountain, compared with those which would, infallibly, be the result of the loss of general liberty, and that happiness men enjoy under a frugal, free, and mild government."[39]

By contrast, what the Federalists really wanted, charged the Anti-Federalists, what their Constitution *really* ordained, was a government that swept up all the local and state powers into one national consolidated government. "To form a consolidated, or one entire government, there must be no state, or local governments, but all things, persons and property, must be subject to the laws of one legislature alone; to one executive, and one judiciary." Such a government will "operate immediately upon the persons and property of individuals, and not on states. . . . " It is by operating immediately upon the property and lives of individuals that the national government usurps the proper domain of the state and local governments. To prevent this, the national government should only be allowed to relate directly to the states, and the "state governments [should] stand between the union and individuals."[40]

Of course, no Federalist was hoping to create a federal government that would usurp all of the states' powers and prerogatives. Rather, they were trying, through the Constitution, to give enough power to the federal government to do its appointed tasks. That having been said, we recall that the Federalist Hamilton thought the national government should be strengthened by acting directly on the people, and the more it intertwined itself with the daily lives of individuals, the more individuals would depend directly on the federal, rather than state and local, government. *That* is precisely what the Anti-Federalists feared most, and given the ever-extending reach of our federal government over the minutest aspects of our daily lives today, we must say that their fears were more than justified.

Our federal government is indeed consolidating all powers unto itself. Moreover, the situation is, if anything, worse than the Anti-Federalists feared, because state governments *themselves* have become direct dependents on Washington. They have yielded their autonomy by taking ever greater mounds of federal dollars for state and local projects and concerns. The national legislature thereby rules all state legislatures, supplanting them rather than supplementing them.

Whom shall we blame? In great part, ourselves. Our difficulty—recalling Tocqueville—is that we are impatient, too often motivated by envy, and addicted to physical gratification. We want *more* than we can pay for, and we want it *now*. Impatient, envious, and materialistic individuals use credit cards, and run up impossibly large debts. These same individuals demand more state and local services and projects than they are willing to pay for through their state and local taxes. The state and local governments then turn to Washington as the ultimate credit card to give them what their own state citizens want but don't want to pay for. So, the national government engages in reckless deficit spending, sells treasury bills, notes, and bonds, and then prints money so that the president and Congress (in exchange for votes) can give to individuals and states what they want but can't pay for. As a result, rather than being intermediate institutions that provide directly for the daily lives of its people, state and local governments become hopelessly dependent on the national government. This, in turn, puts enormous power in the hands of the national government to dictate the details of the lives of every individual, of every local government, and every state.

How could this situation be remedied? In great part, according to the true conservative, the true republican, Anti-Federalist principle of rebuilding ourselves economically from the ground up, that is, on the familial, local, and state levels. That will restore true independence. First things first. If a family cannot rule itself economically, and runs up hopeless debts, there is no hope for reducing the national debt. One most effective way of doing this is called the "envelope system," which my wife champions. Each month you have a budgeted amount set for all major categories of expenditure (mortgage, food, utilities, gas, etc.). Some items are paid for by check (mortgage, utilities); other items are paid for out of actual cash set aside in envelopes labeled accordingly (food, gas). Credit cards are cut up. No money is spent beyond what is budgeted. Extra money is ploughed back into debt reduction. That's pay-as-you-go family economy. You get exactly what you can pay for, and no more.

The same pay-as-you-go plan must be embraced by local and state governments. Budgets must be set in stone and paid for directly by local and state revenue. All projects, all improvements, all services should arise from and be paid for on the local and state level. Loosening the hold of the national government can only occur through a gradual but steady decrease in dependence on federal dollars. The decrease in dependence can only occur through local and state governments providing for their own general welfare through their own money. Local and state taxpayers must be content to live with what they will actually pay for, rather than looking to the federal government to provide things paid for by federal income tax (i.e., other people's money) or deficit spending (our children's children's money) or printing fiat currency (play money).

In short, the ultimate choice rests with us. Do we want a federal union of state republics or one giant consolidated national government? Here, we must be excruciatingly clear that the issue is not merely a contest between two different *sizes* of government, state and national, but two qualitatively different *kinds* of government with entirely different *aims*. Again, the Anti-Federalists were profoundly conservative in wanting to defend human social life as it grows from the ground up, from the family, to the village, the city, the county, and the state. Much like Aristotle, they considered the state to be the natural size-limit of good government. Anything beyond that, because it was too far removed from local concerns, loves, needs, and particular aspirations of the people, could only be a top-down despotism that disregarded the real concerns of the people in the pursuit of the glories of its national empire or its *own* vision of what constitutes happiness and the general welfare.

The Anti-Federalists passionately fought for, and won, a Bill of Rights. They believed that only if these enumerated rights were staunchly and explicitly protected would the built-in tendencies toward the consolidation of national power in the Constitution be kept in check. The problem is, of course, that the usurpations of power by the Supreme Court and Congress, predicted so cogently by the Anti-Federalist Brutus, have either twisted or all but erased the enumerated rights. We have lost the original tension between Federalist and Anti-Federalist arguments that really defined our founding, and we have become, willingly or unwillingly, the very worst kind of Federalists feared by the Anti-Federalists: complete dependents on an increasingly despotic federal government.

Part III
The Place of Economics
for Conservatives

THERE IS A LAMENTABLE TENDENCY AMONG SOME CONSERVATIVES to reduce conservatism to mere economic considerations, as if to be conservative meant only to conserve free economic markets. It might awaken them to recall that it was Marx who reduced all the glory of man to *homo economicus*. For Marx, everything about human nature, from morality to art, to philosophy to religion, and every aspect of our political life, was reducible to each society's economic modes of production. To say the least, that is a stunted view of our humanity, and there is no reason to accep this Marxist principle.

Conservatism must conserve the whole man, and that is why our treatment of economics comes now, after much deeper and wider reflections on deeper and wider conservative principles. We are indeed an economic animal, but we are also a rational, moral, political, and religious animal, and it is this full complexity of our humanity that conservatism properly conserves. Interestingly enough, Aristotle did note that human beings were economic animals—but then again, so were moles, mice, ants, bees, and even octopi.[1] The mere fact alone that through our labor we must build shelter and procure food, store it, and dispense it does not distinguish us as human beings. Nor, for that matter, does our being political. Many other animals live a common, integrated life. (Aristotle mentions bees, wasps, ants, and even cranes as also political animals.[2]) Our rational, moral, and religious capacities are what make the human animal distinct, what define us as human, and hence what determine how we are to be economic and political. For a conservative, that means that the economic (and political) aspects of our life are subordinate to the rational, moral, and religious.

CHAPTER NINE

The Servile State: Hilaire Belloc

"And as I am upon the whole hopeful that the faith will recover its intimate and guiding place in the heart of Europe, so I believe that this sinking back into our original paganism (for the tendency to the servile state is nothing less) will in due time be halted and reversed."

NOW WE COME TO ECONOMICS, FOR WHICH WE'VE CHOSEN TWO books: Hilaire Belloc's *The Servile State* and Friedrich von Hayek's *The Road to Serfdom.* As their titles indicate, they are prescient warnings, which echo Tocqueville, about soft despotism, where citizens become willing slaves of a centralized power in exchange for comfort and security.

To review, Tocqueville saw in Americans a "passion for material well-being" so intense that the "care of satisfying the least needs of the body and of providing the smallest comforts of life preoccupies minds universally."[1] Since America is a fluid society economically, no one is set in a particular economic class. But precisely this fluidity causes deep anxiety: envy at what others above us have, and perpetual fear of losing what we do have. From this anxiety, envy, and fear arises another desire, the intense desire for stability that still allows us to satisfy our passion for material well-being. That desire, in turn, invites the "soft despotism" of a strong central government that will take all the anxiety out of our passionate desire for both physical gratification and security. Our preoccupation with material comfort leads us along a road to serfdom, wherein we willingly embrace a servile state: security and comfort at the expense of liberty.

The irony is that while a free market creates material wealth, that very material wealth—or more accurately the pursuit of physical gratification that such material wealth can fund—may also create an intemperate population that endangers the virtues of the free market, moral liberty, and self-reliance. *Intemperance* is the fancy name for the vice of people who are wholly enslaved to material pleasures. Such materialism is the death of liberty, because staking our happiness entirely in this-worldly physical gratifications and security brings us to trade our moral liberty to the servile state that promises to provide all our this-worldly wants. It is no accident that the servile state is always a *secular* state, and that modern liberalism tends toward a consolidation of power, an exclusion of religion, and a shrinking of human beings to pleasure-driven creatures easily controlled from above. Belloc was rightly alarmed.

Belloc, the Man

Hilaire Belloc was the son of an English mother and a French father, and claimed both countries as his own. Louis-Marie Belloc and his beloved wife Elizabeth Parkes Belloc lived in La Celle Saint Cloud, a village of Paris. Elizabeth gave birth to a daughter, Marie Elizabeth, in August 1868, and to Joseph Hilaire Pierre on July 27, 1870, during the Franco-Prussian war. As France was rapidly overrun by the Prussian army, Louis-Marie and Elizabeth fled with their children to England. They returned to France in 1871, after its capitulation to Prussia, only to find their home had been completely ransacked by German troops. In despair, the family decided to make a new home in England, though Hilaire would remain a French patriot, serving in the French army, and harboring a lifelong hatred of the Prussians and the statism he thought they represented. Hilaire's father died in 1872 (on a visit to La Celle Saint Cloud), and so Hilaire was raised by his mother, who devotedly nurtured the family's dual national loyalties, dividing their time between England and France.

Jean Hilaire Delloc, the grandfather for whom Hilaire was named, was a famous painter, good enough to have his work hung in the Louvre. And Jean Hilaire's wife Louise was a moderately successful writer. As for Hilaire's mother, the Parkes' side of the family tended toward the secular, radical, and literary, and Elizabeth counted novelist George Eliot among her close friends. But under the influence of Henry Edward Manning, soon to be Cardinal Manning, she left behind her family's secular radicalism and became an orthodox Catholic.

Even without the father, the Bellocs might have been financially secure if a stockbroker had not lost Elizabeth's £20,000 inheritance—an immense sum, the loss of which dropped them from wealth to poverty. The family moved to the country, to Sussex. Hilaire loved nature and rural life, and later he would make his own home in a grand but run-down country house in Sussex.

Young Hilaire was intellectually precocious, memorizing poetry and composing his own before he was even ten years old. When, at age ten, he entered John Henry Newman's Oratory School, he excelled in every subject, from mathematics to debating to literature, but especially in the classics, Greek and Latin; and he deepened his faith as well. Imagine your own son, at twelve, writing to you about the joys of Virgil and Homer, and the incomparable splendor of reading Cicero's speeches in Latin! He won every possible academic prize at the Oratory.

At seventeen, Belloc enrolled in the Collége Stanislas in Paris, but it proved not to his liking, and he returned to England. Thus began a time of seeking and wandering, reading and writing (for money). In 1890, young Hilaire met an American girl, Elodie Hogan, and fell completely and permanently in love. She had set herself on becoming a nun, but became equally smitten by Belloc. He chased her across the ocean, and then across America to her home in California, only to be rebuffed by her mother. In distress, Belloc returned to France, and volunteered for the French army. After his tour of duty, he returned to England and entered Oxford in 1893. Again, he was first in everything, especially shining in his capacities as an orator. Yet, because he was both Catholic and outspoken in his politics (which were not always to the administration's liking), Oxford denied him a fellowship. With academic life closed to him, he decided to earn his living as a writer and public speaker. Meanwhile, Elodie entered a religious order, the Sisters of Charity, in 1895, but left soon thereafter, finding her calling in marriage instead. She and Belloc were married in Napa, California, in June 1896, and would have a family of five children.

In April 1900, Belloc met a man who would become his great friend and intellectual co-conspirator, G. K. Chesterton. Belloc was delivering a speech against Britain's war against the Boers in South Africa, and Chesterton was in the audience. Chesterton was entirely enchanted with Belloc's political insight and mastery of language, literature, and history. Both men were "Little Englanders," opposed to imperialism and to great powers swallowing up smaller ones. Both men were making their mark in literature as well, Belloc first finding fame with humorous books of verse for children, beginning with *The Bad Child's Book of Beasts* in 1896; and both were finding that literature and freelance journalism were a hard way to make a living.

Belloc tried his hand at politics, and won a seat in the House of Commons as part of the Liberal Party. It soon became clear he was not a liberal in their sense, as he spent much of his time in Parliament from 1906 to 1910 leveling all-too-trenchant criticisms at his own party. One great difficulty was that the Left tended toward socialism as the solution to England's economic and social problems, and Belloc thought socialism was a cure far worse than the disease. He himself was an avid defender of private property and the freedom of the individual to work for himself. The notion of inviting in a nanny-state to fix society's ills horrified him. He made a lot of very fine speeches, but he did not make a very good liberal. He was certainly happy to leave when he was not re-elected in 1910, and he took near immediate revenge when he teamed up with G. K. Chesterton's brother, Cecil, to write *The Party System* (1911), a book-length exposé of the rot, intrigue, and corruption infecting English politics. *The Party System* caused more than a bit of controversy. Loving a good row, Hilaire and Cecil teamed up to write a "radical" weekly, the *Eye-Witness*, to further report on Parliament's misdoings. (Cecil, incidentally, had been a devout socialist, but Belloc talked him out of it, a tribute to his good-humored oratorical and argumentative skills.)

In 1911, the Liberal Party's David Lloyd George, serving as Chancellor of the Exchequer, introduced a National Insurance Bill. Cheered by liberals, it was also cheered by Ramsay MacDonald, leader of the socialist Labour Party. Belloc's reaction, though he had been a liberal himself (albeit in much the same sense that Chesterton regarded himself as a liberal) was profoundly conservative. He saw nationalized health care as a fatal step toward the servile state. The debate between Belloc and MacDonald was printed up in a pamphlet, *Socialism and the Servile State*, but more important, it was recast in a book, *The Servile State* (1912).

What Exactly Is Economics? What Exactly Is Distributism?

Belloc knew that to understand economics we have to start from the beginning. The best place to start is etymology. The word "economics" comes from two Greek words, *oikos* (home) and *nomos* (custom or law), and the Greek term *oikonomia* refers to the management of a household, not to the GDP of Athens or England or anywhere else. Aristotle wrote a treatise entitled *Oikonomikos*,[2] the proper translation of which is *On Home Management*, however much that sounds like a course that girls might have been required to take in high school in the 1950s. But the conservative point is this: as with politics, economics begins in the home; just as we are social animals by nature, so too we are economic animals.

Nature, however, doesn't simply provide for our necessities. We take what nature gives us, as a kind of raw material, and transform it by *labor*. "That special, conscious, and intelligent transformation of the environment which is peculiar to the peculiar intelligence and creative faculty of man we call the production of *wealth*."[3] Belloc is not here referring primarily to gold or, even less, paper currency. He means the kinds of things that are produced first in a natural economy: a garden full of vegetables, a field with grazing cattle, a barn crammed with good hay, cabinets built for the house, a larder full of corn, beans, tomatoes, and meat canned for the winter, lumber sawn and drying for next year's chairs and cabinets, tools crafted to make one's tasks less burdensome.

"Without wealth man cannot exist. The production of it is a necessity for him,"[4] for without it, he and his family would starve. But this provision of necessities, wrought in the family by the cooperation of husband, wife, and children, provides a moral transformation as well. We become what we should be, in part, by laboring to provide what is necessary for the *home*. That is how we become a good husband and wife, and what makes good children good.

That is the fundamental *oikonomia*, and there are few things more fundamental. "Therefore, to control the production of wealth is to control human life itself. To refuse man the opportunity for the production of wealth is to refuse him the opportunity for life," warns Belloc.[5] If the government snatches a man's land, he and his family will perish. If that same government removes the necessity of his working to provide for his family, then his moral nature will shrivel and perish even though he may be well fed by the state. He will never become what he should be, a husband and father.

Wealth accumulates because human beings cannot live immediately off the land all year (so they store goods to eat during the winter, fashion tools that they may use in the future, and purchase supplies that may be needed later), and because labor generally creates a surplus of goods beyond what is actually needed (more corn is grown than can be eaten, more cattle are bred than can be turned into beef on the table, more chairs are made than a family needs). "To such wealth reserved and set aside for the purposes of future production, and not for immediate consumption, whether it be in the form of instruments or tools, or in the form of stores for the maintenance of labor during the process of production, we give the name of *capital*."[6]

That's the core of economics. We *labor* upon *materials* or *land* to produce what we need, and whatever goes beyond that in surplus. Taken all together, that is our *wealth*. Our wealth that is not immediately needed is *capital*. Moreover, the materials and land that we own, along with the wealth we've gotten from our labor upon it, is our *property*.

Note, we have said nothing about money. Money is not itself capital. At best, it represents capital; at worst, it represents nothing at all. Stock in a company represents the company's actual wealth in goods, materials, buildings, machines, personnel; stock in a company that has no real wealth is, when discovered, worth nothing at all. A good way to measure how much capital you really have is to imagine what you would have if the Stock Market crashed, the dollar crashed, and the national economy crashed. If you and your family can still eat, have sufficient clothing and a home you own, and you are still able to work and produce goods with tools and materials that you own, you have real wealth, part of which is real capital.

If that's the core of economics, the core is not the whole. There is further development. Village or town life allows for a division of labor—carpenters, blacksmiths, butchers, cloth makers, shopkeepers—that builds upon and expands the family economy, allowing all in the village to benefit from each other's labor. This complex interdependence grows as townships grow up around towns and unite in counties, and counties unite to form states—to use the American context. The common *wealth* builds accordingly. What the family can't provide, the village can; what the village can't provide economically, the county can; what the county cannot provide economically, the state can. Thus we end up with layers of intermediate economic institutions, each supplementing, not supplanting, the previous.

The principle upon which such wealth builds is solid, first of all, because a family's labor is upon its *own* materials and land, its *own* property, and when it contributes capital through taxation, it benefits first of all its *own* community. What individual communities cannot provide economically, counties can; if not counties, then the state. Supplemental taxation makes sense, because the burdens and benefits remain local. But in no case should the larger economic entity supplant the smaller, either directly or through excessive taxation. It is not the town's job to raise my children and provide them food, clothing, and shelter with someone else's labor while I loll about. It's my job to provide for them. But I can't build or resurface a county road, replace a municipal sewer system, set up and keep repaired electrical wires, provide fire and police protection, and so on. Larger political or economic entities must do these things.

The great danger, of course, is whenever larger political and economic entities take over local responsibilities. You don't want a national police force cruising the streets of your town; you don't want a national welfare system displacing local mothers and fathers; you don't want national bureaucracies deciding what playgrounds or parks are going to be built, nor how your children should be educated. That is totalitarianism, because it wipes out all the intermediate institutions and directs everything from the top-down.

How may we protect ourselves against such economic totalitarianism? Belloc's fundamental conservative economic principle goes by the name of "Distributism," a term to which he and Chesterton are inextricably linked. It is really another name for the principle of subsidiarity, or for Anti-Federalist republicanism, or the Aristotelian understanding of our lives as political animals. It is simply the common sense and conservative principle that economic ownership and responsibility should be distributed throughout the economic order, not gathered at the top. To understand this, you might want to see a movie, and imagine a horror remake.

It's a Wonderful Life (1946), *It's a Miserable Life* (2008)

It's a Wonderful Life (1946) is a truly great movie starring Jimmy Stewart, who plays a truly great American hero, George Bailey, the head of the *local* bank in Bedford Falls. When the people make a run on his bank, George Bailey must explain to the crowd how a bank really works. It doesn't have a big pile of money that directly corresponds to everyone's savings and checking account. "No, but you . . . you . . . you're thinking of this place all wrong. As if I had the money back in a safe. The, the money's not here." Bailey points to one person lined up to withdraw everything, and then another and another. "Well, your money's in Joe's house . . . that's right next to yours . . . and in the Kennedy House, and Mrs. Macklin's house, and, and a hundred others." He continues, "Why, you're lending them the money to build, and then, they're going to pay it back to you as best they can. Now what are you going to do? Foreclose on them?"

There is a lot in this little speech. The money in the bank comes from the local people. Bailey is compassionate, but not with other people's money. In order to stay in business, in order to keep his depositors' assets, he must be careful about giving his loans to people who can actually pay them back. The community members depend on him lending their money responsibly. Bailey consistently acts with admirable charity, and one essential aspect of this is that he doesn't give loans to people with no jobs, whose only qualification for the loan is that they can fog a mirror with their breath; he doesn't give fantastic rates to local people on outlandishly large sums to buy houses well beyond their means. That would destroy everyone's hard-earned wealth in Bedford Falls. He uses the common *wealth* of the community responsibly, to build up the community.

Now, let's imagine a 2008 remake of the movie, *It's a Miserable Life*. In it, certain Congressmen in Washington get the idea that everyone in Bedford Falls should have a house, a big house, even those who don't have jobs. They want to compel Bailey's bank to give loans entirely without regard to qualifications, and indeed, put a quota system on low income/no income subprime mortgages. But Congress wants to go beyond providing houses to low income/no income folks. To stimulate the national economy (which gets them votes), they want everyone to buy houses that are entirely beyond reach, so they provide ridiculously low initial interest rates on adjustable rate mortgages, and pressure banks to give out promiscuously. Bailey knows all this will destroy Bedford Falls, and refuses to participate. But the villain of the movie, the evil financier Mr. Potter (Lionel Barrymore), leaps at the chance because he doesn't care about Bedford Falls, and he knows that he can bundle his bad loans and sell them all back to Fannie Mae and Freddie Mac, or some dupable foreign investor. What does he care? Like the distant but powerful financiers in New York, he doesn't give a flip what effect his financial actions have on local communities, as long as he can make a bundle. Dazzled by the possibilities of living far beyond their means, everyone runs to Potter, and George Bailey's bank closes. At first, housing prices rise quickly and astronomically, given the easy loan money, but soon enough the bubble bursts. House prices deflate and become worth less than loan amounts, even while the interest rates on the adjustable rate mortgages rise. The townsfolk, stretched far beyond their means, begin to have trouble paying their mortgages. Foreclosures soon start to domino. Foreign investors, smelling bad fish, realize Potter is entirely insolvent, and Congress, finally forced to face the music in Bedford Falls and a million other communities, decides to bail out Potter and print money to forestall the inevitable economic collapse.

Do you see what happened in the remake? Instead of having financial institutions on the local level make reasonable loans, loans that the community could financially support, loans that

actually benefitted the local community, distant political and economic powers displaced these local economic institutions and gave
loans to support grand federal political visions, line political pockets, and satisfy the greed of financial quick-richers in faraway banking corporations. Political and banking power was not distributed
throughout society beginning from the bottom. It has gathered at
the top, and at a great distance away, and through collusion,
forced disastrous policies on local communities. This economic
despotism from the top actually ended up increasing the power of
the feds: when everything collapses, the federal government
rushes in to take over. The penalty for our acting irresponsibly is
to become the slave of the federal power that rushes to your rescue, and that brings us closer to the title of Belloc's book.

Slavery and the Servile State

What is the servile state? Let's look at things in a bare bones
way. It should be obvious that the most natural condition for a family is one in which its members apply their own labor to their own
materials or land, and produce their own wealth in a common
effort, as a kind of miniature "common-wealth." The worst condition would be where the entire family is enslaved to someone else.
The family owns no land. They own no materials. The land and
materials are entirely owned by their master. The family labors all
day, not for their own common good, but to produce wealth for
the master, and they receive no other benefit than merely the minimum of food, clothing, and shelter to keep them alive. That is
slavery. That is an entirely servile condition. That allows us to
understand the servile state.

According to Belloc, "That arrangement of society in which so
considerable a number of families and individuals are constrained
by positive law to labor for the advantage of other families and

individuals as to stamp the whole community with the mark of such labor we call the servile state."[7] Simple enough. A state in which a large number of people are compelled to labor for a small number of people is a servile state. The bulk of the people do not receive any of the wealth that is the direct result of their labor. They own no property. They are themselves the property of someone else.

That is exactly what happened in ancient Greek society, and in fact, what has happened in most societies throughout human history. Aristotle, much to our regret, argued that slavery was necessary and good, but then, it was taken for granted as an institution by most societies in most times. We can and should fault him for that, but again, he lived several centuries before Christ, and Christianity, as Belloc argues, is really what made the great effort to remove the blot of slavery.[8]

While Christianity made great headway in eliminating slavery from the West, slavery still exists and is rising in many places around the globe. Belloc argued that it was indeed threatening to return in Europe and America, although in a different form, one that calls to mind Tocqueville's soft despotism: a *willing* enslavement of the population to a central government master that takes control of the entire economic life, owns all wealth and property, dictates exactly how citizens will labor, what they will produce, and what their wages will be, and takes all the excess wealth by force, either through unlawful seizure or lawful seizure through taxation—all in return for providing complete comfort and security to the enslaved populace.

Slavery is not something we left behind, warns Belloc. It is something we're in imminent danger of freely embracing. We'll be well-kept slaves. Comfortable slaves. But slaves nonetheless. How and why could this happen? To understand, we must have some account of socialism and capitalism, as distinct from the servile state.

Capitalism and Socialism According to Belloc

It is very important to understand that Belloc was writing the *Servile State* before the outbreak of World War I, before the abstract doctrines of communism had been given real political teeth and morbid flesh in the Soviet Union. He was also writing in the context of British life. For Belloc, history was moving from capitalism, through socialism, to the servile state. His historical analysis can easily confuse readers today, not only because they forget the context, but also because of the particular way Belloc defines capitalism.

Reading Belloc today, we wonder how it is that he could be so adamantly for private property and against government seizures of private wealth through socialism, and at the same time so critical of capitalism. What else is there? Isn't the world divided between capitalism and socialism? Let's make a beginning of this muddle by looking very carefully at his definition of capitalist society. "A society in which private property in land and capital, that is, the ownership and therefore the control of the means of production, is confined to some number of free citizens not large enough to determine the social mass of the state, while the rest have not such property and are therefore proletarian, we call capitalist." The number of people owning and therefore controlling everything is small enough that "the state as a whole is not characterized by the institution of ownership among free citizens, but by the restriction of ownership to a section markedly less than the whole, or even a small minority." That is, the overwhelming majority must be "propertyless" or "proletarian," mere workers for wages who own nothing, not even their own houses. All the intermediate economic institutions have been swallowed up by a few, extraordinarily wealthy enterprises, and because of this, there is no free economic enterprise for anyone below them.[9]

On this definition, we in the United States do not live in a capitalist society, and never have. Hopefully, we never will. Too many people own private property, too many people own their own businesses, too many people work for themselves, and a relative few are entirely property-less wage-earners. It is precisely because of our essential commitment to a thoroughly *distributed* private property ownership and thoroughly *distributed* private business ownership that we aren't divided into a few owners and a mass of wage slaves. Recalling both Aristotle and Tocqueville, this is precisely because we have a large middle class.

Belloc's situation at the beginning of the 1900s in England was different. First and most obvious, England is a small country in which, unlike the United States, you had a post-aristocratic plutocratic society where a small number of people owned the majority of land. Moreover, in those pre-union days, many workers in everything from coal mines to factories to dockyards were being severely mistreated, given bare subsistence wages, and fired if they complained—a situation that had plagued England from the industrial revolution on. The rich business owners received nearly all the wealth generated by the labor of their workers. The workers, who had barely enough to keep them alive, were little better off than the worst of slaves. True, they were free to quit their jobs, but since they were entirely without property, they would thereby be freely embracing starvation. For Belloc, this deplorable situation was caused by the fact that the ownership of property and of businesses was not thoroughly distributed throughout English society.

As with many others during the nineteenth and early twentieth centuries, Belloc believed that the situation would only worsen until the mass of working poor became so desperate that they would grasp at any solution. One solution, which his own England would later half-embrace, was socialism or collectivism, "in which the means of production" are "in the hands of the political officers of the community."[10] In socialism, property and its use are taken over by the central government as a remedy for the evils brought on by capitalism. The dispossessed and desperate masses demand government control of industry. They themselves have no property to give up, and so they have no qualms about the government seizure of property and industry from the few rich. Socialism, in turn, becomes the servile state because government thereby takes control of the entire economic welfare of the populace, and the populace, in turn, submits to complete regulation by the government.

By Belloc's definition, capitalism, socialism, and the servile state all destroy what we should most value and protect, wide-scale private ownership, private initiative, and private wealth. By contrast, the best condition is when private ownership, private initiative, and private wealth are most widely *distributed* throughout society. Historically, Belloc sees the peak of distribution, in Europe, being in the Middle Ages (not the Middle Ages you'll get from politically correct text books, but the real Middle Ages); and its downfall began with King Henry VIII of England and his seizure of Church property and the property of nobles who opposed him. But that is a long story that need not detain us.[11]

Soft Despotism, Crisis Socialism, and the Welfare State

Belloc's vision is very much focused on England, where he thought capitalism—with wealth concentrated in the hands of a few—would reach a crisis, and desperate workers would embrace socialism and servility. Does that mean we in America, with our large middle class, are in no danger of becoming a servile state?

Well, unfortunately no; because in America, as we've seen with Tocqueville, the democratic danger is that we could become so passionately concerned with material gratification that we might freely walk into servitude. Big businesses want the government to protect them from their own foolish, greedy, and stupid errors, and bail them out for a soft landing. Individuals who bought houses far larger than they could afford demand a government bailout as well. Even more appalling, both big business and small individuals bring upon themselves the kind of economic crises that invite big government to regulate the smallest aspects of their economic and political welfare. General Motors becomes Government Motors. The idea that individuals and corporations should practice virtue, exhibit fiscal prudence, and practice self-reliance is dismissed as old-fashioned and moralistic; government can and should solve all our problems. This is happening now under what we might call liberal "crisis socialism." Since socialism is a step toward the servile state, we would do well to look more closely at Belloc's brilliant analysis of two fundamental kinds of socialist reformers, what we might call the activist and the dreamer.

The activist "regards the public ownership of the means of production (and the consequent compulsion of all citizens to work under the direction of the state) as the only feasible solution of our modern social ills," so that he will "begin by demanding the confiscation of the means of production from the hands of their present owners, and the vesting of them in the state."[12] General Motors can't handle its own affairs. The banks can't handle their own affairs. The government must buy them out and do things right. But the activist at least works from a kind of charity. "He is out to substitute for capitalist society a society in which men shall all be fed, clothed, housed, and in which men shall not live in perpetual jeopardy of the housing, clothing, and food."[13]

The dreamer, on the other hand, "loves the collectivist ideal in itself," and "does not pursue it so much because it is a solution of modern capitalism, as because it is an ordered and regular form of society which appeals to him in itself. He loves to consider the ideal of a state in which land and capital shall be held by public officials who shall order other men about and so preserve them from the consequences of *their* vice, ignorance and folly."[14] He is not truly moved by injustice and human suffering. Rather, he hates the messiness of actual people, the inefficiency of real liberty, and the genuine complexity of human social life. The local yokels should, for their own good, submit to the bureaucratic experts. "Tables, statistics, an exact framework for life—these afford him the food that satisfies his moral appetite; the occupation most congenial to him is the 'running' of men: as a machine is run." Such a man loves abstract order, not real human beings.

> All that human and organic complexity which is the color of any vital society offends him by its infinite differentiation. He is disturbed by multitudinous things; and the prospect of a vast bureaucracy wherein the whole of life shall be scheduled and appointed to certain simple schemes deriving from the coordinate work of public clerks and marshaled by powerful heads of departments gives his small stomach a final satisfaction.[15]

Belloc thought that, ultimately, the only real defense against socialism and the servile state was the Christian faith: only it could rekindle our desire to live freely as moral human beings; only it could successfully affirm that there are higher goods than material comfort; only it could effectively uphold the central importance of moral responsibility in our temporal lives (because of our eternal destinies). It is, in great part, secular materialism that convinces people to surrender their moral liberty and seek their worldly material welfare from a centralized power. The flickering fire of the Christian faith formed the basis of Belloc's hope that the victory of the servile state was impending, but not inevitable.

CHAPTER TEN

The Road to Serfdom: Friedrich August von Hayek

"Nowhere has democracy ever worked well without a great measure of local self-government, providing a school of political training for the people at large as much as for their future leaders. It is only where responsibility can be learned and practiced in affairs with which most people are familiar, where it is the awareness of one's neighbor rather than some theoretical knowledge of the needs of other people which guides action, that the ordinary man can take a real part in public affairs because they concern the world he knows."

How Not to Be Confused about Hayek: A Primer

FRIEDRICH VON HAYEK'S CLASSIC BOOK *THE ROAD TO SERFDOM* IS an easy read, but it has also been easily misunderstood—in part because of Hayek's brilliance as an economist. The chief misunderstanding is that *The Road to Serfdom* is solely about economics. It is not, and a clue to this is that Hayek took the title for his book, not from some economic treatise, but from Tocqueville's *Democracy in America*, and Hayek quotes in particular Tocqueville's passage about soft despotism:

Thus, after taking each individual by turns in its powerful hands and kneading him as it likes, the sovereign extends its arms over society as a whole; it covers its surface with a network of small, complicated, painstaking, uniform rules through which the most original minds and the most vigorous souls cannot clear a way to surpass the crowd; it does not break wills, but it softens them, bends them, and directs them; it rarely forces one to act, but it constantly opposes itself to one's acting; it does not destroy, it prevents things from being born; it does not tyrannize, it hinders, compromises, enervates, extinguishes, dazes, and finally reduces each nation to being nothing more than a herd of timid and industrious animals of which the government is the shepherd.[1]

Another clue is that he begins chapter 7, "Economic Control and Totalitarianism," with a quote from Hilaire Belloc's *The Servile State*, "The control of the production of wealth is the control of human life itself."[2] Hayek's book is not merely an economic book; it is about the dehumanizing effects that a socialist political-economic system has on the individual. Hayek lamented that one of the main points of *The Road to Serfdom* entirely missed by its critics is that "the most important change which extensive government control produces is a psychological change, an alteration in the character of the people,"[3] one that occurs when they willingly yield their freedom to a totalitarian state, even if it is the comfortable servitude of the welfare state. As Hayek also understood, the control of every detail of economic life by the welfare state "is the control of human life itself" (Belloc), and this pervasive control "hinders, compromises, enervates, extinguishes, dazes, and finally reduces each nation to being nothing more than a herd of timid and industrious animals of which the government is the shepherd" (Tocqueville). We might say it this way: the evil of socialism is not its calculable material inefficiency, but its incalculable damage to the soul.

We should not be surprised, then, that the real case to be made for economic freedom is moral. As with Aristotle, the Anti-Federalists, and Belloc, the positive focus, in regard to economic liberty, is on the moral responsibility of the individual to develop his own abilities to provide the necessities of life. That is an essential part of his perfection, his natural development as a human being. And that is why Hayek can state that the government should be a *means*, a mere *instrument*, "to help individuals in the fullest development of their individual personality,"[4] rather than an end in itself. Centralized, pervasive government planning is not only inefficient, but destroys the opportunity for the individual to develop his own intelligence and moral responsibility, to direct his own human potentialities as a sub-creator, and to contribute the fruit of his own particular talents to the common*wealth*. Socialism crushes all such development, and forces the individual to be a passive means or instrument of the state and its goals.

A second point needs to be made with equal clarity. Hayek's rejection of the niggling interventionist nanny state and his affirmation of economic freedom and competition do not mean that he was a doctrinaire libertarian. That is a mistake that both his detractors and all too many of his promoters make. The controversy, for Hayek, is *not* between the extreme positions of complete government intervention and no government intervention. As he explained, *The Road to Serfdom* was not

> about whether the state ought to act or ought not to act at all. The whole effort of my book was to substitute a new distinction for the older silly and vague idea. I had realized that *some* kind of state action is extremely dangerous. Therefore, my whole effort

was to distinguish between legitimate and illegitimate action. I have attempted to do that by saying that, so far as government plans for competition or steps in where competition cannot possibly do the job, there is no objection; but I believe that all other forms of government activity are highly dangerous.[5]

The Road to Serfdom is focused on the kind of state action that Hayek quite prophetically (and in line with Tocqueville and Belloc) saw as extremely dangerous: the pervasive, top-down control of every level of society and the economy advocated by socialism. Hayek's alternative was not libertarian anarchy, but a limited state that provided, through law, a framework within which individual economic activity can flourish. Economic competition, he wrote, "if it is to be made effective, requires a good deal of government activity directed toward making it effective and toward supplementing it where it cannot be made effective.... I am not an anarchist. I do not suggest that a competitive system can work without an effectively enforced and intelligently drawn up legal system."[6]

That is why he distanced himself from "the wooden insistence of some [classical] liberals on...the principle of laissez faire." There is, argued Hayek, "all the difference between deliberately creating a system within which competition will work as beneficially as possible and passively accepting institutions as they are,"[7] as some advocates of *laissez faire* capitalism propose. "The successful use of competition as the principle of social organization precludes certain types of coercive interference with economic life, but it admits of others which sometimes may very considerably assist its work and even requires certain kinds of government action."[8] In accord with the principle of subsidiarity, the government supplements, rather than supplants, individual economic effort.[9]

Nor did Hayek shun the notion of some kind of social safety net. While rejecting the all-pervasive socialist welfare state, Hayek believed that it was only humane that "some minimum of food, shelter, and clothing, sufficient to preserve health and the capacity to work...be assured to everybody," and the state should also render "assistance to the victims of such 'acts of God' as earthquakes and floods." He even believed that "with genuinely insurable risks...the case for the state's helping to organize a comprehensive system of social insurance is very strong," although what Hayek would have in mind is, to say the least, much different than what is envisioned by socialist-minded liberals. These things can be done, argued Hayek, with a limited state and "without endangering general freedom."[10] Hayek was no Ebenezer Scrooge, no Thomas Malthus; he did not believe in ruthlessly letting the poor suffer to extinction.

A third point concerns Hayek and liberalism. Hayek consistently referred to himself as a liberal and in fact denied (with some misgivings and much clarification) that he could be called a conservative, even writing a famous essay, "Why I Am Not a Conservative."[11] Yet Hayek was anything but a liberal in our modern American sense. Hayek was a classical liberal in the European sense—that is, he was concerned with the preservation of responsible individual liberty from state encroachment. Like Chesterton, Hayek rejected the tag "conservative" because it meant for him merely holding onto the present order regardless of its merits. Also like Chesterton, if you had to put Hayek on one side or the other in today's political taxonomy, conservative or liberal, he is unmistakably, overwhelmingly on the conservative side, with only a few philosophical quibbles, and perhaps a theological one; he has virtually nothing in common with the Left save for the belief that change and reform can be good.

And that brings us to a final point before we dig into the text itself. When *The Road to Serfdom* was written, socialism meant the direct government "nationalization of the means of production and the central economic planning which this made possible and necessary." As Hayek himself later noted, that kind of socialism has largely given way to a new form of socialism achieved through a different means, "chiefly the extensive redistribution of incomes through taxation and the institutions of the welfare state." In the socialism of the welfare state, "the effects" of socialism "are brought about more slowly, indirectly, and imperfectly," but are "very much the same" as if there were a direct government takeover.[12] It isn't revolutionary socialism, but socialism where freedom is lost by an almost imperceptible increase in degrees of servitude to the state.

Hayek, the Man

Friedrich August von Hayek was born on May 8, 1899, in Vienna, Austria, the first son of August and Felicitas Hayek. His father was a medical doctor with a passion for botany, and a not very secret desire to be a university professor. His mother came from a wealthy family, and Friedrich was born into comfortable circumstances, if not comfortable times. His parents were, at best, nominal Catholics, and Friedrich himself became an agnostic by the age of fifteen.[13] In one sense, this makes his ultimate economic and philosophical positions more interesting, for in his own words, he ended up a "Burkean Whig,"[14] believing in the importance of morality, tradition, and religion in forming the foundation of a humane political order that defends the inviolable importance of the individual.

Young Hayek was one of those brilliant and precocious boys who had little interest in performing in schools, and was able, with little application, to succeed brilliantly in failing Greek, Latin, and mathematics when he was fourteen. He spent many dismal hours swimming around at the bottom of the class. Hayek was only fifteen when World War I started, and he entered the army in the spring of 1917, serving in Italy, where he was almost killed several times and underwent a nasty bout of malaria. It was while he was in the army that he read his first serious economic treatise.

Needless to say, the Austria to which he returned was in shreds, economically and politically. Hayek decided to enter the University of Vienna and study economics, although he always maintained a keen interest in psychology. At this point, young Hayek was a soft socialist—not a Marxist, but more a Fabian socialist, the nicer English type that tried to impose socialism gradually through democratic means rather than at the point of a bayonet. Socialism made sense. The old order was destroyed by war, and the present disorder was teetering toward total collapse. During his time at the university, the Austrian economy underwent severe inflation, with prices rising by 7,000 percent between October 1921 and August 1922.[15] Wartime made united, centralized efforts by the government feel normal, and indeed an attractive way to rebuild a new political order from the social and economic rubble.

Yet Hayek ultimately rejected the socialist solution, and in large part that was the result of him coming into contact with the Austrian school of economics at Vienna, where Hayek was indirectly influenced by his reading of Carl Menger, and directly influenced by a professor, Friedrich von Wieser, and later, by the mentorship of Ludwig von Mises. During this time, he formed an intellectual discussion group, the *Geistkreis*,[16] which included among its many eminent members Eric Voegelin. Both Voegelin and Hayek attended von Mises' private seminars. And both Voegelin and Hayek rejected the Left's faith in centralized government as a kind of deity that could control society omnisciently and benevolently.

Hayek earned his doctorate in law in 1921 (economics was a subset of the field of law at Vienna), and in political science in 1923. Obviously, Hayek's days as an academic underachiever were over. Having decided that he would be an economist, he went to New York from 1923 to 1924 (with von Mises' help), studying at New York University, and living in near poverty. He did some preliminary work on the Federal Reserve, but the greatest benefit was gaining fluency in English.

Hayek returned from America, married Helene von Fritsche (1926), and with von Mises founded the Austrian Institute for Business Cycle Research in Vienna in 1927. Hayek was strongly influenced by von Mises' conclusion that fiddling with the money supply to stimulate the economy actually causes far more problems than it solves, providing artificially low interest rates, stimulating artificially high spending, encouraging imprudent investment, and setting off inflation. Mises' arguments weaned Hayek completely off Fabian socialism and set him against the kind of economic manipulation favored by John Maynard Keynes (and favored by liberalism since FDR). "We can spend our way out of this crisis" as a battle cry was, for Hayek, a sure way to send an economy into frantic self-destruction.

Hayek offered a series of lectures at the London School of Economics in early 1931, and the following year took up a post there. Ironically, the LSE was founded by the two leading Fabian socialists, Beatrice and Sidney Webb, and Hayek locked horns with the leading socialist of the school, Harold Laski. Fabian socialism called for top-down reconstruction of all society and all societies— Fabians had no difficulty with a kind of liberal imperialism such as is now ensconced at the United Nations. Top-down radical reconstruction assumed that universal benevolence must be armed with political omnipotence, and so Fabian socialism had ineradicable totalitarian tendencies.

After Hitler annexed Austria in March 1938, Hayek decided to become a British citizen. Hayek would ever after point out the connection between nice British socialism and nasty German socialism (do not forget that Nazi stands for National *Socialist* German Worker's Party). In 1944, with World War II still raging, Hayek published *The Road to Serfdom.* Its initial print run in England was a mere 2,000 copies, but more copies were immediately ordered as the book sold rapidly, and the publisher had to scramble because Britain was suffering from a wartime paper shortage. But this was nothing to the book's reception in America. A *New York Times Book Review* by Henry Hazlitt sent the initial American printing from 2,000, to an additional 5,000, and then 10,000, all within a few days. Then a *Reader's Digest* version appeared in 1945, selling well over 600,000 copies through a Book-of-the-Month arrangement, and Hayek undertook a wildly successful lecture tour.[17] Within a matter of months, Hayek had been lifted from academic obscurity to celebrity, and *The Road to Serfdom* became one of the top-selling economic books of the twentieth century. It is also a modern conservative economic masterpiece that deserves our careful attention.

Humility: The Key to Hayek

You will understand the considerable wisdom of Hayek if you get just one profound point. Human beings are not gods. We are not, and can never be, all-knowing. For our own good, we need to accept, with humility, our own human intellectual limitations.

Of course, as an agnostic, that is not quite how Hayek put it, so let's approach it from his angle. Whatever his other quibbles with Aristotle (and he did have some), Hayek was an Aristotelian in regard to his hearty appreciation of one very important virtue, prudence. Hayek understood what governments tend to overlook: no centralized government bureaucracy can possibly know the particular and various needs of society on the local level—particular and various needs that individuals are best left to meet in their own way using their prudence, i.e., their practical experience and a concrete understanding of their own particular situation.

Hayek argues that the "state should confine itself to establishing rules applying to general types of situations and should allow the individuals freedom in everything which depends on the circumstances of time and place, because only the individuals concerned in each instance can fully know these circumstances and adapt their actions to them."[18] His argument for a free market was not based upon greed, but upon a hearty recognition of the inherent limitations of human knowledge. If the general government, in humility, recognizes that it cannot possibly know and judge all these particulars, then it will take a hands-off approach.

But even more, Hayek (like Voegelin) stressed the inherent and irreducible complexity of human nature and hence human choices—a complexity that we must humbly accept. If all human action could be boiled down to one or two simple causes— say, a merely mechanical reaction to hunger, sex, or pain—then it would be possible to come up with a general and exact science of human action, and hence, human economic activity. If such a science were possible, then human economic activity would be entirely predictable and controllable from the top down—a socialist's dream! Against such utopian dreams, Hayek set forth our commonsense, everyday experience of our own complexity, the recognition that our choices, economic and otherwise, arise from a multitude of sources that cannot be boiled down for the convenience of grand socialist economic planners. They arise—to recall Voegelin—from the fullness of our humanity, from man's "participation in the world with his body, soul, intellect, and spirit." A multitude of real, complex human beings choosing a multitude of particular means to provide for themselves and their families economically in their particular circumstances—*that* is the real, natural foundation of economics. In this respect, Hayek's affirmation of the free market was a safeguard against reductionist views of human nature that would replace the natural foundations of economics with artificial schemes imposed by force from above. It was a call for humility on the part of government, a kind of reverence and respect before the wonderful complexity of human nature.

This would all seem to be simple, practical wisdom and good judgment, i.e., prudence. But governments all too often act as though their good intentions can override prudence.

The Road to Serfdom Is Paved with Good Intentions

The problem with a socialist government is that—with every good intention—it tries to write rules for every particular concrete circumstance and direct every last detail of the people. The result is always the same: the people affected feel like the government is pouring concrete on top of them. When bureaucracies apply distant, general rules to local communities, they rob individuals of their proper liberty to judge circumstances and apply their own prudence. The core of the problem is not the evil intention of the bureaucrat; she may have the best of intentions. The evil comes from that "passion for conscious control of everything"[19] that is the essence of totalitarianism.

Socialist government sees itself as a benevolent god; it becomes instead a malevolent tyrant, micromanaging the details of everyone's life with all the blundering inefficiency, confusion, unintended consequences, and plain idiocy (which we politely call "imprudence") that have made the name "bureaucrat" a term of infamy. The bureaucrat truly becomes evil when he comes to believe that local people are too stupid to know what's good for them and are better off ruled with the iron hand of the government's experts.

Against this hard-knuckled nannyism, Hayek asserts that people are best served when they are given the opportunity to serve themselves and their local communities.

The Case for Economic Freedom and Competition

Hayek frames his case for economic freedom in terms of individual moral responsibility. If the government assumes my moral responsibility in economic life, in my work as a provider for myself and my family, or in any other way, it severely limits my capacity to act as a moral being. "What our generation is in danger of forgetting is not only that morals are of necessity a phenomenon of individual conduct but also that they can exist only in the sphere in which the individual is free to decide for himself and is called upon voluntarily to sacrifice personal advantage to the observance of a moral rule."[20] If someone takes that responsibility from us, he has stripped us of our moral nature. "Responsibility, not to a superior, but to one's conscience, the awareness of a duty not exacted by compulsion, the necessity to decide which of the things one values are to be sacrificed to others, and to bear the consequences of one's own decision, are the very essence of any morals which deserve the name."[21] That is what the economic "collectivism" of a socialist-style government destroys. "A movement whose main promise is the relief from responsibility cannot but be antimoral in its effect, however lofty the ideals to which it owes its birth."[22]

To these moral and philosophical considerations, Hayek adds a political dimension about the nature of power. Bureaucratic power is inevitably centralizing power. In Hayek's words, "by uniting in the hands of a single body power formerly exercised independently by many, an amount of power is created infinitely greater than any that existed before, so much more far-reaching as almost to be different in kind."[23] No human being should be trusted with that much power—especially not bureaucrats, because they are appointed not elected.

In order to avoid this kind of insidious concentration of power in the hands of a few, we need to split economic power up. "To split or decentralize power is necessarily to reduce the absolute amount of power, and the competitive system is the only system designed to minimize by decentralization the power exercised by man over man." By *freeing up* local economies from top-down government control, we necessarily split up, diffract, and dilute economic power, putting it in a multitude of private hands. "What is called economic power, while it can be an instrument of coercion, is, in the hands of private individuals, never exclusive or complete power, never power over the whole life of a person. But centralized as an instrument of political power it creates a degree of dependence scarcely distinguishable from slavery."[24]

Governments expand because they do not trust the independent, free judgments of the people, or because leaders have grand personal or national visions to which they hope to marshal all the resources within their grasp, or both. Obviously, such governments need to make the decisions. Precisely here is the painful rub. When bad decisions are made locally, they stay local; when bad decisions are made by centralized government power it multiplies the bad effects a million-fold.

"But," someone might object, "its *good* effects are multiplied a million-fold as well. And since at least *our* government is 'of the people, by the people, and for the people,' we can expect far more good than bad decisions will be made because they will be made *by us.*" Not so, replies Hayek. What actually happens is this: Since the central government has taken upon itself the task of ruling society in all its particulars, it must make very particular plans that try to cover the myriad details in endless areas. No general legislative body, busy with a thousand other tasks, can possibly attend to any such detail, and so the task of writing legislation is passed on to a very few "experts," and the task of concrete implementation and oversight into the hands of unelected bureaucrats.[25] So much for "of the people, by the people, and for the people." Centralizing always means the rule of the few, so that even with popular election, congressmen will be forced to delegate power to a small number of experts and bureaucrats; that is, they "will at best be reduced to choosing the persons who are to have practically absolute power."[26]

Since the "experts" are often hand-picked from industry or some other special interest—who just happen to have contributed to certain election campaigns—it shouldn't surprise us that we end up with a conspiracy of Congress with special interests. That is not the free market, but the market controlled by a collusion between industry and government, which is the chief source of economic monopolies.[27]

So is there no role for government in the economy? Hayek allows that government should assure that prices aren't fixed by collusion, that monopolies don't crush competition, and that obvious dangers are avoided and some regulatory safeguards imposed: "To prohibit the use of certain poisonous substances or to require special precautions in their use, to limit working hours or to require certain sanitary arrangements, is fully compatible with the preservation of competition. . . . Nor is the preservation of competition incompatible with an extensive system of social services—so long as the organization of these services is not designed in such a way as to make competition ineffective over wide fields."[28] Competition is essential, but it is not the *goal* but rather the *result* of what Hayek is truly trying to preserve, which is free people freely conducting their business without centralized direction.

We aren't surprised, then, that Hayek ends *The Road to Serfdom* sounding very like an Anti-Federalist. Toward the end of World War II, looking over the ruins of Europe caused by the ultimate centralizing effort of Germany to assert itself as a world empire, Hayek said:

> We shall not rebuild civilization on the large scale. It is no accident that on the whole there was more beauty and decency to be found in the life of the small peoples, and that among the large ones there was more happiness and content in proportion as they had avoided the deadly blight of centralization. Least of all shall we preserve democracy or foster its growth if all the power and most of the important decisions rest with an organization far too big for the common man to survey or comprehend. Nowhere has democracy ever worked well without a great measure of local self-government, providing a school of political training for the people at large as much as for their future leaders. It is only where responsibility can be learned and practiced in affairs with which most people are familiar, where it is the awareness of one's neighbor rather than some theoretical knowledge of the needs of other people which guides action, that the ordinary man can take a real part in public affairs because they concern the world he knows.... We shall be the gainers if we create a world fit for small states to live in.[29]

Liberalism, Scientism, and the Utopian Urge

While claiming the classical liberal label for himself, Hayek recognized that socialism's pedigree came from left-liberalism.[30] In the desire to remake the world, to bring about an earthly utopia, left-liberalism aims at complete social, political, and economic reconstruction; and that requires vast, centralized power. This desire is fueled by a belief that science makes such a transformation possible through an omniscient state.

Like Voegelin, Hayek understood that treating politics and economics as if they were branches of physics or chemistry was a dangerous fallacy and a fundamental left-liberal, or socialist, error. "Those who argue that we have to an astounding degree learned to master the forces of nature but are sadly behind in making successful use of the possibilities of social collaboration are quite right so far as this statement goes. But they are mistaken when they carry the comparison further and argue that we must learn to master the forces of society in the same manner in which we have learned to master the forces of nature. This is not only the path to totalitarianism but the path to destruction of our civilization and a certain way to block future progress."[31]

Like C. S. Lewis, Hayek saw the dangers inherent in ever-advancing technology. "While there is nothing in modern technological developments which forces us toward comprehensive economic planning, there is a great deal in them which makes infinitely more dangerous the power a planning authority would possess."[32] To repeat Lewis's warning, we must be ever mindful that "each new power won *by* man is a power *over* man as well."

Hayek won a Nobel Prize for economics, but we should never forget that he believed himself a political and moral philosopher as much as an economist. He knew that the fundamental question is not how we buy and sell, but who we are as human beings, and that is what he wanted to conserve and the key to his conservative approach to economics. But since man is more than *homo economicus*, there is more to our conservative efforts. We will now examine a sadly neglected aspect: the conservative imagination.

Part IV

The Conservative Story, and Conservative Stories

CONSERVATISM AND LIBERALISM TELL TWO DIFFERENT STORIES about nature, human nature, the meaning of good and evil, the purpose of life, and the meaning of death. That's why conservatism is not limited to political theory or economics, but can be found in literature as well. Although there are obviously a great number of works to choose from, for our purposes I've chosen Shakespeare's *Tempest*, Jane Austen's *Sense and Sensibility*, J. R. R. Tolkien's *Lord of the Rings*, and last but certainly not least, a particular translation of the Bible, one Tolkien helped to produce. We will also examine a very popular, and pernicious, literary impostor, Ayn Rand's *Atlas Shrugged*, a story that many take to be conservative but which is, as conservatives like Whittaker Chambers observed long ago, actually at war with the conservative view of the world.

What can possibly be meant by calling a story "conservative" or "liberal"? Liberal stories seek to free us, to liberate us, from conservative conviction that there is a greater reality to which our reason, our will, and our passions must conform: an eternal moral order, a natural law. The defining liberal character trait is pride, an explicit rejection that there is any greater wisdom and goodness beyond what we find in ourselves and what we make. The defining conservative virtue is humility, deference to wisdom and experience, and the conviction that there really is a moral law, good and evil, and we violate that law at our peril.

CHAPTER ELEVEN

The Tempest:
William Shakespeare

"'Ban, 'Ban, Ca-Caliban
Has a new master, get a new man.
Freedom, high-day! High-day, freedom! Freedom, high-day, freedom!"

Gulielmus filius Johannes Shakspere

SO READS THE BAPTISMAL RECORD AT HOLY TRINITY CHURCH OF Stratford, England, a small market town on the river Avon. It tells us, in Latin, of the Holy Sacrament's application on April 26, 1564, to William, son of John Shakspere (spelling in the Elizabethan era being, happily, an art that allowed some creative leeway). *Gulielmus* is the Latin form of the popular English name William, a name that entered England thanks to the earlier invasion in 1066 of William the Conqueror.

Nestled in the rich agricultural county of Warwickshire, Stratford was a comfortably sized town of about 1,500 people, just the right size for solid general self-sufficiency and familiarity. Robert Shakespeare, William's grandfather, was a farmer, living in tenancy on Robert Arden's estate, some four miles from Stratford. By his hard work he was able to accumulate a modest purse by his death. John built upon that wealth, first by marrying Robert Arden's daughter, Mary, and then moving into Stratford, and setting up shop as a tanner and retailer of leather goods and agricultural produce. Young William's house on Henley Street was therefore rather considerable.

For whatever reason, John's rise to prominence in Stratford took a sudden dive around 1577, and we find records of him mortgaging his wife's property, tangled in litigation, and paying off substantial fines. The reasons for his troubles are lost to us, but we do know the Shakespeares did not disappear into destitution or ignominy. John Shakespeare held civic positions in the town, and William went to school at King's New School of Stratford (named after King Edward VI, the sickly son of Henry VIII and Henry's third wife, Jane Seymour). He studied there from the age of seven to fourteen. The school day ran from seven in the morning to five at night. It was a rigorous liberal arts curriculum covering not just the basics of reading and writing, but Latin and grammar, the catechism, and the great ancient authors, their poetry, histories, comedies, tragedies, speeches, and philosophical discourses.

Yoked to Shakespeare's genius, this literary training helped create the greatest playwright in human history. It is too often asserted, by envious academics, that Shakespeare did not write the plays attributed to his name; only an aristocrat, they say, could have created such literary wonders. But experience might teach us that God distributes gifts with a casual disregard for human propriety and social standing.

William married Anne Hathaway in the winter of 1582, when she was twenty-six and he only eighteen. Their first child, Susanna, was born in May 1583, and twins, Hamnet (not Hamlet) and Judith, followed in 1585. We then hear nothing of Shakespeare in any records for some time, so we know next to nothing about his twenties, although one might repeat rumors that he became a schoolteacher's aide, butcher's apprentice, or, having fallen into bad company, a deer and rabbit poacher.

The first we hear of him again, Shakespeare is being pilloried by one Robert Greene for stealing actors for his rival company. In 1594, we find him a member of The Lord Chamberlain's Men, a theatrical company under the patronage of Baron Hunsdon, then of his son and heir, and then of the king (King James I of England) who turned the troupe into The King's Men. By 1594, Shakespeare had already written as many as a dozen of his plays, including *Comedy of Errors, Two Gentlemen of Verona,* and perhaps even *Romeo and Juliet.* He was a literary man of note, and unlike many literary men, fairly prosperous, investing in real estate. His son Hamnet died in 1596, the same year William applied to become a gentleman with his own coat of arms (granted in 1599). By the turn of the century, he was famous enough to be plagiarized for profit by unscrupulous printers. Today, too many think of Shakespeare as fit only for plodding scholars and reluctant schoolboys. But in his own time, he was *popular*, his plays were as successful with the meanest groundlings as they were with the most educated noblemen.

In 1601 Shakespeare purchased a share in the newly built Globe Theater in London, and this stage became his world; it was here he wrote and produced some of his most famous plays, including *Hamlet, Othello,* and *King Lear. The Tempest,* a comedy-romance reputed to be his last play, was first produced in 1611. Shakespeare died on April 23, 1616, after revising his will to take account of his daughter Judith's marriage (his other daughter Susanna had married in 1607 and given him a grandchild named Elizabeth). He was just over fifty-two years old.

Why *The Tempest*?

Everything Shakespeare wrote is worthy of attention, but *The Tempest* is an absolute jewel of conservative wisdom.

The plot is relatively simple. Prospero, the rightful Duke of Milan, and his daughter Miranda are stranded on an island, having been exiled by Prospero's usurping brother, Antonio (who was aided by Alonso, King of Naples). By providence, in their twelfth year on the island, a ship bearing Antonio, Alonso, Alonso's scheming brother Sebastian, Alonso's son Ferdinand, and several others, comes close by, and Prospero uses his magic powers to create a storm to shipwreck them on the island. While on the island, he further uses magic to bring about the remorse and moral redemption of the villains, Antonio, Alonso, and Sebastian, the marriage of Ferdinand and Miranda, and the moral transformation of the other characters insofar as that can be achieved. In the end, all are reconciled and they sail back to Italy, Prospero leaving his magic robe and staff behind.

Simple enough, but in that simple plot Shakespeare embeds concentrated wisdom about God and man. Unfortunately, we haven't the luxury of walking, line by line, through the play. We'll have to be satisfied with making several general points, beginning with a review of the cast of characters, which itself reveals Shakespeare's wisdom about human things.

The Anti-Utopian Wisdom of Shakespeare

Here is a quick chart of the main characters.

ALREADY ON THE ISLAND:
Prospero (the usurped Duke of Milan)
Miranda (his daughter)
Caliban (a deformed savage, son of Sycorax, a witch)

Ariel (a spirit, imprisoned by the evil witch Sycorax but freed by Prospero's magic)

NEWLY SHIPWRECKED:
Antonio (Prospero's brother, usurper, exiler).
Alonso (the King of Naples)
Ferdinand (Alonso's good son)
Sebastian (Alonso's brother)
Gonzalo (a former political counselor to Prospero)
Trinculo (a jester)
Stephano (a drunken butler)

While well-drawn and realistic, the characters form recognizable types. Miranda, for instance, is a young woman of fifteen— innocent in both her moral purity and her naïveté about human nature. Gonzalo is kindly, honest, and loyal, but, like Miranda, foolishly assumes that others are as well-intentioned as he is. Then we have Antonio, Alonso, and Sebastian. Aristocratic and ambitious, they are quite willing to do whatever evil is necessary to gain and maintain power. After their usurpation, Antonio and Alonso had no remorse about putting Prospero and his three-year-old daughter Miranda on a boat so decrepit "the very rats instinctively... quit it."[1] Only by a miracle of Providence were their lives saved by landing on the island. On the other end of the scale, we have Trinculo the fool and Stephano the drunkard, filled with petty ambition; they are the slaves of their own passions. At the lowest end is Caliban, offspring of a witch, half-human and half-beast, a creature whose outward deformity matches his inward deformity, and who is quite willing to become the slave of the first man who offers him pleasure and ease, and to kill the man who tries to save him from his own depravity.

Standing apart from all these and above them is Prospero. Prospero is a man of learning, "the liberal arts" he says, "being all my study."[2] Yet Prospero's passion for learning led him to neglect his dukedom, and allowed Antonio to seize it. It was, then, Prospero's imprudent neglect of politics and his search for wisdom in the seclusion of his study were then responsible for his and Miranda's exile. But it has also given him the power of magic, which, because of his wisdom and virtue, he only uses for good.

In gathering all these characters together on one island, Shakespeare shows that, contrary to what liberals would have us believe, circumstances don't in and of themselves make men evil. Evil is the result of imperfections, failings, and corruptions of human nature (or sin). It is politically disastrous to ignore this truth, as Gonzalo so foolishly illustrates. Gonzalo—good but not wise—rhapsodizes about the beauty and bounty of the island and the "commonwealth" he could create on it.

> I' th' commonwealth I would by contraries
> Execute all things; for no kind of traffic
> Would I admit; no name of magistrate;
> Letters should not be known; riches, poverty,
> And use of service, none; contract, succession,
> Bourne, bound of land, tilth
> vineyard, none;
> No use of metal, corn, or wine, or oil;
> No occupation; all men idle, all,
> And women too, but innocent and pure;
> No sovereignty...
> All things in common nature should produce
> Without sweat or endeavor. Treason, felony,
> Sword, pike, knife, gun, or need of any engine,

Would I not have; but nature should bring forth,

Of its own kind, all foison, all abundance,

To feed my innocent people. . . .

I would with such perfection govern, sir,

T' excel the golden age.[3]

In Gonzalo's vision, evil is caused by the struggle to provide for oneself and one's family, and the consequent development of private property. So, when there is a natural abundance, people will be naturally good, toil and trade will be unnecessary, and there will be no need for distinctions of wealth and property, no need for laws or arms to protect property because everything will be held in common, and no need for technical development because no labor is necessary. Political harmony, he believes, will spring forth as spontaneously as the food on the island.

Good-hearted Gonzalo makes a fundamental error in all this. For him, evil is caused by everything *but* sin. And that, for Shakespeare, is the greatest foolishness. A natural paradise does not cure human evil. Indeed, after Gonzalo's speech, Antonio and Sebastian plan to kill him (and Alonso too).[4] There are already snakes in Gonzalo's misty new Eden.

Clearly, Gonzalo's speech teaches us that utopian visions did not begin with Marx, though one can certainly see Marxist parallels. Many a man has shared Gonzalo's softheaded theorizing about utopia. When Europeans began discovering new lands, the utopian imagination was given new life—here, it was thought, we will find human innocence unsoiled by the degradations of civilization; here we can make a new beginning; here we will have an earthly paradise. Of course, it never turns out that way.

In *The Tempest*, Shakespeare takes up the utopian themes of his day, and offers his anti-utopian wisdom as antidote. From it, we learn why, when utopians do gain power, the men at the helm always resemble the ruthless Sebastian, why they are supported by well-intentioned counselors like Gonzalo, and why they are surrounded by drunks, jesters, and barbaric half-men. Any utopian project begins, not from a clean slate and a pure heart, but from human beings as we find them—a mix of innocents, drunkards, ambitious intriguers, rakes, cads, cowards, the wise and half-wise, the virtuous and half-virtuous, the vicious and the foolish. When the dust settles and the revolutionary vanguard has finally cleared the way for a Communist paradise, when the socialist government has finally removed power from those who oppose progress, there will still be naïve Mirandas, scheming Alonsos, fratricidal Sebastians, ambitious Antonios, honest-fool Gonzalos, jester Trinculos, drunkard Stephanos, and barbaric and irredeemable Calibans. Such is the cast of characters we are always faced with.

Magic, Political Power, and Technology

This same point is emphasized in a different way by the presence of magic in the play. The quickest way to see Shakespeare's wisdom is to ask, "What would _____ do if he found Prospero's magic cape and wand?" Which is another way to ask, "What would _____ do if he quite suddenly gained complete political power?" The answer is, "He would use the power in accordance with his character, for better or worse." Whatever corruptive influence power itself might have, the main problem is the corruption that *already exists* in the soul of the person who gains power. Power magnifies a man's character. For some, it magnifies wisdom and virtue, even while testing them. For most, it merely amplifies flaws, confusions, petty and profound vices, and downright foolishness. That is why conservatives have such a healthy fear of the concentration of political power: the greater the concentration, the more likely that power will be wielded like a magic wand in the hands of a madman.

What would Antonio do if he had it? We know that earlier he had stolen his brother's dukedom. While on the island, he enters into intrigue with Sebastian to kill Alonso, the king who had once been his ally, and the kind and innocent counselor Gonzalo who remains loyal to Prospero. Wicked men seek power and use it wickedly.

What would the drunkard Stephano do? He would rule for the meanest pleasures, drinking and carousing. On the island, thinking that the king and all the nobles have been drowned in the storm, he plots, with Trinculo and Caliban, to kill Prospero, have his way with Miranda, and become the drunken king of the island paradise.[5]

Caliban? He has already tried to rape Miranda, and, showing no remorse, would do it again at the least opportunity.[6] He is the perfect lackey, ready to be a tool to any tyrant that promises to fill his gullet. Having been given a drink of wine by Stephano, he declares Stephano to be a "brave god," gratefully adding that "I'll swear upon that bottle to be thy true subject, for the liquor is not earthly." To this bibulous deity, Caliban offers the whole island and his own servitude, and convinces Stephano and Trinculo to kill Prospero, and thus release him from Prospero's magic powers. He would rather be the slave of a drunkard than a servant of a wise man. Like his new master, he believes that freedom means doing whatever you want, and so sings out gaily as he goes to kill Prospero, "'Ban, 'Ban, Ca-Caliban, Has a new master, get a new man. Freedom, high-day! High-day, freedom! Freedom, high-day, freedom!"[7] Caliban does not represent unspoiled natural goodness, as some analysts of Shakespeare have maintained. Rather, he is the picture of moral degeneration, when men become slaves to passions, and willing lackeys to drunken demagogues who promise them a pleasure paradise free from any moral restriction or penalty. His "freedom song" is the anthem of the most corrupt in an extreme democracy. It takes little imagination to guess what Caliban would do with Prospero's magic wand.

What about Miranda? Miranda is certainly the most morally pure character in the play. Her moral innocence is the result of her isolation on the island and her father's prudent care in her upbringing. Her only brush with evil has been with the entirely repugnant Caliban, and so her naïveté about human goodness and human evil is extremely dangerous. She is much like the person who, having been raised by kind parents and prudently kept from bad society, thinks that the world is divided between all the good people and a few Nazis—the evil people easily recognizable by their menacing uniforms and harsh accents.

The dangers of her naïveté, and the dangers of that naïveté linked to power, are illustrated at two key instances. First, on seeing the ship caught in the storm, Miranda bursts forth in an effusion of pity that she wishes she had the power of her father to "Have sunk the sea within the earth" to save them.[8] But such pity linked to power would have negated the moral regeneration of the people on the ship that Prospero achieves through shipwreck, and made impossible her and her father's return to Milan. Second, in her naïveté, when Miranda finally sees all the men from the ship she utters her famous exclamation, "O, wonder! How many goodly creatures are there here! How beauteous mankind is! O brave new world, That has such people in't!" (to which Prospero wisely replies, "'Tis new to thee").[9] While they might be physically handsome, especially in comparison to Caliban, the men from the ship represent nearly every stage of evil, from fraternal usurpers and fratricides, to drunkards and fools who were ready to murder her father. If Miranda had the power of her father, she would be a doormat for every scheming rogue in the rogue's gallery now inhabiting the island.

As with the others, magic would only magnify Miranda's imprudent innocence. Magical power, like political power, does not save us from our faults, but instead amplifies their ill effects. This is, by the way, the great conservative argument (such as we found it in Lewis) *against* the simple and simple-minded praise of technical progress. As technical power increases our control over the elements, over nature, it approaches nearer and nearer to magic. The problem is the same: technological power is distinct from wisdom and goodness. Anyone can use it, regardless of his moral worth. Because power is distinct from wisdom and goodness, technical superiority and moral barbarity can and do all too easily unite. That is, once again, the wisdom behind Lewis's warning about technology that "each new power won by man is a power over man as well." The advance of technical power would be an unmixed blessing only if wisdom and goodness advanced at least one step ahead. And what did Shakespeare think the chances of that happening were? He has the god-like but mortal Prospero break his magic staff and throw his books into the sea before returning to Milan.[10] That helps us understand something very important about God and Shakespeare.

God and Shakespeare

"If *I* had a magic wand, I'd _____." "If *I* were king, I'd _____." "If *I* were the President, I'd _____." These three statements are, in essence, ways of saying, "If *I* were God, I'd _____." They all assume that I already have the wisdom and goodness, and that all I lack is the power to put things right. That is the essential human error, the error that *The Tempest* was written to correct.

To understand why this is the essential error, we may stand back from the play and ask, "What is the most dangerous mistake made by all the characters?" The answer would be, the confusion between what they happen to *desire* and what is actually *good* for them. Prospero desired only to be left alone to study, and he lost his dukedom. Alonso and Antonio desired political power, but were quite willing to cast aside moral goodness. Miranda desires to help people on the strength of her pity, but their intentions are evil and threaten her own life. Gonzalo desires a political utopia, but doesn't see that it would require a tyrannical iron hand to set it up and maintain it. Stephano desires endless rivers of wine. Caliban desires the violation of Miranda, and slavery to drink and drunkards.

The distinction between what people happen to desire and what is good for them creates the fundamental political problem, the problem that causes the further distinction that Aristotle gave us between the good and bad forms of government. A king rules for what is truly good for his people; a tyrant for what he desires. Aristocratic rule aims at what is good; oligarchic rule aims for what the oligarchs in power happen to desire. A republic is ordered to what is good; a democracy is ordered to what the majority happen to desire. Most governments for most of human history have been aimed at, defined by, the desire of those in power.

On a more profound level, one connected to the level of politics even while going beyond it, people create a worldview according to what they desire. That is the real meaning of saying, "If *I* were God, I'd _____." We live our lives as if the world conformed to our desires. When the world doesn't play along, we condemn it and live our lives dreaming of the way the world *should* be, *would* be, if *we* were in charge of things. Modern liberalism is the singular attempt to stop dreaming and start acting on this hubristic ambition. At its best, it follows Gonzalo, creating a nanny state government dedicated to ensuring a comfortable, secure life for its citizens, whose lives are to be filled with material pleasures, and devoid of pain and toil. At its worst, it becomes as savage as Antonio, ruthlessly eliminating those who don't fit its grand vision. But in either case, totalitarian force is necessary to recreate the world. That is why liberalism seeks both technological mastery over nature and absolute political power to achieve its utopian visions. It seeks the power of a god, and in doing so, it must take God's place. Liberalism is secular in precisely this sense: it aims at godlike power through politics.

Properly understood, *The Tempest* breaks the spell of such visions, and Shakespeare does it by putting Prospero in the place of God. Prospero uses his magic to bring about the repentance and moral regeneration of those whom he causes to shipwreck on the island. He doesn't give them what they desire, but what they need to become good, even though it brings great pain and distress. Prospero causes a storm, putting them in fear of death, as the beginning of their moral renewal. He separates Alonso from his son Ferdinand so that Alonso grieves for the son whom he believes to be drowned—a grief that brings him to repent of having put Prospero and Miranda on a rotten boat, setting them adrift to almost certain death at sea. He divides young Ferdinand from his daughter Miranda, giving him the unpleasant task of hauling wood, to test his moral purity and resolve in taking his precious daughter's hand in marriage. He frightens Alonso, Sebastian, and Antonio with a pageant of spirits so as to heighten their remorse, and give them a fear of supernatural powers that see the evil schemes and deeds they've hidden from others. He has Ariel lead Stephano, Trinculo, and Caliban (on their way to kill Prospero) through thorns and into a fetid swamp, thereby giving them painful justice that leads to their repentance—an act of mercy that keeps them from committing the mortal sin of murder. From the perspective of the characters, what they suffer is in direct contradiction to what they desire, but what they desire is either self-destructive or evil.

These kinds of trials are the very things that real human beings suffer in this life. In the play, we see that without these trials and tribulations, the happy outcome of *The Tempest* would not have been possible—the repentance of Alonso, the return of the dukedom to Prospero, the good marriage of Ferdinand and Miranda, the restoration of all loyal Gonzalo's best hopes, even the return of Caliban to a good master. Prospero uses magic because he lacks one power—or at least, refuses to use it—direct power over the will of others. He cannot directly force them to desire something, but only create circumstances where they are more likely to change their own wills.

And so we are led to ask this. Perhaps the very things that we think are so horrible—from acts of nature that sometimes threaten our very lives, the frustration of romantic desires, and the foiling of our plans, to the possible or actual loss of loved ones—may be the only means that a wise and benevolent God has of bringing us to a happy end. They are made necessary because God will not violate our wills, even though He does put us in circumstances where we are more likely to change our own wills. And, as with Prospero's dealings with those on the island, these difficult, painful, frustrating, or frightening circumstances may be the very things that save us from hurtling to our own and others' destruction. If this is true, then we are brought to the possibility that "bad things" happening in the world are not caused by the failure of a deity, or the lack of a deity, so that the classic argument among liberals for denying the existence of God is shown to be faulty. As in *The Tempest*, the bad things are the dual result of our own human wickedness and the Providential attempts at our moral regeneration.

And this brings us to a very surprising recognition. As God is to the world and Prospero is to the island, so also is Shakespeare to the theater. Shakespeare, by his art, takes the audience through the trials of the people on the island, and in doing so, plays on their fears, their passions, their moral imperfections, their confusion, their naïveté and their foolishness, reforming them through their immersion in the plot and the characters of the play. It is he, not the magician, who has the power of Prospero to create a world in the Globe Theater, a world of illusions, of fairies and demons, storms and shipwrecks, to bend and reform the passions, the imagination, and the minds of his audience. It is he who has the wisdom and goodness to use his dramatic art like Prospero for the moral regeneration of those under his spell. Shakespeare is the most sublime example of a dramatic artist understanding the moral responsibility of the theater. Today, alas, the technical power of the dramatic artist is not in the hands of the heirs of Shakespeare, but in the hands of, at best, the heirs of Gonzalo, at worst, the heirs of Caliban.

Shakespeare would have no part of the cant "Art for art's sake," which for him, would be like someone saying "Magic for magic's sake," or "Political power for political power's sake." Every art is an act of creation; and every act of literary creation brings with it a need for moral responsibility. And if it be true art, it will reveal not only technical mastery; it will be a union of wisdom, goodness, and dramatic power. It will, in other words, be the work of a Prospero, or a Shakespeare, or, as we'll see, a Jane Austen.

CHAPTER TWELVE

Sense and Sensibility: Jane Austen

"Elinor... possessed a strength of understanding, and coolness of judgment.... She had an excellent heart;—her disposition was affectionate, and her feelings strong; but she knew how to govern them: it was a knowledge which her mother had yet to learn, and which one of her sisters had resolved never to be taught."

Jane Austen: A Conservative Life

NO ONE CAN GAINSAY JANE AUSTEN'S LITERARY STATUS. SHE IS EASily one of the most respected, most read, most beloved English authors of all time. We do not have to say "the best *woman* writer," as if she could only win in a category defined by her sex. She was also the consummate conservative, both in her life and in her writing. As opposed to the great destroyers of male and female, marriage and the family, she remains one of the great defenders of what Russell Kirk called "the permanent things."

The Austens were devout Tories and equally devout Anglicans. The Reverend George Austen had risen through Oxford to become a Fellow, and then a priest of the Anglican Church. He married Cassandra Leigh, who was a bit higher up the social ladder. They were a loving and fruitful couple, and provided a very happy home for their children—thereby disproving the foolish notion that one has to be miserable or have a miserable childhood to be a great writer. Jane, born on December 16, 1775, was one of eight children, six boys and two girls. The sisters, Cassandra and Jane, were the deepest life-long friends.

The Austens were of the lower English gentry. The Reverend Austen had two parishes to provide his income. They lived at the Steventon Rectory, Steventon being a small village in Hampshire. The parson and his wife were far from the grand social heights of Mr. Darcy in *Pride and Prejudice.* But the family did mingle in the company of those who were, primarily because one of their sons, Francis, was "adopted" or taken under the patronage of a very wealthy cousin, Thomas Knight, the master of the beautiful God-mersham estate (a far more impressive estate than Darcy's Pem-berley, at least as it is shown in the elegant BBC version of 1996). But the Austens never lacked for anything, and like the young women of Jane's later novels, Cassandra and Jane spent a good amount of time becoming "accomplished"—playing the piano, reading, writing witty letters, visiting, planning for dances, and most of all, hoping to meet eligible bachelors who would make them into wives and mistresses of their own households.

The two sisters were sent off to school in 1783, Jane the younger being only seven. They first went to a rather awful boarding school run by a Mrs. Cawley, and then, two years later, to a much better one, the Abbey School in Reading. They were finished with their schooling by 1786. This rudimentary formal education was slight as compared to the kind of intellectual, moral, and spiritual direc-tion she received at home from her father, and from the "school" of her family. Jane was well-read, but not promiscuously so, and as is obvious from her writings, she was ever alert to the nuances and propensities of character of those whom she met in her daily life.

Most of all, she had a gentle, satiric eye. It shone even in the stories she wrote as a young girl. By 1790, not yet fifteen, she determined that she would be a writer.

As with her female characters, Jane fell in love, her first inamorato being a 20-year-old Irishman named Tom Lefroy. Jane was the same age. During this heady time, 1795 to 1796, she was also at work on two novels, *Elinor and Marianne* and *First Impressions*, or as they came to be later titled, *Sense and Sensibility* and *Pride and Prejudice*. Mr. Lefroy moved on, but Jane's sense of vocation did not. She continued work on these two novels and soon added another, *Susan*, which eventually became *Northanger Abbey*.

During this period, Jane's sister fell in love with a clergyman, a former student of her father's, Thomas Fowle. Hoping to earn more money and better provide for his marriage to Cassandra, Fowle went to the West Indies as a regimental chaplain. Unfortunately, he contracted yellow fever and died in 1797. In 1798, Jane became romantically attached to the Reverend Samuel Blackall, but it, like her previous romance, proved abortive. Prospects of marriage for the Austen daughters were fast disappearing, and they prepared themselves for a future as Aunt Cassandra and Aunt Jane. England at that time was full of dedicated aunts; they were practically a social caste—lively, loving, unmarried women who threw themselves into the lives of their brother's families and became favorites of their children.

Upon his retirement, the Reverend Austen moved his family away from the tranquil countryside in 1801 to the noise and agitation of the city of Bath, a move that Jane detested but bore as cheerfully she could. That same year, another romance was enkindled—this time with a man Jane met while on holiday at the seaside. But this ended with his tragic death, and history does not even record his name. The next year, in December, Jane received and accepted a formal proposal from Harris Bigg-Wither. It would have been, as they say, a prudent marriage, as Mr. Bigg-Wither had a considerable estate, but there was no love on Jane's side. The morning after she accepted his proposal, she informed him that she must, in good conscience, reject it. Jane was to remain Miss Austen.

The Reverend Austen died in early 1806, and after some moving around, the Austen family settled at Chawton House (in 1809), a cottage provided by their very well-off brother, Francis. Here, Jane set about reworking her novels. The first to be published was *Sense and Sensibility* in 1811. As with all her novels published during her lifetime, it would be appear anonymously. It was only after her death in 1817, at age forty-one, that the name of the authoress of *Sense and Sensibility, Pride and Prejudice, Northanger Abbey, Emma,* and the rest of her novels, was revealed.

Neither in her life, nor in her writings, was Jane Austen a rebel. Her chief concern was virtue, not rebellion, and against the liberal attempt to erase the distinctions between man and woman, Jane always distinguished between the particular virtues appropriate to men and women, as well as their particular vices and follies. As Elizabeth Kantor, in her book *The Politically Incorrect Guide™ to English and American Literature*, states,

> Jane Austen's novels show the failure of female self-control, on the one hand, and men's abdication of their proper responsibility, on the other, as the chief causes of women's unhappiness. Far from being "subversive" of traditional gender roles, Jane Austen's novels celebrate them. This is one area where she's comparable to Shakespeare, and, arguably, outdoes him: her novels are masterful celebrations of marriage. Jane Austen paints what now has to be called old-fashioned marriage—the institution into which a woman entered expecting to be guided and

protected by her husband, to look up to and please him, and to be responsible for the management of a household and the nurture of children—as both the most usual and the most intense source of female happiness.[1]

In the delineation, celebration, and protection of the real differences and responsibilities of men and women, Jane Austen forms the moral imagination of readers in the most conservative way. Like Aristotle, she takes us back to the first principle of all society, the union of male and female that creates the family, and shows us the real romance and firm moral contours of this original, natural source of all else good that follows. In doing so, she is a particularly potent enemy to liberalism, a woman author of the first rank who defends both manhood and womanhood.

Time to Rent a Movie

Jane Austen has been popular with filmmakers. Some of these adaptations have been less than satisfying (e.g., the 2005 version of *Pride and Prejudice* starring Keira Knightley), and some absolutely brilliant (e.g., the 1995 version of *Persuasion* with Amanda Root, the 1999 version of *Emma* with Gwyneth Paltrow, or the above-mentioned 1996 version of *Pride and Prejudice*). By far the best adaptation of *Sense and Sensibility* is Emma Thompson's 1995 version.

Odd as this advice might seem, I strongly suggest seeing the movie version of *Sense and Sensibility* before reading the book. We live in a visual, not a verbal, age, and young people especially might find it useful preparation (though Jane Austen is quite easy reading, albeit not in ways we're used to now) to see the drama portrayed before they read it in print. There is another benefit, too: watching this extraordinarily well-done movie (and it merits repeated viewings) will set for you and your family a standard of cinematic excellence that will deny the enchantment of lesser fare. A good movie has depth of character, plot, and technique that are only discovered slowly, after many viewings. When we successively discover them, we not only come to appreciate the art of good movie-making, but also gain a greater appreciation of the real depth of human existence itself, of our own drama. Good drama is not only a training to weed out bad drama, it is, more importantly, an education of the mind, imagination, senses, and emotions.

There is yet another reason to watch the movie several times: *Sense and Sensibility* is a banquet to savor, not fast food to stuff and run. The act of reading it constitutes a cure for the damage done by our vulgar culture—it is the exact opposite of television, the Internet, magazines, and the snap and buzz of our twitterdom. Escaping twitterdom, however, can be hard. An excellent movie helps. It sets the mood, prepares you for the tempo, and helps you to appreciate the layers of meaning that are to be found in Austen's work. Read today, Austen's novels would help bring about a conservative reclamation of the mind and imagination, and hence the culture.

The Moral Worlds of *Sense and Sensibility*

Austen's book could well have been titled *Reason and Emotion*, or *Moral Duty and Self-Absorption*, or *Tradition and Romantic Anarchy*, or, *Conservative and Liberal*. But she chose to call it *Sense and Sensibility*, and these two traits are represented in the respective characters of Elinor and Marianne Dashwood. These same traits are also expressed among other characters. Joining Elinor to represent good sense, we have Edward Ferrars and Colonel Brandon. On the other side, representing with Marianne strong feelings unguided by wisdom (sensibility), we have her mother, Mrs. Dashwood, and the seducing romantic rogue, John Willoughby. Those of sense are guided by reason and the prudent traditions of society. They are not unfeeling, but realize feelings need guidance. Those drenched in sensibility live a life defined by the passions of the moment. For them, to feel is everything. Those defined by sense are Tory Anglicans: conservatives of their place and time. Those defined by sensibility are the Romantics—not real romance, but the Romantic movement of the late eighteenth and early nineteenth centuries.

As a culture, we have taken the side of sensibility to its logical and dark conclusion. Or, to say it from a different angle, contemporary liberalism represents the culmination of the Romantic movement, that is, the victory of sensibility over sense, the passions over reason, self-absorption over moral duty, romantic anarchy over tradition. Miss Austen would be rightly horrified at our not heeding her warning, but unsurprised by the results.

Sadly, both original species presented by Austen are largely extinct. Women like Elinor have been driven out of the culture by force or ridicule, and the Mariannes have given way to something even more alarming. The Romantics might have been destructive of themselves and others (as they are in Austen's novels), but Romanticism has been replaced by something far worse, nihilism— what is really the fulfillment of Romanticism and liberalism. The victory of sensibility over sense leads to vulgar insensibility and the elevation of nonsense; the victory of passion over reason leads to the exaltation of irrationality; the victory of self-absorption over moral duty leads to narcissism; and the victory of romantic anarchy over tradition leads to a passion for violence. Flip to a movie broadcast on any cable channel and you'll likely be thrust into a world of dark and horrible violence and vulgar sexuality from which all traces of goodness (certainly as Austen would know it) have been largely extinguished. There are exceptions, of course, but it is on the whole fair to say that in our drama as in our culture, we have lost the moral world of Jane Austen. But that doesn't mean all is lost. If our minds, imaginations, and passions are assaulted by a nihilistic world, we can repair them by immersing ourselves in the moral world of Jane Austen's great novels, in particular *Sense and Sensibility*.

Cast of Characters and Plot

As with Shakespeare, we will be much better off having in front of us a list of the main characters, and a short account of the plot (which is more complex than *The Tempest*). Let's begin with a who's who.

THE DASHWOODS

Henry Dashwood (heir of Norland Park; dies at the beginning of the novel)

Mrs. Dashwood (Henry's second wife, his first having died)

John Dashwood (the son of Henry by his first wife; he inherits the Norland Park estate)

Fanny Dashwood (the wife of John Dashwood; maiden name, *Ferrars*)

Elinor, Marianne, and Margaret Dashwood (the daughters of Henry and his second wife; at the opening of the novel they are nineteen, sixteen, and thirteen respectively; Elinor falls in love with Edward Ferrars; Marianne falls for the aristocratic rake, John Willoughby, but ends up marrying Colonel Brandon)

THE FERRARS

Mrs. Ferrars (matriarch of the Ferrars family; her husband is dead, and she has full control of the considerable estate)

Edward Ferrars (eldest son of Mrs. Ferrars; he falls in love with Elinor Dashwood, but he's already promised to marry Lucy Steele)

Robert Ferrars (second son of Mrs. Ferrars; ends up marrying Lucy Steele)

Fanny Ferrars (now Mrs. John Dashwood)

OTHERS

Colonel Brandon (retired military officer and owner of Delaford Estate; falls in love with and, after much struggle, marries Marianne Dashwood at the end of the novel)

Eliza Williams (Colonel Brandon's first love who was forced to marry his brother; she dies under tragic circumstances)

Eliza (the daughter of Eliza Williams, offspring of an illicit affair; she is seduced by John Willoughby, and bears him a child)

John Willoughby (aristocratic heir of Combe Magna Estate; a romantic rake who seduces Eliza and then woos Marianne Dashwood, but ends up marrying the wealthy Miss Sophia Grey)

Mrs. Smith (the current elderly owner of Combe Magna Estate who disinherits Willoughby for fathering a child out of wedlock with Eliza and then refusing to marry her)

Mrs. Jennings (a kindly but rather vulgar matriarch who befriends the Dashwood sisters; the mother of Lady Middleton, John Middleton's wife, and Mrs. Charlotte Palmer)

Sir John Middleton (a distant relation of the Dashwoods; kindly offers the dispossessed Dashwoods a cottage on his estate, Barton Park)

Lucy Steele (secretly engaged to Edward Ferrars for several years; a scheming social climber who ends up dumping Edward for his brother Robert when she learns that Robert is to receive the full inheritance of the Ferrars estate)

Already in the cast of characters I've given some hint of the complexity of the plot. The novel begins with the death of Henry

Dashwood. The Norland Park estate was given to him by his uncle, whose will stipulated that it be passed on, in turn, to John Dashwood, Henry's son by his first wife. This leaves his current wife and daughters with a pittance. On his deathbed, Henry begs his son to take care of them, which he promises to do. But when Henry dies, John Dashwood's cold-hearted and controlling wife Fanny convinces him not to give them anything, and the John Dashwoods proceed to move into Norland Park immediately, making it clear that the current Mrs. Dashwood and her three daughters, Elinor, Marianne, and Margaret, are not welcome there.

While they are looking for another home, Fanny Dashwood's brother Edward Ferrars visits Norland Park, and Edward and Elinor fall in love. (Unbeknownst to everyone but Edward, a few years back he had already promised to marry one Lucy Steele.) The Dashwoods then receive an offer from a distant relation, Sir John Middleton, of a cottage on his estate, Barton Park, some distance from Norland Park.

Mrs. Dashwood and her daughters settle in at Barton cottage, a very modest home, suitable to their much-reduced financial situation. The daughters now have no substantial dowry. Edward, for reasons unknown to the Dashwoods, does not come to visit Elinor, but Marianne begins to receive the attentions of Colonel Brandon, a prudent, solid man who is almost twenty years her senior. She reminds him of his first love, Eliza Williams, now dead. Much to Brandon's displeasure, Marianne is swept away by the dashing, young, romantic aristocrat John Willoughby, whose intended estate Combe Magna is close by. If I am correct in my calculations, and have sorted out the timeframe accurately, Willoughby has already seduced and abandoned Eliza William's daughter, also named Eliza, by the time he meets Marianne.

Willoughby and Marianne act with such passion and intimacy that everyone assumes, including Marianne, that they will be married. But one day, Willoughby shows up at Barton Cottage and informs the Dashwoods that he has been called immediately to London by Mrs. Smith, the heiress of Combe Magna, who holds Willoughby's entire financial future in her hands. While the Dashwoods think the elderly Mrs. Smith objects to him marrying Marianne because she is a girl with no money, the truth is that she has given him an honorable ultimatum: marry Eliza or be disinherited. Willoughby refuses to marry the girl, and ends up betrothed to the very rich Miss Sophia Grey. When he meets Marianne in London, he treats her coldly, and writes her a letter telling her that he never intended to marry her. She is entirely crushed.

Meanwhile, the Dashwoods have met Lucy Steele. About four years prior, the young and imprudent Edward had promised to marry her. Unlike Willoughby, Edward is a man of honor, and will not break that promise even though he loves Elinor. Lucy, realizing all this, does her best to befriend and vex Elinor. As it turns out, when the engagement is discovered, Mrs. Ferrars disinherits Edward, whom she had intended for marriage to someone of his own class, and the estate is legally bound to his younger brother, Robert. Soon enough, Lucy dumps Edward after having charmed Robert, and Robert and Lucy marry. This frees the noble Edward, who proposes to Elinor, and she blissfully accepts. Marianne also accepts the offer of Colonel Brandon, and they also marry. The Dashwoods end up happy after all.

Elinor and Marianne

Now that we've got the characters and general plot, we may look more closely at the two main representatives of sense and sensibility. There are no better words than Austen's.

> Elinor...possessed a strength of understanding, and coolness of
> judgment, which qualified her, though only nineteen, to be the

counsellor of her mother, and enabled her frequently to counteract, to the advantage of them all, that eagerness of mind in Mrs Dashwood which must generally have led to imprudence. She had an excellent heart;—her disposition was affectionate, and her feelings strong; but she knew how to govern them: it was a knowledge which her mother had yet to learn, and which one of her sisters [Marianne] had resolved never to be taught.

Austen makes clear that Elinor is a woman who has learned to govern and guide her passions by reason. Her sister Marianne allows hers free reign. "Marianne's abilities were, in many respects, quite equal to Elinor's. She was sensible and clever; but eager in every thing; her sorrows, her joys, could have no moderation. She was generous, amiable, interesting: she was everything but prudent."[2]

Prudence is good moral judgment in our particular circumstances; it means training feelings by habit and reason. As C. S. Lewis pointed out, the question is not what feelings anyone *happens* to have, but what feelings he *should* have, and so the great task of education is to train our thoughts and feelings to correctly reflect the actual moral order.

Marianne rejects prudence because for her it smacks of prudishness. Passion is the thing. Feelings must take the place of judgment. It is all too easy for her, because of their similarity of character, to immediately throw herself at Willoughby. When Elinor objects, prudently stating that they have known each other for a very short time, and so she can have no real knowledge of his character, Marianne proclaims,

You are mistaken, Elinor... in supposing I know very little of Willoughby. I have not known him long indeed, but I am much better acquainted with him, than with any other creature in the world, except yourself and mama. It is not time or opportunity that is to determine intimacy;—it is disposition alone. Seven years would be insufficient to make some people acquainted with each other, and seven days are more than enough for others... of Willoughby my judgement has long been formed.[3]

Her errors in judgment about Willoughby have a natural source. She rightly believes that romantic attention *means* marriage, and therefore gives her young heart away to Willoughby as a prelude to giving her body to him in marriage. She allows no possibility that he is merely a seducer, a man who plays upon a woman's natural desire for marriage as an instrument to lure her into bed.

Nothing shows Marianne's imprudence more clearly than an episode early on. Colonel Brandon has invited the Dashwoods, Mrs. Jennings, Sir John Middleton, and Willoughby to a picnic, commencing from Barton Park. But just as they are about to set off, Brandon gets a letter that causes him great agitation. Concealing the contents of the missive, he declares that he must set off to London immediately.

This allows Willoughby yet another occasion for expressing his habitual mockery of Colonel Brandon. He speaks in "a low voice to Marianne, 'There are some people who cannot bear a party of pleasure. Brandon is one of them. He was afraid of catching cold I dare say, and invented this trick for getting out of it. I would lay fifty guineas the letter was of his own writing.'" To which Marianne replies, "I have no doubt of it."[4]

The mysterious letter is the very one informing Colonel Brandon that the young Eliza has suddenly reappeared—and is with child, in fact, Willoughby's child, although Brandon doesn't know it yet. As Brandon later relates the incident to Elinor,

Little did Mr. Willoughby imagine, I suppose, when his looks censured me for incivility in breaking up the party, that I was called away to the relief of one, whom he had made poor and miserable; but *had* he known it, what would it have availed? Would he have been less gay or less happy in the smiles of your sister? No, he had already done that, which no man who *can* feel for another, would do. He had left the girl whose youth and innocence he had seduced, in a situation of the utmost distress, with no creditable home, no help, no friends, ignorant of his address! He had left her promising to return; he neither returned, nor wrote, nor relieved her.[5]

The day of the picnic, after Brandon hastily leaves, Willoughby drives off with Marianne alone, and takes her—unescorted— through every room of Combe Magna. She sees no impropriety in this because, being a creature of sensibility, she has no sense. The reality is that she put herself into the hands of a seducer, one quite willing to leave his prey to destitution once conquered. Marianne, innocently but imprudently, believes that Willoughby gives her the tour of his estate because he intends to marry her, even though he has never actually, formally proposed.

When Elinor learns of this, she points out the impropriety of going unescorted with Willoughby. Marianne replies, "If there had been any real impropriety in what I did, I should have been sensible of it at the time, for we always know when we are acting wrong, and with such conviction I could have had no pleasure." In other words, it didn't *feel* wrong, so it could not *be* wrong.

But again, the basis of her feeling is her belief that Willoughby fully intends to make her his wife, and hence mistress of Combe Magna. She is entirely wrong about everything. When Mrs. Smith finds out about young Eliza, she gives Willoughby an ultimatum. As Willoughby later relates to Elinor, Mrs. Smith

> offered to forgive the past, if I would marry Eliza. That could not be—and I was formally dismissed from her favour and her house. The night following this affair [i.e., the disinheritance]... was spent by me in deliberating on what my future conduct should be. The struggle was great—but it ended too soon. My affection for Marianne, my thorough conviction of her attachment to me—it was all insufficient to outweigh that dread of poverty, or get the better of those false ideas of the necessity of riches, which I was naturally inclined to feel, and expensive society increased. I had reason to believe myself secure of my present wife [Sophia Grey], if I chose to address her, and I persuaded myself to think that nothing else in common prudence remained for me to do.[6]

In sum, Willoughby refused to do the honorable thing, and marry Eliza. Now that he was disinherited, he would not marry Marianne, a girl with little money. And so he trots off to woo and marry the very rich Sophia Grey. That is the *real* Willoughby, who even in his tearful, drunken confession to Elinor, manages to try to make himself appear an object of her pity, a victim of circumstances and forgivable weaknesses. (Unfortunately, Willoughby's self-absorbed and self-indulgent "confession" to Elinor near the end of the book did not make it into Thompson's movie version of *Sense and Sensibility*—a great shame, since it reveals the true depth of his debased character.)

Everything that Marianne *feels* about Willoughby turns out to be false. His dashing appearance and manners, the very things that charmed her Romantic sensibility, hide an inner corruption. In terms of character, Willoughby is the exact opposite of Edward Ferrars, Elinor's true love, and Colonel Brandon, whom Marianne marries after her Romantic world comes crashing down.

Unlike Willoughby, Edward Ferrars will not use a woman; he will not make a promise to her heart, and then break his promise *and* her heart. He is the man of honor, and when Elinor finds out he was engaged to Lucy, and against the wishes of his heart, remains engaged to her, she is of course heartbroken. But she also recognizes that he *is* the kind of man she would want to marry precisely because he *is* the kind of man whose moral integrity won't allow him to dump Lucy for her. She loves him for his character, and so, ironically and against her feelings, approves of his stalwart intention to marry Lucy. And while she has a broken heart, completely unlike Marianne, she refuses to wallow in Romantic emotional self-pity.

When all this is revealed to Marianne, she cannot at first understand: "and yet you loved him!" But Elinor replies, "Yes. But I did not love only him;—and while the comfort of others was dear to me, I was glad to spare them from knowing how much I felt....I would not have you suffer on my account." Elinor bore her great pain and disappointment, but unlike the Romantic Marianne, she did not give in to her emotions and drag her family into her self-absorbed misery. Marianne took Elinor to be cold; in truth, she was suffering *for* Marianne and the rest of the family. This was an act done out of love for them, the very opposite of the self-absorbed, emotional "love" of Romanticism. Marianne finally sees the truth, "Oh! Elinor...you have made me hate myself for ever.— How barbarous have I been to you!—you, who have been my only comfort, who have borne with me in all my misery, who have seemed to be only suffering for me!"[7]

Yet, Marianne is not so easily cured. She is still tinged with self-absorption, as evidenced by her later indulgence at the Palmer estate. She insists on going out for twilight Romantic walks, getting her feet wet, and imprudently sitting about afterwards "in her wet shoes and stockings."[8] She catches a cold that from seemingly innocuous beginnings soon becomes life-threatening. She eventually recovers, but with this lesson: Romantic trifles can turn into a real tragedy, not only for oneself but for those who worry and care about you. We owe it to others even to take care of ourselves.

> My illness has made me think—It has given me leisure and calmness for serious recollection. Long before I was enough recovered to talk, I was perfectly able to reflect. I considered the past; I saw in my own behaviour since the beginning of our acquaintance with him [Willoughby] last autumn, nothing but a series of imprudence [*sic*] towards myself, and want of kindness to others. I saw that my own feelings had prepared my sufferings, and that my want of fortitude under them had almost led me to the grave. My illness, I well knew, had been entirely brought on by myself, by such negligence of my own health, as I had felt even at the time to be wrong. Had I died,—it would have been self destruction. I did not know my danger till the danger was removed; but with such feelings as these reflections gave me, I wonder at my recovery,—wonder that the very eagerness of my desire to live, to have time for atonement to my God, and to you all, did not kill me at once. Had I died,—in what peculiar misery should I have left you, my nurse, my friend, my sister!. . . I cannot express my own abhorrence of myself. Whenever I looked towards the past, I saw some duty neglected, or some failing indulged. Every body seemed injured by me.[9]

The Importance of Miss Austen

Elinor's character is certainly reminiscent of Austen's own. She embodies all the virtues that Austen understood to be the essential constituents of good moral character, as against the self-absorbed, reckless, and self-indulgent revolution of Romanticism that threatened to destroy a world that, through tradition, was still largely defined by prudence. Austen was not a feminist; she not only accepted patriarchy, but was quite fond of it; and she was a brilliant literary artist, a novelist whose deep understanding of human nature and human character has justly been compared to Shakespeare.

Many modern literary critics, however, detest Austen's conservatism, her gentle, loving treatment of English hierarchical society, but even more, her fundamental assumption, upon which the delicate, penetrating, and ingenious plots are built, that the union of man and woman in marriage is the great and natural goal of male and female. As Elizabeth Kantor notes, "The one possibility that the feminists refuse on principle to consider is that the traditional differences between male and female roles are necessitated by the real, natural, and ineradicable differences between men and women." Feminists who loathe Austen, distrust "the patriarchy," and repudiate tradition, and therefore assume the liberal conviction that *structures* (in this case, sex roles, marriage, and so on) are the cause of evil and misery.

Austen, a stellar conservative, assumed that *sin* was the cause of evil. Sin affects everyone, male and female, in every station, from the noble to the peasant, and so (continues Kantor) Austen's novels are defined by this fundamental conviction "that every member of the human race, male or female, is capable of vice and folly and has a duty to struggle against them. This struggle—not the war between the sexes or a campaign of subversive resistance to the patriarchy—provides the drama in Jane Austen's novels."[10]

We could well imagine a Willoughby holding forth to a rapt audience on the rights of women to break the chains of patriarchy, cast aside the remnants of tradition, free themselves from sexual repression, and throw themselves into the spontaneity of passion. Willoughby is the archetypical sexual revolutionary who leaves a trail of wrecked lives behind him. There are plenty of Willoughbys and Elizas in our culture, and perhaps a few Mariannes yet unfallen, but where are the Elinors? They, unfortunately, are increasingly rare, thanks to liberalism's war on tradition, virtue (including the virtues of honor and self-denial), and the primacy of family. One of the great gifts of Jane Austen is that, through the power of her literary art, she cuts through the cant of the Willoughbys, which is really, in a political sense, the all-too-familiar rhetoric of liberalism.

CHAPTER THIRTEEN

The Lord of the Rings:
J. R. R. Tolkien

"Other evils there are that may come; for Sauron is himself but a servant or emissary. Yet it is not our part to master all the tides of the world, but to do what is in us for the succor of those years wherein we are set, uprooting the evil in the fields that we know, so that those who live after may have clean earth to till. What weather they shall have is not ours to rule."

"I am in fact a hobbit."

JOHN RONALD REUEL TOLKIEN WAS BORN ON JANUARY 3, 1892, IN the Orange Free State near the southern tip of Africa.[1] His father, Arthur Tolkien, a manager at the England's Bank of Africa in Bloemfontein, had come to South Africa in the wake of gold and diamond discoveries. His mother, Mabel Suffield Tolkien, had followed Arthur from England as soon as he could establish himself financially, and they were married at the Cape Town Cathedral in April 1891. John was their first son, his parents always calling him by his second name, Ronald. Another son, Hilary Arthur Reuel Tolkien, arrived on February 17, 1894. There were to be no more Tolkiens. In February 1896, while Mabel and her two sons were visiting in England, Arthur Tolkien died, his health destroyed by a bout of rheumatic fever.

The Tolkiens, sans father, settled in Birmingham, England. A new widow of little means with two small children, Mabel scraped together enough money to rent a cottage in the country hamlet of Sarehole, a mile outside the city. This was, for young Ronald and his brother, a golden time, and he was forever after in his heart a man of the rural hamlet against the grime and greyness of the industrial city, a champion of the shire towns of Hobbits over the dark towers and fiendish ironworks of Saruman.

Mabel became, through default, her boys' teacher, and a good one she was, helping Ronald learn Latin, French, penmanship, drawing, and botany. She also had them read the classics—a home-schooling mother many decades before the movement took hold in America. Ronald was especially taken with the fairy books of Andrew Lang, which awakened in him the same kind of mysteri-ous pull that the northern sagas exercised on Lewis. The Tolkiens went to church each Sunday—though their church changed, as they converted from Anglicanism to Catholicism, a move that alienated them from other members of their family.

At seven, Ronald entered King Edward's school, and Mabel realized that they would have to move into town again to be near it. Ronald was a good student, but hated the city, missing Sarehole as his Arcadian paradise. By far, his favorite subject was language. Both boys were next enrolled at St. Philip's, a Catholic school established by the great English convert, John Henry Cardinal Newman, but Ronald was soon back at King Edward's again, thanks to a scholarship. In 1904, Mabel caught pneumonia—and was also diagnosed with Type 1 diabetes. A family friend, Father Francis Morgan, invited the Tolkiens to stay at a Worcestershire country cottage—built by Cardinal Newman as a retreat house for the clergy of his Oratory—to help her recuperate. The boys, removed from the grit of the city, blossomed again; sadly, Mabel did not. She died in the middle of November, and Father Francis Morgan became the boys' guardian. Ronald was only twelve.

Father Morgan settled the boys with their widowed aunt, Beatrice Suffield, which meant going back to the city. In many ways, Hilary and Ronald were quite ordinary. Both were altar boys, and Ronald had a passion for Rugby. But Ronald's interest in languages, especially their inner construction, set him apart. In addition to the required Greek and Latin, he took up Old English (reading *Beowulf*), Middle English (focusing on *Sir Gawain and the Green Knight*), Old Norse, and Gothic. As a young man of sixteen, he could easily participate in school debates in Latin, as was the custom, but could just as easily slip into fluent Greek. On occasion, he surprised the audience by expounding in Gothic or Anglo-Saxon. He also had a passion for making up his own languages, complete with their own grammar and alphabet.

Philology allowed the peculiar thrill of crawling backwards in history, through a language's development, to glimpse the birth of a people. Tolkien loved to take language apart and puzzle out the etymological lines. In making up his own languages, he came at things from the opposite end, creating the words *before* the world they fit and then creating the world to fit his language. That creative philological impulse would later bear fruit in *The Lord of the Rings*.

Ronald was only sixteen when Father Morgan moved the two boys to a house belonging to a Mrs. Faulkner. Another lodger at the Faulkners' was Edith Bratt, with whom Ronald soon fell in love. At nineteen, she was three years his senior, and her family background was troubled (she had been born out of wedlock). Father Morgan thought Ronald should be keeping his mind on his books and so forbade him to see her. Edith moved away; Ronald's affections didn't. But for the time being, he dedicated himself to qualifying for entry into Oxford.

He entered Exeter College at Oxford in the fall of 1911 to study Classics. On the whole, he was more interested in fun than study, but that was in great part because Classics bored him. He arrived with an advanced knowledge of Greek and Latin, and could survive without much effort. A class in Comparative Philology was the only one that really interested him.

Tolkien turned twenty-one in January 1913, and that meant he was free to seek out the hand of his beloved Edith, the only sticking point being that, in his enforced absence, she had become engaged to someone else. In the letter informing poor Ronald of her attachment, she made it known that, were he to pursue, she would break her engagement. He charged off immediately, arriving by train at Cheltenham. By the end of the day, Edith was won back again. They were formally betrothed a year later, after Edith entered the Roman Catholic Church.

In the meantime, Tolkien continued with his studies at Oxford. While he was supposed to be working on his Greek and Latin, he was instead immersing himself in the Germanic origins of the English language, and, in the summer of 1913, he transferred from the study of the Classics to the School of English Language and Literature. He was particularly taken with the early Anglo-Saxon Christian poet Cynewulf, especially a line from his *Crist*: "*Eala Earendel engla beorhtast / ofer middangeard monnum sended,*" "Hail Earendel, brightest of angels / above the middle earth sent unto men."[2] Earendel was Venus, "the morning star," (also known as "the evening star"), the last planet to be seen as dawn approaches, because of its brightness. As the morning star, it announces the approach of the greater light, the sun. In *Crist*, Earendel stands for John the Baptist who presages Christ.

Haunted by the lines from Cynewulf's *Crist*, Tolkien wrote a poem in late summer 1914, "The Voyage of Earendel the Evening

Star." It was the origin of the mythology that would fit his created languages, eventually set out by Tolkien in his *Silmarillion*. The mythology, in turn, provided the primordial background of his epic trilogy, *The Lord of the Rings*. We hear of Eärendil (as Tolkien came to spell it) early in the first book of the trilogy, *The Fellowship of the Ring*, when the great king Aragorn, disguised as Strider, sings an ancient Elven song to the Hobbits.[3] The wise, ageless elf Elrond of Rivendell is the son of Eärendil and Elwing, and the father of Arwen, who becomes the brides of King Aragorn near the end of the third book of the trilogy, *The Return of the King*.[4] Language, mythology, epic history—such would be the unfolding of Tolkien's creative art.

But the full creation of that world was as yet a long way off. During World War I, Tolkien signed up with the Lancashire Fusiliers. On March 22, 1916, he married Edith, and in June he was shipped off to France. Lice saved his life, infecting him with Trench Fever severe enough that in November he was sent back to England to recuperate. During his long convalescence, he began work on the details of the mythology that eventually swelled into *The Silmarillion*.

Other wonders were created during the last year of the war. The Tolkiens' first child was born in November 1917, John Francis Reuel. In 1919, the year after the end of the war, Tolkien received his MA from Oxford, and in 1920 he took up a position at Leeds University. A second son, Michael, arrived that same year, and another, Christopher, in 1924. The following year, Tolkien was awarded a position as teacher of Anglo-Saxon at Oxford, and he became an Oxford don. In May 1926, he met another don, the newly elected Fellow and Tutor in English Language and Literature, a Mr. C. S. Lewis, and a deep friendship soon blossomed. It was, in great part, Tolkien who patiently but firmly broke the ice of Lewis's atheism, and through long talks and long walks melted him to theism by the summer of 1929, and Christianity by the fall of 1931 (though the fact that Lewis did not embrace Catholicism remained a source of some irritation to Tolkien).

In 1929, Priscilla Tolkien was born. The following year, a strange creature emerged from a hole in the ground—or, more accurately, from Tolkien's imagination while he was bleakly trudging through student examinations. "In a hole in the ground there lived a hobbit" scribbled Tolkien on a blank page of a student's test booklet. His novel *The Hobbit*, which his publishers marketed as juvenile fiction from a very bookish don, became an immediate success when it was published in 1937. "I am in fact a hobbit," Tolkien later explained, "in all but size. I like gardens, trees, and unmechanized farmlands; I smoke a pipe, and like good plain food. . . . I like, and even dare to wear in these dull days, ornamental waistcoats. I am fond of mushrooms (out of a field); have a very simple sense of humour (which even my appreciative critics find tiresome); I go to bed late and get up late (when possible). I do not travel much."[5]

Tolkien was pressed to write a sequel. The publisher merely wanted another nice children's story about Hobbits, but Tolkien could not bring himself to produce it, however hard he tried. The expansive world-creation and mythology of his *Silmarillion* kept intruding. Something far grander, more brilliant and full of light, more threatening and wracked by evil, was brewing in Tolkien's imagination, something of biblical proportions, a fantasy so powerfully contrived that it both drew its readers within its world by enchantment and lifted the veil draped over the reality of our own world. It was born in the first tremors of World War II, but it was not an allegory of that awful struggle between flickering light and devouring darkness. Rather, *The Lord of the Rings* revealed the real nature of the battle between good and evil, hidden beneath the veil of history wherever it occurred. As Lewis rightly understood, *The Lord of the Rings* was "not devised to reflect any particular situation in the real world. It was the other way around; real events began, horribly, to conform to the pattern he had freely invented."[6]

The first two books of the trilogy, *The Fellowship of the Ring* and *The Two Towers*, were published in 1954, and the final book, *The Return of the King*, in 1955. They were at first moderately successful and over time became wildly successful. While Tolkien remained the archetypical don, immersed in the arcane of academia, he was also the world famous creator of one of the greatest works of literature in the English language. Or any language.

The Key to *The Lord of the Rings*

For my own family, the key to *The Lord of the Rings* was the three magnificently produced movies that drew us into reading the book. We watched them over and over, and, at the same time, read the trilogy out loud in the evenings. For quite a few months, the book and the movies formed our imaginations, our intellects, our family discussions, our reading and our viewing pleasure, our jokes, our quips, and our insights. The movies are great; the book is far, far greater.

The greatest insight was uttered by my wife, who before the movies wanted nothing to do with "elf stories," but came to be entranced by both the book and films. One day she said, quite simply, "*The Lord of the Rings* lifts the veil." Tolkien, looking down, would be proud. That is exactly what he created it to do, as he makes wonderfully clear in one of the most important, intellectually thrilling essays I've ever read, "On Fairy Stories." As Tolkien relates, this essay was "written in the same period (1938–1939) when *The Lord of the Rings* was beginning to unroll itself and to unfold prospects of labour and exploration in yet unknown country as daunting to me as to the hobbits."[7] *The Lord of the Rings* is a fairy tale, perhaps the second best one ever told. The best one, maintains Tolkien, is the Bible, in particular the Gospels.

The use of the term "fairy tale" might seem provocative in this context, but Tolkien, the Catholic believer, tells us that the proper effect of a fairy story is precisely this: it lifts the veils covering our eyes and lets us see what is really true, what is really there. That is why the best fairy stories last, handed down from generation to generation. And one fairy story in particular, despite its fantastic nature, actually happened: the story related in the New Testament. This startling notion is central to my analysis of *The Lord of the Rings* and the Bible (and the conservative literary imagination), and so we had better spend some time in sorting out exactly what Tolkien means.

On Fairy Tales

We recall Chesterton remarking about the importance of fairy stories, especially for us sophisticated moderns. Fairy tales contain more truth, said Chesterton, than the dry, grey world of the materialists, who deny ordinary miracles (like free will, or love, or joy) and splutter that extraordinary things can't happen (when they quite obviously do). Unfortunately, our grasp of the truths of fairy tales is hindered by confusion about what a fairy tale really is. As Tolkien explains at great length in his essay, the modern notion of fairies as delicate little creatures flitting about from flower to flower is a great aberration. The word "fairy" actually is the equivalent of "elf," and elves, in mythology and legend, are human-sized creatures of great power. They are not to be trifled with. They are, in fact, the image of unfallen man. Created by man's imagination, they are "freed from those limitations which he feels most to press upon him. They are immortal, and their will is directly effective for the achievement of imagination and desire."[8] That is why the elves in *Lord of the Rings* are both great warriors and great musicians, exceedingly wise as well as whimsical; they seem angelic in their ethereal purity and more substantial than humans in their physicality; their art and architecture blend seamlessly with nature even while bringing it to effortless exaltation; their food is simple, yet makes every other food taste like mud by comparison, and has almost miraculous restorative properties. They are creatures of our imagination that represent all that was possible and wonderful in our nature had it not been wounded by sin. They are creations of man's art that shed great light on the origins and deepest aspirations of man.

Tolkien's great art is, as he termed it, "sub-creation," the creation of a world in which elves, hobbits, wizards, dwarves, trolls, and malignant spirits exist along with men. He draws readers from their "Primary World" into his "Secondary World" by the power of his words so that while we are reading we are truly, in our imagination, living in that Secondary World. He is Shakespeare's Prospero, creating illusions for the enchantment of his audience, a strange new world in which his readers can live and learn while the spell lasts.

Such enchantment is not, argues Tolkien, the result of a "willing suspension of disbelief," but a total immersion in the story *as real*, and a consequent deep desire to believe, to have and experience *as real*, the wonders we find within. Fairy stories "open a door on Other Time, and if we pass through, though only for a moment, we stand outside our own time, outside Time itself, maybe."[9]

Rather like Tocqueville, we become a foreigner seeing our world and our time from another world and Other Time. The effect of this enchantment of our mind, our will, our passions, even our senses that occurs while immersed in the Secondary World provides an awakening to the extraordinary nature of reality in our

Primary World. We recover our natural wonder, our natural sense of adventure, our natural joy in finding ourselves alive and surrounded by the truly startling reality of our Primary World. Life becomes a gift. We become enchanted and amazed once again by what we may call the permanent things, the primary things—sitting by a fire, singing a song, composing and reciting poetry, the smell of a forest, feasting, the love of husband and wife, the joy of children, the invigoration of working with our hands and minds, friendship, the courage of battle. "It was in fairy-stories," remarked Tolkien, "that I first divined the potency of the words, and the wonder of the things, such as stone, and wood, and iron; tree and grass; house and fire; bread and wine."[10] The passing enchantment of the story allows us to regain "a clear view," to "clean our windows; so that the things seen clearly may be freed from the drab blur of triteness or familiarity," so that we may again enjoy "seeing things as we are (or were) meant to see them."[11] These permanent things at the foundation of human life are what conservatism properly conserves, what it defends against all attacks, what it promotes against all odds and orcs (orcs being the demons of Tolkien's Middle Earth).

That is why the entire epic of *The Lord of the Rings* is built around the simple life of hobbits in the towns of their Shire. In the Shire, we find a life worth living and worth defending against every evil. How to evoke what the Shire means? I shall never forget one evening, when dusk had brought in a low-lying mist that rested upon the bottom land and lapped at the hill leading up to our cabin. As I sat down below by the stream, I watched the goats crop the grass on the hillside and the fog drift over the pumpkin patch. My family was safe in the cabin, bustling about after supper, and my eldest daughter came out to sit on the porch and play the theme music of the Shire from the movie on her cheap pennywhistle.

Because our house nests in a hollow, the notes were naturally amplified and so seemed to come up from the ground itself. May God grant you, reader, one such moment of peace and contentment. These are the primary things: family, home, food, music, the enchanted beauty of creation—the heart of the Shire.

I hope it is clear—or can become clear through reading *The Lord of the Rings*—that it is just such things that the Anti-Federalists were fighting for. Hear Tolkien's description of the ordering of the hobbits' Shire: "The Shire at this time had hardly any 'government.' Families for the most part managed their own affairs. Growing food and eating it occupied most of their time. In other matters they were, as a rule, generous and not greedy, but contented and moderate, so that estates, farms, workshops, and small trades tended to remain unchanged for generations."[12] Hobbits are true conservatives, the Anti-Federalists of Middle Earth.

The Shire: The Life Worth Living and Dying For

The entire adventure of the *Lord of the Rings* is actually about the defense of the hobbits' Shire. It begins with the Shire and ends with the Shire. What is a shire? A shire is an English county, but the hobbits' Shire is about the size of a large American county or a very small state. As with Aristotle and the Anti-Federalists, the towns of the Shire are the bedrock of human life; hobbit life grows from the family outward to the town, and the many towns constitute the Shire. It is economically and politically self-sufficient and contented; the simple way of life is embedded in the change of seasons and the moderate enjoyment of the permanent things.

There is no false and abstract universality. Hobbits are not all alike. As with all good things, there is blessed variation and stubborn particularity, and so we find "somewhat different breeds" of hobbits, the Harfoots, Stoors, and Fallohides, each with his own signal traits and habits.[13] The hobbits and their Shire are part of Middle Earth, containing other peoples and their own beloved lands—dwarves, elves, men, and even more fantastic creatures. There is no super-government trying to rule them from a distant location—until the time of Sauron's arising.

The blessed life of the Shire is interrupted by the presence of a ring that had been forged ages ago by the evil Sauron who meant to rule all of Middle Earth by its malignant power. The Ring had been lost for some ages until an adventurous hobbit, Mr. Bilbo Baggins, happened upon it (as recounted in *The Hobbit*). Bilbo has no idea of its origin, power, or evil nature; he only knows that it makes him invisible. At the opening of *The Lord of the Rings*, the Ring of Power passes to Frodo Baggins, who was adopted by Bilbo upon the death of Frodo's parents. They live in the town of Hobbiton.

The grand adventure begins when the evil Nazgûl—men corrupted and transformed by the power of Sauron—come at Sauron's bidding to recapture the Ring. If they find it, Sauron's power will have no limits. The Shire and all of Middle Earth will be entirely under his dark tyranny, and all its denizens his miserable slaves. The only way to avoid this dismal end is to destroy the Ring in the fires of Mount Doom, unhappily located in Mordor, Sauron's own land. By providence, Frodo is chosen to bear the Ring to Mount Doom, and this journey, with all its perils, battles, and triumphant and horrible moments, constitutes the adventure of *The Lord of the Rings*. The free and peaceful lives of everyone in Middle Earth, and especially Frodo's Shire, depend upon the success of this seemingly hopeless task.

I will not attempt to recreate the story before the reader's imagination. There is only one way into the enchanted world of Tolkien, and that is to let the spell of his words work its magic and draw you in. I shall instead concentrate on those central points we have been stressing in our analysis all along.

The Real Hero

Of course, there are many heroes in the story. Along with Frodo we have Aragorn the great king, Gimli the brave dwarf, Legolas the dauntless elf, Théoden the noble king of Rohan, and others. But the greatest hero is Frodo's gardener and loyal companion, Samwise Gamgee, the "foot soldier" who looks after Frodo, who literally carries him through to Mount Doom. As Tolkien later related, Sam's character was based upon the solid soldiers of the war, the privates rather than their aristocratic officers. "My 'Sam Gamgee' is indeed a reflexion of the English soldier, of the privates and batmen I knew in the 1914 war, and recognised as so far superior to myself."[14] A "batman" for the Brits is a soldier-valet assigned to a commissioned officer to look after him and his things, just as Sam Gamgee looked after Frodo.

Sam is about as common a hobbit as one can imagine, unsure of himself, exceedingly humble and a bit of a bumbler, but sure of his devotion to Frodo and the Shire, and of the fundamental difference between good and evil. It is just this devotion, the courage that arises from it, and his plain common sense and humility that ultimately save Middle Earth. He is the common man, the man of good sense, the man of the soil whose virtues arise from the simplicity and integrity of his way of life and his character. He is precisely the kind of creature despised by great planners in far off locations, who want to impose their rule upon a hapless yokel population. He is a hater of tyranny and a lover of ordered liberty—a dangerous hobbit indeed.

One particularly poignant scene is well worth visiting because it reveals the way Tolkien, and any conservative, understands good stories to work. Finding himself at the very heart of a real adventure, with real danger, real death, and real evil, Samwise realizes that all the great tales he loved in his childhood were preparing him for the drama in which he now finds himself. That is an essential point about good stories: they prepare us for the real battles. As he and Frodo, along with the misshapen, Caliban-like Gollum, climb ever closer to their destination, Sam reflects on the connection between the great stories of his youth and the great drama of his present life in the context of their dismal journey through the ruined lands of Sauron. "I don't like anything here at all," remarks Frodo disconsolately, "step or stone, breath or bone. Earth, air and water all seem accursed. But so our path is laid." Sam replies,

> Yes, that's so. . . . And we shouldn't be here at all, if we'd known more about it before we started. But I suppose it's often that way. The brave things in the old tales and songs, Mr. Frodo: adventures, as I used to call them. I used to think that they were things the wonderful folk of the stories went out and looked for, because they wanted them, because they were exciting and life was a bit dull, a kind of a sport, as you might say. But that's not the way of it with the tales that really mattered, or the ones that stay in the mind. Folk seem to have been just landed in them, usually—their paths were laid that way, as you put it. But I expect they had lots of chances, like us, of turning back, only they didn't. And if they had, we shouldn't know, because they'd have been forgotten. We hear about those as just went on—and not all to a good end, mind you; at least not to what folk inside a story and not outside it call a good end. You know, coming home, and finding things all right, though not quite the same— like old Mr. Bilbo. But those aren't always the best tales to hear,

though they may be the best tales to get landed in! I wonder what sort of tale we've fallen into?[15]

That is what we all have to wonder, especially when we find ourselves in similarly dark times. As a friend of mine once said, regarding the condition of our culture, "The orcs are in the Shire!" Orcs, again, are the demon creatures of Middle Earth, the willing slaves of Sauron, the polar opposite to elves. They live for destruction, hate beauty, and worship power over nature and over others. They are the very picture of our deepest corruption, just as the elves are the vision of our lost natural innocence and power.

To battle orcs we must, like Samwise Gamgee, gather strength from the great tales. We find ourselves in a particular place and time, confronting real evils that must be dealt with. We have the freedom to turn back, to try to continue a life of ease and make the best of it as the sky darkens. But we also have the freedom to trudge on and do what we must. The freedom we do not have, however, is to be neutral or be in another time. We shall be judged by God and others by what we did or didn't do in the face of the evils that confront us, by what kind of world we leave those that live after us. As Gandalf the wizard later counsels, "Other evils there are that may come; for Sauron is himself but a servant or emissary. Yet it is not our part to master all the tides of the world, but to do what is in us for the succor of those years wherein we are set, uprooting the evil in the fields that we know, so that those who live after may have clean earth to till. What weather they shall have is not ours to rule."[16]

After the Ring is destroyed and the great adventure is complete, Sam returns with the other hobbits, Frodo, Merry, and Pippin, to Hobbiton in the Shire. Unfortunately, the writers of the film saw fit to cut out Chapter VIII of *The Return of the King*, "The Scouring of the Shire," which is a brilliant presentation of the attempt to "bureaucratize" the Shire through fear by ruffians and lickspittles of the fallen wizard Saruman (renamed "Sharkey"). "The Scouring of the Shire" is a must-read for conservatives, because it so vividly portrays the kind of fear that causes good folks to cower and acquiesce, the kind of damage to the good life that petty tyranny brings, and the kind of bravery necessary to throw it off.

After a battle in the Shire, good order is restored. Samwise marries his love, Rose Cotton, has thirteen children, and because of his great bravery, fame, goodness, and wisdom, is elected Mayor of Hobbiton seven times. He is known as Master Samwise, but still tends his own garden. But while Samwise the Great is certainly a hero, he is not the only hero in the book.

Men with Chests, and Kings with Crowns

The Lord of the Rings is a book of men with chests—or more exactly hobbits, elves, dwarves, and men with chests. It's not a book for the likes of Gaius and Titius who, deathly afraid of the horrors of war, seek to make men without chests and peace at any cost. There are times when the evil is such that we must fight, and battle demands men *with* chests, noble men, great men, both wise and strong. If there is one single virtue that stands out in Tolkien's masterpiece, it is courage, the manly virtue of those who must fight against those who would enslave them and turn to ruin all they love.

In portraying manly courage, the three films are extraordinary: the battles are grand, the trials are harrowing, the danger is palpable, and the intensity of the bravery of the main characters swells the hearts of the viewers. Every boy who hopes to become a man, every man who strives to become a better man, and every woman who yearns to know what a real man is should throw themselves into the movies.

That having been said, there is one central and serious defect in the films' portrayal of the character of Aragorn. In the film, he is an extraordinary and extremely brave man; in the book he is a magnificent king, so glorious that when he chooses to reveal himself fully, both friend and enemy shrink in his sight. To cite a vivid example, in the film, when Aragorn, Gimli the dwarf, and Legolas the elf are come upon by Éomer and the noble Riders of Rohan, Aragorn reacts submissively to Éomer's challenge. In the book, Aragorn does no such thing. Rather, he reveals his true identity, with quite the opposite effect.

> Aragorn threw back his cloak. The elven-sheath glittered as he grasped it, and the bright blade of Andúril [his legendary sword] shone like a sudden flame as he swept it out. "Elendil!" he cried. "I am Aragorn son of Arathorn, and am called Elessar, the Elfstone, Dúnadan, the heir of Isildur Elendil's son of Gondor. Here is the Sword that was Broken and is forged again! Will you aid me or thwart me? Choose swiftly!"
>
> Gimli and Legolas looked at their companion in amazement, for they had not seen him in this mood before. He seemed to have grown in stature while Éomer shrunk; and in his living face they caught a brief vision of the power and majesty of kings of stone. For a moment it seemed to the eyes of Legolas that a white flame flickered on the brows of Aragorn like a shining crown.
>
> Éomer stepped back and a look of awe was in his face. He cast down his proud eyes. "These are indeed strange days," he muttered. "Dreams and legends spring to life out of the grass."[17]

Here is revealed a true king, not just an ordinary man, but something of legend, like King Arthur, who suddenly appears. The entire drive of the third book, *The Return of the King*, depends on this vision of a great king, a thing of seeming myth that suddenly intrudes into real life to fulfill an age-old prophecy. To reduce him merely to a brave man, as the film does, tarnishes the crowning of the book, the climactic coronation of Aragorn at Gondor. In the film, Aragorn takes up his kingship with all the sheepishness of a man who really believes that kings should be replaced, at best, by presidents. In the book, things are much different when the crown is placed on Aragorn's head.

> But when Aragorn arose all that beheld him gazed in silence, for it seemed to them that he was revealed to them now for the first time. Tall as the sea-kings of old, he stood above all that were near; ancient of days he seemed and yet in the flower of manhood; and wisdom sat upon his brow, and strength and healing were in his hands, and a light was about him.[18]

The failure to capture the true glory of the king is a major flaw in an otherwise very good adaptation of the book. But it is a very great flaw, one that goes beyond cheapening the inner grandeur of Tolkien's imaginary world and unfits us for two essential truths.

The first comes from Aristotle. We live in a democratic age, one that is all too easily tarnished by envy, so that we find it hard to believe that there is extraordinary goodness, courage, and wisdom. This leads us to a fundamentally confused view of kingship: that all kings are tyrants. But recall that Aristotle argued, quite reasonably, that we can distinguish between good and bad kings, true kings and tyrants, just as we can distinguish, in regard to majority rule, between the majority that rules for the true common good and the majority that rules for its own selfish interests, republican and democratic rule. Even more startling and reasonable, for Aristotle it was better to live under the rule of a good king, than in an oligarchy or a democracy. But even more unsettling to us, remember that Aristotle stated quite soberly that if there were one person, preeminent in virtue, a man of supreme goodness, it would be good for "everyone to obey such a person gladly" as their king. If there *were* a man like Aragorn, as the book presents him, we should welcome him as king. If you cannot feel that, deep down, then *The Lord of the Rings* will be entirely lost on you.

Outlandish? No Jew or Christian can deny it, and further, if you cannot feel it deep down, the Bible as well will be entirely lost on you. The Bible is a great epic drama centered around kingship: the kingship of God, the kingship of David, and the culmination of the deepest desire for the return of the king, the fulfilling of all prophecies of one who is to come, as if out of legend, the king of kings, heir of David. That will be part of our theme when we look at the Bible in the next chapter, but we have one more aspect of *The Lord of the Rings* we must look into: the Ring itself.

"One Ring to rule them all..."

In the mythology of Middle Earth, there are actually many more rings than the One Ring—nine rings for men, seven for dwarves, and three for the elves. Shortly after the original forging of these Rings of Power, the evil Sauron made the "One Ring to rule them all, One Ring to find them, / One Ring to bring them all and in the darkness bind them / In the Land of Mordor where the Shadows lie." The evil Ring is the ring of greatest power, but its very making was defined by malevolence. It is a power that cannot be used for good, no matter how good the intentions of the wearer, no matter how great the peril from which such power could deliver good people. That is why it presents the greatest temptation for those who face the evil Sauron. That is why it must be destroyed.

The presence of the One Ring represents many subtle facets of evil, but three are particularly worth our attention.

First, it represents an evil deeper and far darker than mere hobbits can understand, just as the battle between good and evil extends far beyond the level of the Shire to unimagined heights and depths of reality. Aragorn is greater, Gandalf the Wizard is greater, Sauron is greater, the battle for Middle Earth is greater. As the hobbit Pippin says to Merry after the "Battle of Pelennor Fields," referring to Aragorn,

> "Was there ever any one like him?...except Gandalf, of course.... Dear me!...we can't live long on the heights."
>
> "No," said Merry, "I can't. Not yet, at any rate. But at least, Pippin, we can now see them, and honour them. It is best to love first what you are fitted to love, I suppose: you must start somewhere and have some roots, and the soil of the Shire is deep. Still there are things deeper and higher; and not a gaffer could tend his garden in what he calls peace but for them, whether he knows about them or not. I am glad that I know about them, a little."[19]

The evil they face, the evil they fight against for the sake of the Shire, reaches far beyond their reckoning, just as the good that ultimately protects it. Yet, the very ordinary hobbits were essential in the overthrow of the evil, essential in the battle on the side of the good that rose above their vision as well. We hobbits must recognize that we are part of a far larger cosmic battle.

Second, the One Ring represents the essential, and often painful, self-limitation of the good man who *could* use an evil means to a seemingly good end, who is sorely tempted to use an evil means to a noble end, but forces himself to turn away. This is the courage of a true conservative when faced with moral limits, limits that could be transgressed and grant us some great benefit, but which, once transgressed, turn upon and corrupt the will that crossed the sacred boundary. If we could save a man's life by harvesting live organs from human beings raised for this purpose, produced through *in vitro* fertilization and kept in a kind of warehouse, should we? If we could save a woman embarrassment and hardships by helping her have an abortion, should we? If we could improve the genetic strength and future health of our race by systematically eliminating the less genetically endowed through prenatal screening, should we? A true conservative says no. Good can never be purchased with evil; the conservative accepts moral limits as a matter of honor and duty and even prudence. The liberal, however, brushes these limits aside, laughing at old-fashioned notions of good and evil, and rushes forward on a path of presumed progress, using the magic wand of technology and the force of law to remake man as he thinks he should be made.

Finally, we must not overlook the obvious. The Ring is a single entity, a single power that ultimately resides in a single source, Sauron in Mordor. With it, he desires to rule all of Middle Earth, bending everything to his will. He presents the very essence of totalitarianism: the desire to override all the real wills of real persons, in all their intractable variety and local color, and reform all that is below him into one master plan. He imposes government from the top-down, crushing everything in his path as of no consequence. The Shire and all its lovely towns, as well Lothlórien, the land of the Elves, and Gondor, the home of men—these and all the other places of independent peoples and particular ways of life must be destroyed or reduced to servitude. One cannot fail to see, in this great struggle of Middle Earth, and in the dark designs of Sauron, the familiar contours of twentieth century totalitarianism and the grave possibility that its threat extends into the twenty-first.

I am not suggesting that liberalism, in its desire to centralize power in the federal government and then in a world government, partakes of the malice of Hitler, Stalin, or Sauron. But what they all do share is a desire to use power to dominate others. Liberals fail to realize a central moral lesson of *The Lord of the Rings*: such power itself will take even the best of intentions to the darkest of ends.

CHAPTER FOURTEEN

The Jerusalem Bible

"Who do men say that I am?"

Why This Translation?

NEARLY EVERYONE HAS A FAVORITE TRANSLATION OF THE BIBLE, usually the one he grew up reading. I have little interest in putting forth the Jerusalem Bible as the best and only translation, but great interest in its being the most unfamiliar, for the whole aim of this chapter is to get readers to discover the Bible as if it were a story they'd never read.

A familiar translation breeds, not contempt perhaps, but a kind of coziness that makes our minds less awake. To rediscover the story of the Bible, we cannot tread its pages like a well-worn path. It must become an adventure again. We must become enchanted by the story *as* a story in just the same way that, with Tolkien, we become enchanted by the Secondary World he created in *The Lord of the Rings.* We must enter the biblical world as a strange and fascinating Secondary World.

Why? Precisely because we are generally guilty of confusing our world—that is, our world as defined by our contemporary culture—with the world of the Bible. We envision Abraham, Sarah, Isaac, Joshua, Saul, Samuel, King David, Isaiah, John the Baptist, Mary, and Joseph in our imagination as white people with bathrobes who would quite comfortably fit into a suburban afternoon of backyard grilling and light conversation on the patio. In truth, if Abraham or Sarah showed up at your door on a Saturday afternoon you would call the police. The ancient Jews are as alien to us—in look, in speech, in what they considered important, in how they understood reality—as the elves or dwarves of Tolkien's Middle Earth.

The biblical world was a world of tribes and tribal deities, of people defined by families and clans; a world of extraordinary brutality and even more extraordinary hospitality, where life was lived close to the soil, completely dependent on rain and sun, the health of the herd, the luck of the hunt; a world where a man's worth was measured by the strength of his sword and the number of sheep and goats he could call his own; a world in which shepherds could become kings.

The King James version of the Bible, however great its literary merits, was written in seventeenth-century English, and certainly to our ears sounds elegant and ornate, and a little obscure, but it is not the language of an ancient tribe. Modern Americanese translations that press the Bible into our parlance have the effect of entirely removing the great distance separating our way of life, our way of thinking, from that of the ancient Jews, the result being that we are not looking into the depths of history but into the shallow reflection of a mirror.

But the Jerusalem Bible, while not perfect, is certainly unfamiliar to most of us. It is also, I would argue, much closer to the straight-forward epic language of the original. By "epic" I don't mean flowery, but simple and at times almost brutal, the tongue of the tribal warrior, a language much more akin to what we find in the *Iliad* or the *Lord of the Rings*. That is because the ancient Jew's way of life was closer to the way of life portrayed in Homer or Tolkien.

At its best, the Jerusalem Bible evokes the speech of a tribe with its tribal deity, the speech of men with swords, strong, powerful, proud fighters led by kings—cunning, wise, foolish, ruthless, arrogant, humbled, holy, and profane kings; the speech of harrowing and strange prophets who continually struck at kings and the people in the name of the tribal deity, laying upon them the most violent and effective curses, the most outrageous threats, and setting before them impossibly good rewards; the speech of real priests, blood-sacrificing, smoke and incense, stone-altar priests. That is not our world, but it is the world we need to enter.

Now it is a very interesting fact that J. R. R. Tolkien is listed among the "principal collaborators in translation and literary revision" of the Jerusalem Bible—the 1966 version, not the later and lesser one, the New Jerusalem Bible. As it turns out, the general editor, Alexander Jones, contacted Tolkien because of Tolkien's impressive command of the English language as evidenced in *The Lord of the Rings*. It is interesting to me, anyway, since it was only after reading *The Lord of the Rings* aloud with my family and watching the three movies that I was finally able to read the Bible. By "read" I mean "read with real excitement, deep understanding, and fascination"—or, in a word, with "enchantment." As you may have guessed, the Jerusalem Bible was the translation through which this enchantment was effected.

Hear, for example, the beginning of Psalm 28: "I cry to you, Yahweh, / my Rock! Do not be deaf to me, / for if you are silent, I shall go / down to the Pit like the rest." Or Genesis 2:5–7: "At the time when Yahweh God made earth and heaven there was as yet no wild bush on the earth nor had any wild plant sprung up, for Yahweh God had not sent rain on the earth, nor was there any man to till the soil. However, a flood was rising from the earth and watering all the surface of the soil. Yahweh God fashioned man of dust from the soil. Then he breathed into his nostrils a breath of life, and thus man became a living being." Or the victory song sung after crossing the Red Sea, Exodus 15:13: "Yahweh I sing: he has covered himself in glory, / horse and rider he has thrown into the sea. / Yah is my strength, my song, / he is my salvation. / This is my God, I praise him; / the God of my father, I extol him. / Yahweh is a warrior; / Yahweh is his name." (Yah is another form of Yahweh.)

To dwell on the obvious, the Jerusalem Bible is not only very direct and simple, it dares to print the name chosen by God Himself, Yahweh, His name for "all time," the name by which He "shall be invoked for all generations to come" (Ex 3:15). The effect created, at least in me, was startling since, along with everyone else, I had always read the circumspect "LORD" which is politely inserted into the text wherever Yahweh actually appears. But when you read a translation that prints Yahweh where it occurs, you suddenly realize how many times one actually finds it in the Old Testament. As a consequence, you feel far more deeply, with the personal name, the very personal relationship the Jews had with the Almighty. It is like the difference between the generic name Lord, which could apply even to human beings, and the personal name, Jesus (or Yeshua, from Yehoshua, "Yahweh saves").

Moreover, substituting LORD obscures essential prophetic connections. Isaiah says, "A voice cries, 'Prepare in the wilderness a way for Yahweh. Make a straight highway for our God across the desert." The prophetic fulfillment duplicated in Matthew to announce the coming of Jesus reads, "A voice cries in the wilderness: Prepare a way for the Lord [Greek, *kurios*], make his paths straight." The Greek word for lord or master, *kurios*, is used by the New Testament writers to stand for Yahweh in deference to the commendable Hebrew custom of never pronouncing the name "Yahweh" when it appeared in the Old Testament. But in putting LORD in the passage in Isaiah, we lose the startling assertion that Matthew is making to the Jews of his day: This man Jesus *is* Yahweh "our God," Yahweh in the flesh.

To return to a previous point, I don't mean to overestimate the place of Tolkien in the making of the Jerusalem Bible. In fact, he worked only on the translation of Jonah. But obviously the general editor, in inviting Tolkien, was affirming the kind of English style he thought best represented the simplicity and directness of the original languages, a style he himself had encountered in reading *The Lord of the Rings*, a style that can jolt us out of complacent familiarity with the Bible, so that we once again read it in wonder as a story.

The Bible as Story

What I needed, in reading the Bible, was to enter another world, leaving my own behind. That kind of literary effect was exactly what Tolkien had in mind in creating the Secondary World of *Lord of the Rings*, a self-contained cosmos, integrally woven with marvelous skeins, a world in which even what is familiar becomes strange. Again, what I ask of readers is simply this: for once in your life read the Bible as a *story*, as you would *The Lord of the Rings*. Lay aside the familiar translation, the familiar ideas of what you think is going on, the familiar themes, and enter into the Bible as an epic drama, a great piece of literature. Read it as having a deep, integrated, unfolding plot, rather than from the standpoint of belief or unbelief. Become immersed in it exactly as you would any other great piece of literature where you find yourself, through your captured imagination, experiencing the story *from within*, as the characters themselves experience it—not digging around to find out whether this or that thing is an actual fact, or how what this or that character says applies to you or your time, but living *in* the story itself, and following out all the myriad entwined threads that trace the intricacies of the plot as they unfold around you.

What I am trying to exclude are all the kinds of questions and attitudes that would block our imaginative immersion into the text as a Secondary World. We would not ask, on reading Charles Dickens's *A Christmas Carol,* "Well, *was* there really a Jacob Marley?" or remark with a snort, "This is a silly, childish book. It begins with a doorknocker that changes into a ghastly image of a man long dead!" Nor would we engage in questions about why Dickens wrote it, or try to boil the whole thing down to the cultural context, or snuffle around looking for bits and pieces of the story in previous works by different authors so as to show our own cleverness in discovering its unoriginality. These are the ways that "scholars" ruin the story, for themselves and everyone else.

So, to the scholar and skeptic, I say just read it as you would *A Christmas Carol.* In reading Dickens, we accept that in this story there *are* ghosts, several of them, and that the appearance of Marley's face on Scrooge's doorknocker is entirely appropriate and integral to the plot. If we do not feel the terror of the ghosts, and even more, the inner moral horror of Ebenezer Scrooge slowly revealed to him by these ghosts, the greatness of the story and the truths it teaches will be lost on us. The primary truth served is not the tasteless moral pabulum, "Be nice to poor people." Rather, it is the horrifying experience of a damned soul, and the exhilarating

experience of its redemption. That is not a truth we understand outside the story, as if the moral could be written on an index card or
a bumper sticker. It's an experience that we have through immersion in the story as real while we are reading it.

So also, when reading the Bible, we must accept that in this story
a terrible deity does create merely by speaking things into existence, that he reveals himself in fire to a man named Moses, that
water does spring from a rock on command, that the outcome of
battles does depend on whose tribal deity is real, and that a seemingly ordinary man does cure lepers with a word, and demons
shriek in terror at his presence. If we do not accept these things,
we will never experience the truths the Bible reveals.

And I'm speaking here not just to skeptics. Too often, believers
are searching the Bible for a set of moral or theological dicta that,
once found, count as *the* revelation. The obvious ill effect of this
approach is that the biblical story doesn't really matter. It is merely
a vehicle on which slogans are painted; once the key didactic passages have been picked out, one can safely dispense with the story
itself. But if *that* were all God wanted to say, and indeed *how* He
wanted to say it, the Bible would have been a considerably shorter
and easier text.

To experience the Bible as a story, by contrast, means that we
allow ourselves to enter into the wonders, terrors, miracles, bru-
talities, uncertainties, triumphs, tragedies, the joy, and the anguish
experienced by the characters. We must go into battle with them,
cry alone on our beds with them, thrash ourselves for our moral
failures, experience the terror of a prophecy of doom settling upon
us, and the unnamable ecstasy of a glorious prophecy beyond our
wildest hopes taking shape in our midst. But above all we must let
the story unfold *as* a story—that is, as it was written, rather than
spot reading for juicy bits or jumping around as if the plot were

entirely inconsequential. As with any novel, the deeper meaning of what happens at the end depends upon how well we, as readers, attend to the beginning and middle.

To take the most important instance, who Jesus is in the New Testament cannot be understood apart from the successive revelation of who Yahweh is in the Old Testament. Jesus the man actually appears in the way that the Jews, from all their prophecies, had expected Yahweh to come—except that the very last thing they expected was that the metaphorical language about God in the Old Testament (Yahweh having arms, legs, eyes, and a mouth, and so on), was going to be taken with shocking literalness in the Incarnation. Jesus fulfils the prophecies of Yahweh's entrance into Jerusalem, but in a way the Jews did not imagine—as a Jewish man, as a son who no doubt bore a significant resemblance to his mother Mary, and in whose veins ran the blood of Jewish kings and shepherds. He bore in himself all the particularities of the Jews' long history. He is, in sum, the flesh and blood culmination of all the previous chapters leading up to Him, the culmination of Yahweh's revelation about Himself.

The literary threads that connect Yahweh with Jesus are everywhere for patient readers of the whole story. In Malachi (3:1) the prophet, speaking in the name of Yahweh, says, "Look, I am going to send my messenger to prepare a way before me. And the Lord you are seeking will suddenly enter his Temple; and the angel of the covenant whom you are longing for, yes, he is coming, says Yahweh Sabaoth." This entry will not be pleasant; Malachi is speaking of the dread Day of Yahweh, when He will come to purge the Temple. In Matthew, Jesus identifies the messenger with John the Baptist, and hence Yahweh with Himself (Mt 11:10). Of course, this prophetic utterance is the context for understanding Jesus' later stormy entry into the Temple, cleansing it of money-changers (Mt 21:12–14). There, He cures the blind and the lame ("Yahweh restores sight to the blind" Psalm 146:8). In response to these wonders, the children shout, "Hosanna to the Son of David," which makes the chief priests and scribes indignant. But Jesus answers, "Have you never read this: 'By the mouths of children, babes in arms, you have made sure of praise?'" which is a reference to Psalm 8, "Yahweh, our Lord, how great your name throughout the earth! Above the heavens is your majesty chanted by the mouths of children, babes in arms." The Temple dignitaries only want to accuse Jesus of taking on the title of kingly messiah. Jesus does them one better by identifying Himself with Yahweh.

But the identity of Yahweh and Jesus in the story is even more mysterious, because it also includes the identity of Jesus as a Jew. Let's go to a few related scenes in the drama, starting with one of the strangest and most terrifying. Yahweh appears to the childless Abram (not yet renamed Abraham) in a vision, saying, "Have no fear, Abram, I am your shield; your reward will be very great." "But," Abram replies, "You have given me no descendants." Yahweh then promises him descendants that number as many as the stars, and the Promised Land itself. "My Lord Yahweh," Abram says, "How am I to know that I shall inherit it?" (Gen 15:2–6).

Yahweh's response is a frightening ancient ritual. We cannot approach this scene from our world. We must enter a world in which a man's vow was considered absolutely sacred and binding, a thing so serious that only bloody sacrifice could seal it.

Yahweh has Abram get a heifer, a goat, a ram, a turtledove, and a young pigeon, and cut them in half. In this ritual, two men make a covenant, a binding promise, by each walking between the split carcasses of animals, calling down upon themselves the same gruesome fate if they break their vows. Abram does as he is told (but for some reason doesn't cut the birds in half). And then he waits. "Birds of prey came down on the carcasses but Abram drove them off."[1] And still he waited until "as the sun was setting Abram fell into a deep sleep, and terror seized him.... When the sun had set and darkness had fallen, there appeared a smoking furnace and a firebrand that went between the halves" (Gen 15:7–18). We must wait there with Abram and imagine ourselves the witnesses of a ghastly and ominous scene.

But what can this dark and horrible scene mean? How could Yahweh enter a two-sided covenant, one that seemed to imply that he could be slaughtered if He doesn't fulfill his end of it? And why didn't Abram walk through? At this point in the story, it is all a complete mystery, but that is exactly how stories work.

Perhaps an even more horrifying scene takes place when this same deity commands Abraham to slaughter his own son Isaac on an altar, and then burn up the corpse as if he were making a food offering of a sacrificial animal (Gen 22:1–19). What kind of a god would ask a man to sacrifice his son? Of course, that was precisely what many of the pagan deities did. Even as a kind of test of Abraham's fidelity to Yahweh, or perhaps especially as a kind of test, it seems not only barbaric but even more, contradictory, since it is through Isaac that the promises to Abraham have been made. Kill Isaac, and the covenant promise of endless descendants is killed as well. And here we must understand that the same voice, the same powerful vision with the same irresistible authority that revealed to Abram that he would be blessed through this son, also said, "Take your son ... your only child Isaac, whom you love, and go to the land of Moriah. There you shall offer him as a burnt offering, on a mountain I will point out to you" (Gen 22:1–2). What can it mean? How can Yahweh ask such a thing?

Many centuries later, Israel has been dragged into exile, torn from the Promised Land, abandoned by Yahweh for breaking the covenant. Yet, to these Jews in Babylon, the prophet Isaiah speaks words of unimaginable hope, "A voice cries, 'Prepare in the wilderness a way for Yahweh'" (Isaiah 40:1). Israel herself, the servant of Yahweh, is crushed in exile, nearly torn in two. "See, my servant will prosper, he shall be lifted up, exalted, rise to great heights," Yahweh promises through the inspired Isaiah. But then:

> [T]he crowds were appalled on seeing him—so disfigured did he look that he seemed no longer human . . . a thing despised and rejected by men, a man of sorrows and familiar with suffering, a man to make people screen their faces; he was despised and we took no account of him. And yet ours were the sufferings he bore, ours the sorrows he carried. But we, we thought of him as someone punished, struck by God, and brought low. Yet he was pierced through for our faults, crushed for our sins. On him lies a punishment that brings us peace, and through his wounds we are healed (Isaiah 52:13–53:5).

In the New Testament story, the various seeming contradictions and mysteries are resolved, if even in a greater mystery. We now understand why only Yahweh passed between the bloody carcasses. In the flesh, Jesus is the descendant of Abraham and mercifully takes upon Himself, as a Jew, the terrible punishment that results from Israel breaking her side of the covenant; yet He is Yahweh.

The plot thickens even more. Jesus, Yahweh-Saves, is revealed as the Son of the Father. We therefore find out what kind of a deity could ask that a man's only son be slaughtered as a way to fulfill the covenant and open up the Promised Land; at the same time, He bears the full punishment for breaking the covenant. It is not accidental that the crucifixion takes place on a hill, that Jesus carries his cross as Isaac carried wood up the mountain for his own sacrifice, and that the same kind of eerie darkness accompanies the crucifixion as the original bloody covenant between Yahweh and Abram.

But since this is a masterful story, we have only begun to touch the multiple strands of meaning that unfold in the plot: the prophecies, the details of kingship, the wisdom literature that leads to the Incarnation of wisdom itself.

Note one important thing about all this. On the literary level, all these connections are in the text. In one sense it doesn't matter whether we believe them. To understand the Bible as a story, all that matters is that we follow out all the connections and discover the full meaning intended. But, of course, the obvious question is: is it a true story? Or is it a fairy story? Or is it both?

Is the Bible a Fairy Story?

It is certainly right to call the Bible a fairy story in Tolkien's sense of the term, for it is a great adventure filled to overflowing with the fantastic. As with Dickens's *A Christmas Carol,* which I think qualifies as one of the greatest modern fairy stories, our experience of its truths depends on how deeply we experience the story as real. In fact, the most salutary effect of *A Christmas Carol* is that we wish ghosts *did* come to haunt the near-damned.[2] We'd all be a lot better off.

With the Bible, there is this difference, *the* difference. It is the one fantastic story that actually happened. In this case, story is history. We need to experience the Bible as real through our imagination, and *then* realize that much of what we have just read testifies to actual incidents that truly occurred and that are as well recorded as many other historical events of the Ancient World that we take for granted. But note the movement. First, we lose ourselves in the story, just as we would any other great story, like *A Christmas Carol.* Second, we are hit, slowly or suddenly, with the truths revealed *through* the story. And then third, we realize that in fact what we have just read is in large part an historical account.[3]

I stress "in large part." The Bible is written from a variety of styles and angles, using straight-out description, metaphor, parables, proverbs, poetry, and didacticism. The ancient Jews, like most ancient people, were not history-journalists in the modern sense; for them, the way one describes what really happened needs to reflect the full complexity of what really happened and their understanding of it—and sometimes (as often happens with fairy stories) that requires poetry rather than prose, or a parable rather than a descriptive paragraph.

And so, perhaps we can be somewhat less shocked at Tolkien saying that:

> The Gospels contain a fairy-story, or a story of a larger kind which embraces all the essence of fairy stories.... But this story has entered History and the primary world;... There is no tale ever told that men would rather find was true, and one which so many skeptical men have accepted as true on its own merits. For the Art of it has the supremely convincing tone of Primary Art, that is, of Creation. To reject it leads either to sadness or to wrath.
>
> It is not difficult to imagine the peculiar excitement and joy that one would feel, if any specially beautiful fairy-story were found to be "primarily" true, its narrative to be history, without thereby necessarily losing the mythical or allegorical significance it had possessed.... But this story [in the Gospels] is supreme; and it is true. Art has been verified. God is the Lord, of angels, and of men—and elves. Legend and History have met and fused.[4]

We end this section on an obvious note, and a sour one at that. The modern case against fairy stories in general, and the Bible in particular, is that miracles cannot happen. Fantastic things are impossible, we are told. Therefore, the Bible is a fairy story in the worst sense: it is the one fairy story which, in most foolish pretence, claims to be true, and hence is most laughable.

Miracles cannot happen, the materialists tell us, because all events are materially determined. Of course, materialists, by the same argument, say that we don't exist—at least not in the way that you or I think we do: as thinking, conscious, acting beings rather than as a series of biochemical reactions.

More important in this context, though, is the circular confusion in the skeptical materialist's reasoning. The claim that miracles *do not* happen is based upon the assumption that they *cannot* happen. That is entirely non-scientific, arguing not from evidence but ideology. The real question is whether miracles *do* happen. If they do occur, then our science would have to include that fact, even if it can't explain it. (That is basically what happens when, in the Catholic Church's investigations into the cause of canonization of a saint, every effort of the latest science is bent on proving the non-miraculous nature of alleged miracles.) Once we accept that miracles can and do happen, the fantastic in the Bible is no longer an obstacle to our understanding the story as real. We might even wonder if the explicit rejection of the miraculous has, at its source, not evidence that miracles are impossible, but the deep desire to deny the reality of the biblical story.

The Story of Liberalism vs. the Biblical Story

Readers should not think that I've stepped beyond the themes of this book. At its heart, liberalism is secular. That is, it rejects the possibility that the Bible is a true story, and does so on two related grounds: that materialism (which liberalism generally accepts) forbids the miraculous; and that religion, especially the religion of the Bible, is dangerous, leading to war and a morbid preoccupation with otherworldly heaven and hell when we should be thinking of this-worldly comfort and peace.

Ironically, in rejecting Christianity, it takes over its themes. Consequently, the story of liberalism is a story of "progress" *away* from religion *through* the ministrations of miracle-producing science *toward* a world of peace, comfort, and plenty, a kind of new Eden. It is, if we compare it to the Bible, the great anti-Biblical fairy story, filled with tales of astounding scientific discoveries that manifest a new kind of magic power over nature, and promises of even more fantastic magic in the utopian future.

Not surprisingly, this secular utopianism self-consciously inverts the biblical relationship of creature to creator. Liberalism, as fundamentally secular, sees itself as fundamentally creative, and human beings as raw material to be recreated. Liberalism is, then, perhaps less fairy story than science fiction; the liberal goal is utopia, the brave new world, where man is not created in the likeness of God, but rather man can be recreated in whatever likeness he pleases, if he wields sufficient technical power. In this utopia, good and evil are not objective, but each can define them for himself. In the liberal anti-Biblical story, moral evil is not the violation of human *nature* as defined by a Creator, but the suppression of any human *desire*, any desire, as defined by the individual. Since goodness in this story is defined by "what I desire," the point of government, and even religion as it is co-opted by liberalism, is to satisfy whatever desires individuals happen to have.

There are other essential differences between the biblical and liberalism's stories. In the Bible, human social life does not begin in a "state," but in a family, with the union of male and female, so intimately designed for each other that they become as one flesh. In this fusion of two into one, a child is created. Everything good for human beings that comes after depends upon this fundamental union; anything that is evil in some way violates and profanes it. The central importance of this familial origin is seen clearly in the precedence that family has throughout the story. Yahweh does not make nations from social contracts or abstract principles. He does not make Israel from even Jews, but from Abraham and Sarah. Marriage is so important, so primary, that it is the main metaphor Yahweh uses in relationship to Israel—He the bridegroom, Israel the bride. His demand of obedience takes the form of a demand for marital fidelity. The Incarnation occurs, not in the sudden appearance of a resplendent and terrifying king, but in a stable as the baby in the family of Mary and Joseph. When this child is, upon growing up, asked about the negation of marriage in divorce, he responds, "Have you not read that the creator from the beginning made them male and female and that he said: This is why a man must leave father and mother, and cling to his wife, and the two become one body? They are no longer two, therefore, but one body. So then, what God has united, man must not divide" (Mt 19:4–6). This is not merely a denial of divorce as allowed by religious leaders; it is a denial of the right of any man, or the state, to transgress the nature of marriage. For our purposes, it is important to note that the family is prior to the state in every sense.

Again, we have the opposite flow in liberalism. From its inception in Thomas Hobbes, the twin foci of liberalism have been the individual and the state, both to the exclusion of the family. Whereas the Bible quite naturally considers individuals to come from families, and the nation as something that grows from families, liberalism begins with individuals and the state as if actual natural families were a kind of bothersome afterthought, or even an interference with the desires of individuals and the designs of the state. One ill effect of this has been the ironic liberal notion that the state is just one big family, a way of offsetting the equally unpleasant effects of considering the state to be a mere collection of isolated, desire-driven individuals. The elevation of the individual above the family has another interesting effect: blindness to the obvious fact that there is no such thing as an abstract, nondescript, asexual "individual." There are only very concrete males and females. Individuals do not get married; men and women do. Individuals do not have children; fathers and mothers do. Children are not "individuals"; they are boys and girls. The liberal war against the natural distinction between the sexes and the natural family is the result of its elevation of the entirely artificial, abstract "individual."

To keep those individuals in check, the liberal needs power, and liberals believe that knowledge and technical mastery are tools to achieving power. Conservatives take a more biblical view. They believe that the beginning of knowledge is "the fear of Yahweh," or to put it another way, knowledge comes from understanding and respecting the natural moral order as defined by the Creator.

The biblical passage, "The fear of Yahweh is the beginning of knowledge; fools spurn wisdom and discipline" (Proverbs 1:7) cannot be read as a mere familiar bromide; rather, it must be understood as a real fear, the proper reaction of coming to direct experience of an all powerful being, *the* all-powerful Being. This is such an essential point about the nature of biblical revelation—and hence the question of how we should read the Bible—that we must pause for its further consideration. I realize that our imaginations are feeble, that the power of revelation is hard to grasp, but to read the Bible we need to imaginatively recreate the experience of the story. When we read, "Yahweh said to Abram, 'Leave your country, your family and your father's house, for the land I will show you. I will make you a great nation; I will bless you and make your name so famous that it will be used as a blessing'" (Gen 12:1–2), the voice or vision must be understood to have been of such personal authority and power, that it penetrated straight to the marrow of Abraham's soul. He was immediately and completely drawn into the presence of a greater reality, such that, when the vision and voice faded and he slipped back into the everyday, his normal existence seemed paltry, cheap, a mere mist by comparison. Just the kind of experience of transcendence that C. S. Lewis reported, only far more powerful.

Throughout the Old Testament, Yahweh speaks with this authority; it is the presence of this same authority that explains why the fishermen apostles drop their nets and follow Jesus. The moral contours of the Bible come from the extraordinary experience of the presence of Yahweh. The point with Moses coming down with the tablet from Mount Sinai is not that a very loud and ostentatious deity is handing down a clean-up list of thou shalts and thou shalt nots. The moral response comes from the revelatory encounter with Yahweh. In such encounters, Yahweh is felt, is known, as "the supreme and only important object of desire," to use Lewis's phrase about his own glimmer of transcendent joy.

In political terms, that means that we should have no other gods, like an omnipotent state, before Yahweh. But that is exactly what liberalism seeks to do: to put the state in the place of God. To liberals, a god above the state is too dangerous. Transcendence must not be allowed. We can trace a direct line of liberal animosity to biblical revelation from the seventeenth century to our own day. Seventeenth and eighteenth century liberals like Thomas Hobbes, Benedict Spinoza, John Locke, and the Deists permitted religion as an obsequious servant of the state. This quite naturally led to a religion *of* the state in the nineteenth and twentieth centuries, a worship of the state as the bearer of all meaning, purpose, and human fulfillment. The elevation of the state as a secular religious idol is, historically, the result of denying that God revealed Himself in history and that this revelation puts in perspective and judges all human political activity beneath it.

This brings us again to the question of morality. In the Bible, the experience of God *as* pure and *as* holy results in the human quest for purity and holiness. That is why the Ten Commandments begin with our relationship to God, and then go on to our relationship with other human beings. The bridge between these two types of commandments, religious and moral, is that we are somehow made in the image of Yahweh. We do not kill, but love our neighbor, because somehow our neighbor is made in the image of "the supreme and only important object of desire." It is in worshiping God that we keep from killing our neighbor as we would any other animal.[5]

In our own very secular time, of course, the reverse is happening; we are increasingly treating human beings as mere animals. I refer here not only to the horrific butcheries conducted by the National Socialists and Communists of the twentieth century—putting human beings on cattle cars to be slaughtered—but to the similarly insidious insinuations of the same thinking in so-called progressive democracies: "putting down" people when they get old, sick, or inconvenient; getting ourselves spayed and neutered; thinking about human procreation in terms of breeding fit or unfit specimens. Christianity claims that man is a creature standing somewhere between God and mere animals. Liberalism proceeds to make him an animal and, in doing so, sets him free to treat himself however he wants. There is no sin. The liberal denial of sin, and its effect on the political realm, contrasts sharply with the biblical story. The overall drama of the Old Testament is tragic. The Jews are a chosen people and promised a land of milk and honey. Yet despite their best efforts, human sin keeps them from setting themselves up permanently and blissfully in the Promised Land. It is not that Israel itself is especially bad, or that its forms of government are worse than others. Rather, the lesson of the Bible is that if the chosen people cannot bring about a political promised land because of the ravages of sin, then no one will be able to create a political utopia. If God Himself, as incarnate king, declares that His kingdom is not of this world, then no merely human attempt to establish a heaven on earth is possible.

Here, we see Voegelin's point about modern liberalism as a Christian heresy, Christianity without God. Liberalism assumes that there is no fundamental defect in the human soul, but that what ails us can be cured by some new kind of political arrangement, or by a hitherto unprecedented application of technical or political power. The state becomes the redeemer, and the heady assumption is *that the state cannot sin.* The practical effect, of course, is that those who actually wield political power are given license to act as if they could not sin. All actions are justified if they are directed to bringing about an earthly political utopia.

The Bible tells a quite different story, one that, after the horrors of the twentieth century, should seem eminently wise to even the greatest skeptics.

Conservative Wisdom and Biblical Wisdom

We can see, I hope, the obvious connections between biblical wisdom and conservative wisdom. That does not mean, of course, that the two are to be identified. Conservative wisdom is open to all human beings as human. It is, we might say, natural wisdom. That is why it is found among the ancient Jews and the ancient Greeks, and why the Jewish wisdom literature bears so many striking connections to other ancient near-east wisdom literature, as well as to things we find in Confucius or the Stoics. While the wisdom found in the Bible includes natural wisdom, it also reveals truths about the source of that wisdom that exceed our merely human capacities to discover, and in great part, to fully understand.

That is why the Bible can never be reduced to conservatism, even while it may act to clarify and reinforce conservatism's principles. Recovering biblical wisdom will certainly aid the conservative cause, but must never be identified with it. Conservative wisdom is open to all, because it is natural wisdom, human wisdom, the wisdom available to our natural powers of understanding. Since God is the creator of nature (including human nature as made in the image of God), biblical wisdom includes conservative wisdom, but rises far beyond, to divine wisdom.

The Bible contains both kinds of wisdom, as the Wisdom Literature well illustrates. It doesn't seem to take any kind of special revelation to grasp much that is found in Proverbs: "Gathering in summer is the mark of the prudent, sleeping at harvest is the sign of the shameless" (10:5); or "Worry makes a man's heart heavy, a kindly word makes it glad" (12:25); or "A worker's appetite works on his behalf, his hungry mouth drives him on" (16:26). These are wise words gathered through ordinary experience, the watchwords of prudence.

Yet we also find in Proverbs wisdom being personified, calling aloud in the streets and at the city gates, for people to come to her (1:20–33), "You ignorant ones! Study discretion; and you fools, come to your senses!" (8:3–5). She promises, "I love those who love me; those who seek me eagerly shall find me" (8:17). Wisdom is personified as created by Yahweh "before the oldest of his works," and in the creation of all else, wisdom reveals, "I was by his side, a master craftsman, delighting him day after day..." (8:22–31). The wisdom by which nature was created calls everyone to a banquet: "Come and eat my bread, drink the wine I have prepared! Leave your folly and you will live, walk in the ways of perception" (9:5–6).

Wisdom is the food of the soul, personified as a kind of active presence in creation, portrayed as feminine and a creature to distinguish it from Yahweh. Yet, it is also understood as embodied in the Law, as Baruch later makes clear when speaking of God the creator, "It is he who is our God, no other can compare with him. He has grasped the whole way of knowledge, and confided it to his servant Jacob, to Israel his well-beloved; so causing her to appear on earth and move among men" (Bar 3:36–38). Baruch is speaking here of the revealed Law, the wisdom of God made known to the Jews, and the self-revelation of Yahweh—that is why he can use the feminine "she." In Ecclesiasticus (or Sirach), Jesus Ben Sira unites God's creative wisdom and the Law in one personification. He has her proclaim, "They who eat me will hunger for more, they who drink me will thirst for more" (24:21). God's wisdom is infinite; there is always more.

Insofar as we understand all these passages as merely poetic, as metaphors meant to vivify the deep appreciation of the Jews for the wisdom of God found in creation, we shall remain in the realm of natural or conservative wisdom. Insofar as we begin to grasp the active presence of wisdom in God's revealed Law, and the way it fills the soul with a wisdom deeper than natural and moves history toward some mysterious and fantastic culmination, we are going beyond natural to supernatural wisdom, and hence what can be claimed as conservative wisdom available to all.

The New Testament takes us even further beyond, to what quite properly shocked the Jews, the incarnation of what was meant as a poetic, metaphorical stretch to capture the ineffable in Yahweh. With the Incarnation, as the beginning of the Gospel of John reveals, wisdom becomes flesh, appears on earth and moves among men, not as a woman, but a Son. Even stranger and more mysterious, the metaphorical picture of eating wisdom, wisdom as the life-giving food of the soul offered at a banquet ("Come and eat my bread, drink the wine I have prepared!"), is made flesh as well. Jesus declares of Himself, as wisdom actually personified, "I am the bread of life. He who comes to me will never be hungry; he who believes in me will never thirst." Here is God's wisdom made flesh—there is no wisdom beyond. Real flesh; with the Incarnation, the metaphorical becomes actual. "I tell you most solemnly, if you do not eat the flesh of the Son of Man and drink his blood, you will not have life in you. Anyone who does eat my flesh and drink my blood has eternal life, and I shall raise him up on the last day. For my flesh is real food and my blood is real drink. He who eats my flesh and drinks my blood lives in me and I live in him" (John 6:35, 53–56). Here, we have entered a realm of supernatural wisdom, an otherworldly kingdom, into which mere conservative wisdom cannot enter without the transformations effected by divine grace.

CHAPTER FIFTEEN

Atlas Shrugged: Ayn Rand

"I swear—by my life and my love of it—that I will never live for the sake of another man, nor ask another man to live for mine."

Rand's Anti-Conservatism

I WILL NO DOUBT RAISE THE HACKLES OF MANY CONSERVATIVES BY including Ayn Rand as the impostor, but I have this in my favor: Ayn Rand would have agreed that she was no conservative. After having first cuddled up to conservatives when she came to America, she definitively rejected conservatism and sharpened her own philosophy, Objectivism, against it. Her conscious break with conservatives had three related causes.

First, Rand was a devout atheist. Her contemptuous dismissal of religion in general and Christianity in particular was, in large part, the cause of the famous and deep antagonism that quickly developed between Rand and William F. Buckley and his *National Review.*

Second, Rand's insistence on pure selfishness as the root and branch of her moral system proved irreconcilable with true conservative moral principles, as she herself made amply clear in her work and in her personal life.

Third, her defense of the free market was based on the idea of a few heroic Nietzschean figures satisfying their creative and pecuniary impulses; it was not based on the conservative understanding of the free market as primarily about freedom for families and communities to provide for themselves in their own way, unhindered by government interference.

"Objectivists are *not* 'conservatives,'" she declared in her *Objectivist Newsletter*. "We are *radicals for capitalism*."[1] More accurately, as we'll see, Objectivists are radicals for Objectivism, Ayn Rand's philosophy.

In her earlier years, Rand did make common cause with conservatives and the Republican Party. She was an adamant critic of Franklin Roosevelt and the New Deal, and worked on the Wendell Willkie campaign in 1940 to unseat FDR. She worked hard for Barry Goldwater in his 1964 bid for president. But by the time Ronald Reagan was battling it out with Gerald Ford for the nomination of the Republican Party in 1976, Rand declared to her disciples, "I urge you, as emphatically as I can, not to support the candidacy of Ronald Reagan," whom she deemed a conservative in "the worst sense of the word."[2] She considered Friedrich Hayek another false conservative, writing in the margin of her copy of *The Road to Serfdom*, "The man is an ass, with no conception of a free society at all."[3] Rand biographer Jennifer Burns, who thoroughly documents Rand's conscious break with conservatives, is surely dead-on in maintaining that Rand's *Atlas Shrugged* is a novel written both as an explication of her Objectivism and a rejection of conservatism.[4]

Yet, Rand's *Atlas Shrugged* is still heartily admired among conservatives, although it appeals more to libertarians (whom Rand also rejected as defective, calling them "scum," "intellectual cranks," and "plagiarists"[5]). Rand's popularity has shot up since the Obama administration jerked the country back into the FDR Great Society mode. With the disintegration of the economy and the feverish attempts of Washington liberals to spend their way out through massive centralized government largesse, it seems to many as if Rand's *Atlas Shrugged* has proven to be prophetic fiction.[6] Sales hit 200,000 in 2008, and over 500,000 in 2009.[7]

Almost thirty years after her death and more than fifty years since the publication of *Atlas Shrugged*, Rand is hitting a raw nerve. Many conservatives are attracted to her message, and there is something of substance in it. In fact, Rand goes deeper than defending capitalism, excoriating welfare liberalism, and attacking intellectual skepticism. That having been said, there is a dark side to Rand, and it is exceedingly dark. As with our other chapters, we begin with biography.

Alissa Rosenbaum, Alias, Ayn Rand

If anyone wished to demonize Ayn Rand, the most efficient way would be through biography. One can scarcely read about her personal life without, at some particularly ugly parts, wanting to dig her up and drive a stake through her heart (just to make sure), or if we are far holier, praying for her morbidly tainted soul. All macabre excesses to the side, no one should read only *Atlas Shrugged*, or any of her other, lesser novels, without reading at least Barbara Branden's *The Passion of Ayn Rand*, Jennifer Burns's *Goddess of the Market: Ayn Rand and the American Right*, and Anne Heller's *Ayn Rand and the World She Made*.[8]

In saying this, I am not making the case that her awful personal life discredits her most important novel, but I am making the case that we will misunderstand exactly what Rand means to say in *Atlas Shrugged* if we do not firmly grasp that her life was an illustration of her philosophy. "My personal life," stated Rand, "is a postscript to my novels; it consists of the sentence: '*And I mean it.*' I have always lived by the philosophy I present in my books—and it has worked for me, as it works for my characters. The concretes differ, the abstractions are the same."[9] I am not out to demonize Rand through her biography, but to make very clear that one cannot judge her philosophy independently of her life.

Alissa Zinovievna Rosenbaum was born on February 2, 1905, in St. Petersburg, Russia. Her father, Zinovy (Zelman Wolf Zakharovich Rosenbaum), and mother, Anna (Khana Berkovna Kaplan), were married the year before. The Rosenbaums were Jewish, or more accurately, her father was a secular Jew while her mother retained some Jewish practices.

Zinovy was able to climb the Russian social ladder by getting a degree in chemistry at the University of Warsaw, and then working his way up from manager to owner of a successful apothecary. The Rosenbaums were well-off members of the bourgeoisie, living in a fine apartment with a cook, maid, nurse, and governess. As Jews, they were surrounded by the general air of Russian anti-Semitism, although St. Petersburg was safer than most places. As successful Jewish entrepreneurs, they were both envied and hated by those below them socially. The notion that Jews were "greedy entrepreneurs, rabid industrialists, and ruthless bankers" fueled anti-Semitism, and certainly contributed to Rand's life-long disgust with leftist tirades against greed, industry, and money.[10]

Alissa, the Rosenbaum's first child, was generally ignored by her father and disliked by her mother, who would erupt into fits of temper, "on one occasion breaking the legs of Alissa's favorite doll," and on another screaming at all the Rosenbaum daughters, Alissa, Natasha, and Nora, "I never wanted children at all! I look after you because it's my duty to do so."[11] As Rand later recalled, "She disapproved of me in every respect except one: she was proud of my intelligence and proud to show me off to the rest of the family."[12] Given that the only positive attention she received when she was young was related to her intelligence, it is small surprise that she prized her reason above all things. Nor are we surprised that Rand later reminisced, "I did not like being a child, I did not like being attached to a family," and that she decided when she was a mere adolescent against ever having children.[13]

The expression of her intelligence, at home or school, became the only source of positive attention and real joy in Alissa's life. We must emphasize *her* intelligence. She didn't glory in reason, but in *her* reason. From a very early age, Alissa was extremely possessive and opinionated. If she disliked something, it was therefore declared contemptible. If it appealed to her, it was unquestionably good, and off-limits to lesser mortals. As she noted, if she valued something, "I didn't want others to share this value. I felt: This is *my* value, and anyone who shares it has to be extraordinary. I was extremely jealous—it was literal jealousy—of anyone who would pretend to like something I like, if I didn't like that person. I had an almost anxious feeling about it, that it wasn't right. They have no right to admire it, they're unworthy of it."[14] Even as a child, she was argumentative by nature, picking an intellectual fight at the slightest provocation, especially when others transgressed the borders defining her likes and dislikes. She had almost no friends.

This intellectual possessiveness pervaded even the smallest areas of her psyche. At a young age, she heard bandstand music while vacationing with her family on the beaches of the Crimea—happy, bouncy, brassy, plinky-tinky stuff, one of the tunes being "It's a Long Way to Tipperary."[15] The problem wasn't her merely liking that music; it was that she invested it with all the profundity of the greatest classical music *because* she happened to like it, and she defended it as such. Later she latched onto Chopin and Rachmaninoff, but cast aside Mozart, Beethoven, Bach, and Handel.[16] Once she decided that she disliked the latter four, they were declared morally reprehensible. If any of her followers dared to admit a liking for them, they were treated as moral reprobates with psychological problems, and Ayn would spend hours grilling them about the most personal aspects of their lives to discover the malignant source of their aesthetic crimes.[17]

An even more important instance illustrating how the early "likes" of Alissa Rosenbaum turned into the philosophical desiderata of Ayn Rand, was the young girl's fascination with a French pulp adventure, *The Mysterious Valley* by Maurice Champagne (1914). Of the dashing main character Cyrus Paltons, Rand later declared him to be "a *personal* inspiration," that is, "a concrete [instance] of what one should be like. He was a man of action who was totally self-confident, and no one could stand in his way. No matter what the circumstances, he'd always find a solution. He helped me to concretize what I called 'my kind of man'....Intelligence, independence, courage. The heroic man."[18]

That story became the template of her mature philosophy, the source of the ideal, heroic man that largely defined, for Rand, what it was to be human. As she later proclaimed,

> I have held the same philosophy I now hold, for as far back as
> I can remember. I have learned a great deal through the years
> and expanded my knowledge of details, of specific issues, of def-
> initions, of applications . . . but I never had to change any of my

fundamentals. My philosophy, in essence, is the concept of man as a heroic being, with his own happiness as the moral purpose of his life, with productive achievement as his noblest activity, and reason as his only absolute.[19]

Howard Roark, the hero-architect of *The Fountainhead*, but more important, Francisco d'Anconia, Ragnar Danneskjöld, Hank Rearden, and John Galt in *Atlas Shrugged*, were all philosophical amplifications and developments of her childhood adventure hero. It was as if a young girl's heart had been won by seeing an Indiana Jones movie, and forever after, her perceptions were defined by this childhood encounter with a larger-than-life fictional character. Her later fascination with Friedrich Nietzsche and his *übermensch* was an elaboration of her worship of the heroic fictional figure, Cyrus. In saying that her philosophy had never changed, Rand was admitting far more than she realized.

The signal importance of *The Mysterious Valley* also helps to account for the "action adventure" quality of her fiction, especially evident in *Atlas Shrugged*. Her stories read like adventure movie scripts. It is no coincidence whatsoever that Alissa was enamored with American movies, and when, as Ayn Rand, she crossed the Atlantic, she made her way straight to Hollywood and started working in the blossoming movie industry as a script reviewer and writer. A defining goal of her writing career was getting her books made into movies; she died in the midst of writing a television script for *Atlas Shrugged*.

But we are getting ahead of ourselves. As noted, Alissa's family was originally fairly well off in Russia. World War I (and far more, the Russian Revolution) would change that. From the balcony of the Rosenbaum apartment in St. Petersburg, on her twelfth birthday, Alissa watched the Czar's forces open fire on angry and hungry protesters. The revolution had begun. Alexander Kerensky rose to power as head of a moderate republican government, but was ousted by Lenin and the Bolsheviks. Soon after, Communist thugs muscled their way into her father's shop and declared it nationalized. All that Zinovy had worked to build up was brutally torn from him and handed over to parasitic incompetents who claimed to rule in the name of the people. The fruit of *his* work became the property of the state, and soon the state reduced his shop and all of Russia to grim, collective poverty. Later, when Zinovy was allowed to open his shop again and his business began to prosper, the Communists again descended upon it and nationalized it.

Alissa saw the real and ugly face of communism: blockheaded propaganda, confiscation of private property, starvation, firing squads, destitution, destruction of the economy, complete moral corruption, and all the while, the endless spouting of declarations about taking the moral high road that looked down scornfully at the greedy capitalists.

It is no wonder that Ayn Rand, once she arrived in America, had the greatest contempt for leftist intellectuals comfortably and stupidly proclaiming the glories of the Soviets and the evils of capitalist America. Under the Bolsheviks, her family lost everything. The Rosenbaums were soon wearing rags, and literally starving. How could she—who had once collapsed on the floor out of hunger, begging her mother for one more dried pea[20]—not be filled with the deepest loathing when she heard the comfortable and deluded Left praising the bountiful Communist paradise of her homeland? She had known the devilry first hand, she had seen thriving cities quickly decay into lifeless skeletal grey remains; she had rubbed kerosene in her hair to ward off the lice that carried typhus; she had experienced the stab of pain when a courageous student (for whom Rand had a secret love) was dragged off to die in Siberia for speaking out against the Communists.[21] Even amidst the greatest deprivations and depravations, Alissa continued to attend school, finding in the academic rigors her only consolation. In 1914, before the revolution, she had entered a top-rate private school, the Stoiunin, a progressive school for the well-off.[22] At the tender age of nine, she had decided to be a writer. By the time she was eleven she had written four adventure novels.[23] She was known as the class brain. After the Communist takeover, she continued to apply herself to her studies and her writing, the only areas of her life the Bolsheviks had not yet been able to ruin.

While her hatred of the Communists grew, she at least shared one central dogma with them. At thirteen years old, she wrote confidently in her diary, "Today, I decided to be an atheist." She was convinced that "the concept of God is degrading to men" because the affirmation that "God is perfect" meant that "man can never be... perfect...." The thought that "man is low and imperfect and that there is something above him," Alissa thought, was simply "wrong." Moreover, "no proof of the existence of God exists," therefore, belief is rationally indefensible.[24] The point to stress here is not so much her atheism, but that, once Alissa decided something was a certain way, there was no arguing her out of it; she held to this decision for the rest of her life. Alissa's intellectual method was to settle on a congenial dogma and then grind out the logical results.

After graduation from high school in 1918, Alissa went to the University of Petrograd to study history and philosophy. Here, she encountered that great conservative, Aristotle, and fell in love with his logic.[25] She later declared the "only philosophical debt I can acknowledge is to Aristotle."[26]

She graduated from college in 1924, and then entered the State Technicum for Screen Arts, a new cinematography school founded to advance Soviet propaganda through movies. Alissa had the dangerous notion that she could use their art against them.

And then, a strange thing happened. More than three decades earlier, family members of the Rosenbaums had given money for some of their relatives' emigration to America. Now they contacted the Rosenbaums again, and Alissa begged her mother to write back and make the arrangements for her to "visit" them—a plan for escape which meant dealing with the slow, difficult, tedious, and suspicious Soviet bureaucracy. The official papers finally arrived, and her mother sold the last of her jewels to finance the trip. Alissa left her family in January 1926, and arrived in Manhattan in mid-February. The first thing she did was go to the movies, and the first book she bought was an English translation of Friedrich Nietzsche's *Thus Spoke Zarathustra*.[27] After a few days, she went on to her extended family in Chicago, the Portnoys, Goldbergs, and Stones.

Ayn Rand had escaped to America. The name "Ayn" (rhymes with "mine") was a Finnish name she adopted because she liked the sound of it. "Rand" is something of a mystery. The original rumor that she got it from her Remington Rand typewriter has been rejected, at least by some scholars.[28]

Immediately upon arriving, Rand began writing movie scripts, banging away at her typewriter during the night, keeping her bewildered hosts awake. When she wasn't pounding the typewriter in the middle of the night, she was loudly running the bathwater for hours—she had a germ phobia, and thought it necessary to clean out the pipes thoroughly to avoid contagions. For the same reason, she would later wash all her dishes in boiling water. The Goldbergs and Stones ended up shuttling Rand between their two homes; when one family couldn't stand her any longer, they sent her to the other.

Happily for the Goldbergs and Stones, Rand stayed only half a year before she left for Hollywood. Her relatives had chipped in one hundred dollars—about $1,200 in today's dollars. Rand never paid it back, nor any of the money they sent her while she was trying to make it in Hollywood.

Through a series of improbabilities, she ended up working for Cecil B. DeMille in the fall of 1926, both as an extra on the set of *The King of Kings* and then as a junior screenwriter. She fell in love at first sight with Frank O'Connor, another extra on the set. They married in spring 1929. The handsome and charming Frank was, for her, the dashing "heroic man" of her dreams—he looked exactly like Cyrus Paltons in René Giffey's illustrations in her beloved *Mysterious Valley*.[29] Ironically, while he was handsome, he was not heroic. He was entirely passive, neither the towering intellectual nor the aggressive, self-confident *übermensch* Rand idolized. Frank was merely a nice, handsome guy, graceful, friendly, likeable, charitable—the exact opposite of Rand herself, who was physically rather dumpy and clunky, supremely aggressive, prickly, and narcissistic to the extreme. For their entire marriage, Ayn insisted that Frank *was* what she wanted him to be, a projection of her romantic ideal, even though he was merely an appendage to her career. He had no life of his own. He ended up drinking himself to death.

For an immigrant who could barely speak a few words of English on her arrival, Rand's success was remarkably quick. She began work on her first novel, *We the Living*, in 1930, became a U. S. citizen the following year, and sold a script, *The Red Pawn*, to Universal Pictures in 1932 (it was not produced). Two years later, the O'Connors moved to New York City. Her play *Night of January 16th* opened on Broadway in the fall of 1935 and was a significant financial success. Her novels *We the Living* and *Anthem* were published in 1936 and 1938 respectively.

So industrious was Ayn that she and Frank made it through the Great Depression relatively unscathed. In one of the great ironies of Rand's life, the very first vote she cast as an American citizen was for Franklin Delano Roosevelt in 1932. She had been attracted by his rejection of prohibition (and he campaigned on a much more conservative platform than he would later govern), but she soon came to believe that his New Deal was Soviet collectivism by another name, and threw herself into the Wendell Willkie campaign to unseat FDR in 1940.

Her first big hit, *The Fountainhead*, was published in 1943, and the O'Connors moved back to Hollywood where Ayn could work on making it into a movie. In 1945, *The Fountainhead* sold an amazing 100,000 copies, and she negotiated the movie rights to Warner Brothers for an astounding $50,000—over a half a million in today's dollars. They were now wealthy enough to buy a thirteen acre ranch in the San Fernando Valley. Ayn hated it—she was always highly uncomfortable with direct contact with nature—but Frank loved it, spending the entire day outdoors as a successful gentleman farmer.

She began *Atlas Shrugged* in early 1945, but it was a long, slow go. She and Frank moved back to New York—a move that devastated Frank—and after much turmoil, *Atlas Shrugged* was published in the fall of 1957. It represents Rand's picture of the destruction of societies and souls wrought by benevolent totalitarianism. Set in America, not the Soviet Union, *Atlas Shrugged* was a warning about the real motives and direction of FDR's Great Society, Progressivism, and left-leaning liberalism in general. It was dedicated to Frank O'Connor and Nathaniel Branden.

Who is Nathaniel Branden? In one sense, he is the answer to *Atlas Shrugged*'s endlessly repeated question, "Who is John Galt?" Branden, whose given name was Nathan Blumenthal, was Rand's heroic ideal in the flesh. Handsome and, unlike Frank, brilliant and aggressive, he was a young psychology student at UCLA who admired Rand's *The Fountainhead.* With his girlfriend and fellow Rand devotee, Barbara Weidman, he made bold to contact her in 1950 so that he could express his deep admiration. They soon became her favored disciples, the ideal man and woman, set upon pedestals above the growing circle of passionately devoted Randites. Unlike Frank, they both really understood Rand's philosophy and could discuss it with her long into the night while Frank sat smiling passively in his chair. In January 1953, Nathaniel and Barbara married. Their union fulfilled Rand's notion of romantic rationalism.

For Rand, it was axiomatic that intellectual ability and physical beauty and attraction should go together: the expression of sexuality was ultimately the culmination of right thinking and an appreciation of intellectual excellence. The mutual affirmation of the truth, a union of the minds, must lead to a union of bodies. Both Nathaniel and Barbara were devoted to Rand's intellectual system, the only true philosophy; Nathaniel was handsome and Barbara was beautiful; therefore, it was only logical that they *had* to get married, and their marriage *had* to be happy.

The interesting thing about the logic of Rand's romantic rationalism is that if one met someone who was intellectually superior, then it was rational to unite with them physically. Barbara was the top woman disciple of Ayn Rand; but Rand was the great teacher. Therefore, it was rational for Rand to have an affair with Nathaniel, a 50-year-old woman with a starry-eyed young man in his early twenties. Frank looked like the heroic ideal, but he was entirely uninterested in the intellectual life. Nathaniel was the heroic ideal, vigorous in mind and in body. Rand had the heroic mind, but was dumpy and square in figure, awkward in motion, and entirely unattractive in face, except for her large, dark eyes. Presumably, at least in Rand's mind, her exceeding intellectual credit made up for her physical debit.

So Ayn, sitting on the couch, hand in hand with Nathaniel, informed Frank and Barbara. "You know what *I* am, you know what Nathan is.... By the total logic of who we are—by the total logic of what love and sex mean—we *had* to love each other.... It's not a threat to you, Frank, or to you, Barbara.... It's something separate, apart from both of you and from our normal lives."[30]

Totally logical, totally rational. To accept Ayn Rand's philosophy as true meant to accept the affair as the proper and rational culmination of Rand's philosophy. Ayn Rand was entirely rational; therefore, to object to the affair was to affirm one's own irrationality. So they would all stay happily married, Rand argued, and the affair could heat up full steam. It was the only rational thing to do, and since rationality was the foundation of morality for Rand, it was the only moral thing to do.

So Rand happily carried on with her rational-sexual fantasy while toiling over the writing of *Atlas Shrugged*, in particular the two-year struggle to write John Galt's speech. She worked long hours, helped out, as she had been since her days of slaving over *The Fountainhead*, with amphetamines (an addiction that lasted over thirty years). For breaks, Nathaniel would come over to the O'Connor apartment, and Frank was shown the door (it was too inconvenient to rent a separate apartment for the frequent trysts). He would go out to a bar and drink himself numb as Ayn and Nathaniel reveled in romantic rationalism.

Barbara was also falling apart during this time, unable to reconcile her intellectual devotion to Rand's philosophy (which affirmed the affair), with her very human revulsion at what seemed self-serving hypocrisy and a violation of the essence of marriage. Always the compassionate one, Ayn would spend hours with Barbara trying to help her work through her irrational feelings and moral defects. One night, while disconsolately walking the streets as Ayn and Nathaniel were enjoying each other's embrace, Barbara called Rand, begging to come over to the apartment and talk. Rand exploded into the phone, "How dare you! Do you think *only* of yourself? Am I *completely* invisible to you? *I* don't ask anyone for help! There's your whole problem in the fact that you called—if you *want* something, that's all you know or care about! Don't dare dream of coming here!"[31]

As readers of her biography will find out on page after page, such narcissistic treatment of everyone, but especially her own disciples, was typical of Rand. She exalted rationality. She believed that she had forged *the* rational philosophy entirely by herself, overlooked by the entire history of philosophers, save a few good bits of logic in Aristotle. Indeed, she believed herself to be the manifestation of rationality. Therefore, what seemed rational and desirable to her *must be* rational, and whatever contradicted her *must be* irrational. Anyone who disagreed with her was either stupid or malicious, and she consequently treated them with utter contempt. Those who dared to disagree within her inner circle of devotees were subjected to a shredding by Rand's formidable logical powers, suffering hours-long interrogations in an effort to uncover their rational errors or moral failings.

As Rand's fame grew, it seemed right to found an organization dedicated to the spread of her philosophy, and so the Nathaniel Branden Institute was formed, with Nathaniel and Barbara in charge. It was immensely successful, and both Nathaniel and Barbara rose to eminence. As the favored disciples, they enjoyed admiration, respect, and intellectual authority second only to Rand herself.

This situation manifests the strange, Svengalian effect Rand had over her devotees. Both Nathaniel and Barbara thought Rand to be the very incarnation of rationality and morality. The great success and respect they received was entirely the result of their devotion to *her* system. Rand couldn't be wrong; their successful lives were defined by her being right. But try as they might, the affair ground down both Nathaniel and Barbara. Even when the physical aspects fizzled out for a period—Ayn's own physical and mental health were in a state of deterioration—there was always the expectation by Rand that the fires would be relit.

By the mid-1960s, Rand was ready for a rekindling of some rational romance. Nathaniel, unable to respond to a woman old enough to be his mother, began to have an affair with Patrecia Gullison, another Rand devotee. Rand, who was now in her early sixties, couldn't understand why Nathaniel's passionate embers were growing cold. Meanwhile, (according to Heller) Barbara had been carrying on a rational romance herself with another Rand disciple while Nathaniel was busy with Patrecia.[32] In 1965 Nathaniel and Barbara separated. Ayn Rand was entirely flummoxed. How could Nathaniel not be inflamed with desire for *her*? How could the perfect Randian couple uncouple?

Barbara, tired of all the hypocrisy and strain, finally broke the news to Ayn that Nathaniel had been "cheating" on her. Rand turned into a cold, hissing snake, and demanded that Nathaniel come immediately to her apartment. "How did you dare aspire to *me*! If you ever, for even a moment, had been the man you pretended to be—you would value me romantically above any woman on earth if I were eighty and in a wheel chair! You'd be blind to all other women!" She slapped Nathaniel three times, ordered him out, and set about to ruin him by publicly disclaiming him as her prototype and intellectual heir and dismantling the Nathaniel Branden Institute. In her journal, *The Objectivist*, she outlined the crimes of Nathaniel—very vaguely; she declined to tell her devoted Randites about the affair, but said only that "Mrs. Branden suddenly confessed that Mr. Branden had been concealing from me certain ugly actions and irrational behavior in his private life, which was [sic] grossly contradictory to Objectivist morality and which she had known about for two years"—and informed her followers that "Nathaniel Branden and Barbara Branden are no longer associated with this magazine, with me or with my philosophy."[33] Their intellectual and moral failures were inexcusable and irredeemable; they must be excommunicated.

This kind of treatment was not something new for Ayn. As all her biographers make clear, Rand left a string of shattered friendships, casting out and cutting off one after another of those who originally had found her Objectivism exciting and groundbreaking. The pattern was always the same. They would find their way into her inner circle. As soon as they expressed any intellectual disagreement or moral misgiving, they were ruthlessly cut off as moral miscreants. To be rational, to be an Objectivist, came only to mean sycophantic agreement with whatever Ayn Rand said.

Again, the point is not that we should reject Rand's philosophy *because* we have discovered hypocrisy in her private life. Rather, her private life reveals what she meant by the exaltation of rationality and of selfishness as a moral principle. As an obvious illustration, her affair with Nathaniel is a parallel to the sexual "progression" of Dagny Taggart, the heroine of *Atlas Shrugged*, from Francisco d'Anconia, to Hank Rearden, and finally to John Galt. Francisco and Hank, who are each presented as perfect expressions of Rand's philosophy, passionately love Dagny, but manfully and rationally affirm that the sexual torch must be passed to the next, higher, and more resplendent hero. To delve a bit into details, the evil parasitic social planners have contrived, through Hank Rearden's wife, Lillian, to blackmail the heroic

industrialist Rearden into handing over the rights to his spectac-
ular Rearden Metal by the threat of exposing his affair with
Dagny. Instead of allowing herself to be cowed, Dagny goes on
the radio and boldly announces, "For two years, I had been Hank
Rearden's mistress. Let there be no misunderstanding about it: I
am saying this, not as a shameful confession, but with the highest sense of pride."[34] Hank hears the confession, especially the use
of the past tense "had been." Even though he had sacrificed
everything for Dagny, he cheerfully recognizes that someone as
supremely rational as Dagny could only speak about him in the
past tense if she had found a greater hero—the mysterious John
Galt. "It's true. I've met the man I love and will always love," she
confesses. Hank calmly replies, "I think I've always known that
you would find him. I knew what you felt for me, I knew how
much it was, but I knew that I was not your final choice. . . . I
can'trebel against it."[35] He cannot rebel because the notion that
affirmation of rational excellence must lead to sexual union was
what ultimately allowed Hank to justify his adultery with Dagny.[36]
Dagny later receives a note from Hank, "I have met him [i.e.,
John Galt]. I don't blame you. H. R."[37] *That* is how Ayn Rand
wanted Frank and Barbara to accept her rational romance with
Nathaniel. Dagny is an obvious projection of Ayn Rand herself,
with the fictional addition of a beautiful body to match her magnificent mind.

The only charge of hypocrisy we can bring against Rand—and
it is considerable—is that she concealed from all her devoted followers the real reason for her break with Nathaniel and Barbara
Branden. But her actions were completely consistent with the
expression of her philosophy in *Atlas Shrugged,* and now that we
have dipped into the story of *Atlas Shrugged,* we had better jump in
the whole way, beginning with the main characters.

The Main Characters

Dagny Taggart (the heroine; the woman who really runs Taggart Transcontinental Railroad)

James Taggart (Dagny's weak, parasitic brother; titular head of Taggart Railroad)

Francisco d'Anconia (heroic heir of the great d'Anconia Copper company; Dagny's first paramour)

Hank Rearden (heroic industrialist-owner of Rearden Metal; Dagny's second paramour)

Lillian Rearden (Hank's parasitic and scheming wife)

John Galt (ideal hero; Dagny's final paramour)

Ragnar Danneskjöld (heroic "pirate," who destroys the attempts of collectivists to steal the wealth of the industrialists)

Dr. Hugh Akston (heroic philosophy professor; teacher of D'Anconia, Danneskjöld, and Galt)

The Basic Plot

The world of *Atlas Shrugged* is divided between the heroic producers, the industrial geniuses who through their talent create the technology and services that lift human life above mere animal existence, and the parasitic non-producers who live off the intellectual, productive capital of the producers, even while they show them the greatest contempt as materialistic dollar-chasers and try to control them through arbitrary government power. In Randian shorthand, it's the capitalists vs. the collectivists, the producers vs. the moochers.

John Galt, the first person to realize the injustice of the situation, vows to "stop the world's motor" by withdrawing all the real producers from society, and letting it cave in under the incompetence of the parasitic non-producers. As the collectivists impose one law after another designed to manipulate industry for this or

310 BOOKS EVERY CONSERVATIVE MUST READ

that social cause, Galt goes about his scheme, drawing after him his philosophy professor, Hugh Akston, and his fellow brilliant students of Akston, Francisco d'Anconia and Ragnar Danneskjöld. The industrial geniuses are "on strike." Galt takes with him a motor he invented that can run on static electricity in the atmosphere; d'Anconia ruins his own copper mines by carrying out collectivist notions to the extreme; Danneskjöld becomes a pirate, stealing from the collectivists and putting the "swag" they've taken from the industrial producers into a secret bank account. All three engage in sabotaging the efforts of the real industrialists to work within the ever more oppressive socialistic system, so that the economy can cave in, teaching the ultimate lesson to the collectivist parasites. One by one, the great industrialists disappear, and as they disappear, the political and economic situation of the country gets more and more desperate and chaotic under the rule of the incompetent collectivists. That is the very lesson Galt wants to teach the world.

Dagny Taggart and Hank Rearden are the last to know about this grand scheme, and originally consider whoever is trying to destroy Taggart Transcontinental and Rearden Steel as their great enemies. But they, too, finally see the light, and withdraw with Galt, Akston, d'Anconia, Danneskjöld, and a small number of other similar geniuses to a hidden "Atlantis" in Colorado, Galt's Gulch. Here, they can start over in a kind of utopia without parasites, and when the lights finally go out on the world, they will emerge and reconstruct civilization.

Rand's Important Insights

In one sense, the entire novel is condensed near the end, in the final, three-hour, sixty-page speech given over the radio by John Galt to the bewildered, dying, collectivist world.[38] Galt's famous speech—which again, it took Rand about two agonizing years to write—contains her entire Objectivist philosophy, and *Atlas Shrugged* is merely a fictional illustration of it. That accounts for the rather heavy-handed and preachy nature of much of the novel: the story is entirely contrived for the sake of her pounding home the points of her philosophy. That having been said, I will refer both to the novel and the speech in bringing out Rand's important and enduring insights, insights both attractive and useful to conservatives.

1. Human Beings Are Rational by Nature, and Truth Is Objective

Ayn Rand was passionately and rightly antagonistic to the reigning intellectual subjectivism of her day—hence, the name of her philosophy, Objectivism. In many ways, her Objectivism hearkens back to Aristotle. And though she would be loath to admit it, it also relies on the natural law tradition best exemplified by St. Thomas Aquinas, who defined human beings as essentially rational animals. In Galt's words,

> Man's mind is his basic tool of survival. Life is given to him, survival is not. His body is given to him, its sustenance is not. His mind is given to him, its content is not. To remain alive, he must act, and before he can act he must know the nature and purpose of his action. He cannot obtain his food without a knowledge of food and of the way to obtain it. He cannot dig a ditch—or build a cyclotron—without a knowledge of his aim and of the means to achieve it. To remain alive, he must think.[39]

Rand overturns subjectivism in a way parallel to Aristotle's overturning of sophism. Aristotle showed that the sophists' moral

relativism was false by pointing to the undeniable natural beginnings of society from which morality arises. Rand attacked modern intellectual skepticism by pointing out the necessity of reason
to man's survival. "Truth is the recognition of reality," declares
Galt. "Reason, man's only means of knowledge, is his only standard of truth."[40]

Her argument goes something like this. Human beings do not
act by instinct. Long before there were ever university philosophy
departments and skeptical professors, human beings had to provide food, clothing, and shelter. In doing so, they were forced to
find out how nature actually works: how different kinds of wood
can be used for building or for burning to keep warm, how different kinds of food can be grown and harvested, how to hunt and
fish, how to cure meat, how to cut and build with stone, how to
smelt iron, and so on.

This practical, productive know-how naturally embeds us in the
real order of nature. We are not skeptical by nature; in fact, skepticism would destroy our ability to survive. In order to survive, we
must gather real, very concrete knowledge of each distinct thing
we use. It is by working with things, making things, growing things
that we discover the intricate layers of "objective reality." The
advance of human technology that raises us up ever higher above
the animal level of mere survival is only possible because the
knowledge upon which it builds is solid.

There are no sophists, no smart-set subjectivists, when questions
of survival press upon us. They arise, in both ancient and modern
times, only after the real producers—farmers, stonemasons, and
carpenters; electricians, chemists, and engineers—are in place, providing for all of society's material needs. Sophism, skepticism, is a
debauched luxury of civilization, not a cause of it. In more Randian

terms, sophistic intellectual skepticism is parasitic, living off the productive host upon which it feeds.

2. THINKERS DEPEND ON MAKERS

It follows from the first point that producers are prior to theoreticians. The men and women who really work with nature, the ones who really know how to grow food, raise cattle, build houses, weave cloth and make clothing, build and sail ships, smelt iron, and forge plows and weapons are prior to philosophers—and this, in two very important (and very Aristotelian) ways. First, producers come before thinkers in time and establish an undeniable practical connection to reality that *should* properly constitute the foundation of all later philosophical thinking (and hence, disallow intellectual skepticism). Second, thinkers depend upon producers all the time to provide them all the necessities of civilized life so they can devote themselves to the life of the mind. Rand's picture of intellectual and moral degradation is a comfortably ensconced university professor (like the despicable Dr. Pritchett in *Atlas Shrugged*) spouting off nostrums of subjectivity and nihilism, and treating with contempt the industrialists who provided the money for his salary and all the materials that built his home, office, and classroom. Her portrait of Pritchett at Hank and Lillian Rearden's party is priceless satire.

> Dr. Pritchett picked a canapé off a crystal dish, held it speared between two straight fingers and deposited it whole into his mouth.
>
> "Man's metaphysical pretensions," he said, "are preposterous. A miserable bit of protoplasm, full of ugly little concepts and mean little emotions—and it imagines itself important! Really, you know, that is the root of all the troubles in the world."[41]

For the intellectually trendy Pritchett, the universe has no intrin-
sically knowable order, and consequently, life is a meaningless
charade, with no intellectual or moral standards. "The purpose of
philosophy," he tells his goggle-eyed admirers at the party, "is not
to help men find the meaning of life, but to prove to them that
there isn't any.... Reason ... is the most naïve of all superstitions."
Those who think that human reason can actually know things,
"suffer from the popular delusion of believing that things can be
understood." They "do not grasp the fact that the universe is a solid
contradiction.... the duty of thinkers is not to explain, but to
demonstrate that nothing can be explained.... The purpose of philosophy is not to seek knowledge, but to prove that knowledge is
impossible to man."[42]

At that same party, Rand offers a menagerie of similar intellectual "parasites" who, together, well represent the kind of thinking
associated with the left-leaning intelligentsia, both then and now.
To take two more examples, there is Balph Eubank, the author,
whose most recent novel is *The Heart Is a Milkman.* He declares that
all literature of the past was "a shallow fraud," a mere mask hiding
the beliefs and social agenda "of the money tycoons whom it
served. Morality, free will, achievement, happy endings, and man
as some sort of heroic being—all that stuff is laughable to us." For
Balph, the real essence of life is "defeat and suffering."[43] Then there
is Bertram Scudder, a newspaper columnist and Marxist muck-
raker whose sole passion is to needle the captains of industry like
Hank Rearden. Pritchett, Eubank, and Scudder are happy to wolf
down the food and drink provided by Hank Rearden at a party
thrown by his wife, even while they sneer at Rearden for being a
"greedy" industrialist. They are second-rate minds with well-fed
stomachs who hypocritically call for the redistribution of income
from wealthy industrialists to the poor and needy, but only so that

they can pose as morally superior. They don't actually engage in any charity themselves.

3. HUNGER CURES BAD PHILOSOPHY

All that it would take to refute the sham, comfortable world of the left-leaning intelligentsia presented by Rand would be to pull out the practical foundation of civilization provided by the industrialists and workers. When the real producers go "on strike," nonproducers will be shown for what they are: parasites who live off the work of others even while they hold them in contempt. Thus, when the industrial heroes go "on strike" in *Atlas Shrugged*, society crumbles into a condition almost exactly like Rand herself experienced when Russia fell into the hands of the Bolsheviks: trains don't run, machinery of all kinds breaks down and no one knows how to fix it, the electricity flickers out, food isn't shipped, people start to starve, gangs of thugs and looters begin to roam the land. The smart-set intellectual relativists, who have no practical knowledge how to do anything from growing a tomato to repairing a motor, find that they are completely helpless without the producers.

The industrialist is thereby shown to be the real hero of society, the Atlas upon whose shoulders civilization rests. When he shrugs and withdraws, society caves in and life returns to the primitive state of brutal survival. In this condition, there are no skeptics, and no high-sounding speeches about suffering. Real suffering, real deprivation cures bad philosophy.

4. THE INDUSTRIALIST AS PHILOSOPHER

The industrialists are not just heroes in the very practical sense of providing the goods and services upon which society rests. They are for Rand intellectual heroes as well, true philosophers. The great industrialists—typified by Galt and his miraculous motor and

Rearden and his Rearden Metal—have their intellects most intimately united to the real order of the natural world. They are the consummate knowers of reality, uniting practical know-how to the theoretical abilities that allow them to make major discoveries and invent new materials and machines. In their demiurgic creative powers, they transform matter by their minds, and so, most closely of all human beings, resemble a creative God—except that, for Rand, God doesn't exist.

5. THE INDUSTRIALIST VS. MATERIALISM

It might seem that Rand the atheist would also be a materialist, but in fact she quite rightly saw materialism at the foundation of modern socialism, collectivism, skepticism, and relativism. Like true conservatives, Rand rejected materialism, arguing that the proof that we human beings are creatures of both soul and body is that we use our mind to actively re-form matter according to our immaterial ideas. Our creative intellectual power clearly manifests our spiritual nature, providing a definitive proof of the power of mind over matter. All the technical, architectural, agricultural, mechanical, electrical artifacts of civilization that help lift us up above mere animal survival are proof-positive that materialism is false. This is the central error of Marxists, whom Galt calls the "savages who stutter that ideas are created by men's means of production. . . ."[44] They do not see that the truth is quite the opposite: ideas create the various modes of production. The industrialists, by virtue of mind, are "the conquerors of matter."[45]

6. THE CENTRAL INJUSTICE OF COLLECTIVISM/SOCIALISM

For Rand, the fundamental moral evil of all collectivist schemes is that the state steals from those who produce and gives handouts to those who don't. In assuming this power, the state also takes to regulating or managing the industrialists. The state's crude and destructive interference with the creativity and success of the producers means the industrialists have less and less reason to be the Atlas for society, as the collectivist government gains more and more control. Ayn's father learned this first-hand in his apothecary. Why bother investing all one's time, intelligence, and energy in building up a business only to have it seized by the state and incompetently run into the ground in short order? Or, to put it more in the American setting, why spend years inventing something if the state will seize the rights to it (as in *Atlas Shrugged* the state does with Rearden Metal) or tax away the legitimate profits of the inventor?

7. A CASE AGAINST MORAL RELATIVISM

Rand rejected moral relativism for the same reason she rejected intellectual relativism: human *life* demands certain moral foundations and actions. To act truly in accordance with intellectual and moral relativism is death. The conditions of life demand that we work to provide for ourselves, and it is through reason that we harness nature. Work, to be productive, demands certain kinds of virtues—intelligence, patience, courage, attention to reality.[46] Capitalism is, for Rand, merely an extension of these original virtues into the marketplace. Buying and selling the goods produced entails justice, and affirms the virtues of the producer as evidenced in his product. As Francisco states in his famous speech against those who consider money the root of all evil, "Money is *made*—before it can be looted or mooched—made by the effort of every honest man, each to the extent of his ability."[47] Money represents an agreement not to take goods by force or fraud, but through mutual agreement. So, for Rand, money represents fundamental moral truths, truths embedded in reality. Those who are satisfied with half-truths and lies about reality will remain dysfunctional savages, and societies that unjustly take from producers and provide handouts to parasites will soon decay.

The Problems with Ayn Rand

There is no doubt that Ayn Rand was a leading intellectual voice against the vacuities of Western progressive intellectuals with roseate views of communism and a quasi-religious devotion to socialism. She championed reason against the skeptics, and a meaningful, purposeful, and moral existence against the nihilists and relativists. She was, in large part, the enemy of conservatism's enemies.

Having given Rand her due, we must be clear-headed about the problems with Rand. Too often conservatives make the mistake of thinking that the enemy of my enemy is my friend.[48] This is a dangerous principle. Sometimes the enemy of our enemy is *also* our enemy. Stalin, for instance, was our ally in the war against Hitler, but he was certainly not our friend. For this reason, we need to be very clear about where Rand went wrong, and this will include some important illumination from her private life.

1. WHERE RATIONALITY LEADS

In Galt's Gulch, Dagny Taggart views the extraordinary power station designed and built by Galt himself, using his miraculous motor. "She thought of this structure, half the size of a boxcar, replacing the power plants of the country, the enormous conglomerations of steel, fuel and effort," the time, energy, and materials its efficiency saved, and especially of "a train pulled by the power of this motor—with all the energy of that weight, that strain, that time replaced and paid for by the energy of a single mind who had known how to make connections of wire follow the connections of his thought."[49] In a similar revelation, Dagny later wonders over the complexity of the train's relay station back in New York. The line of interconnected relay levers, seem "like shelves of books and as much of a monument to human intelligence." In watching the men expertly handle switches that "threw thousands of electric circuits into motion, made thousands of contacts and broke many others, set dozens of switches to clear a chosen course and dozens of signals to light it," she understood vividly the "enormous complexity of thought condensed into one movement of a human hand to set and insure the course of a train."[50] These beautiful passages lead to one, very profound insight: the well-designed technological object is a demonstration of the existence of the spiritual power of the human mind over matter *against* those who (like Marx) would argue that our thoughts are entirely caused by material conditions.

But as we recall, Rand pushed her case for rational objectivity even deeper. Our self-preservation, let alone our astounding technological progress, would not be possible if our minds were incapable of penetrating nature, if there were no order to nature, if there were not definable objective truth. Things are not a mishmash, as the relativists declare. Iron is iron, having its own distinct, intelligible, and determinate properties, and iron is not silver or aluminum; oak is oak, and not maple or mahogany; apples are apples and not potatoes. "A is A," not B. This, Galt proclaims, is "the formula defining the concept of existence and the rule of all knowledge."[51] And here's the problem for Rand. She rightly rejected the notion of people resting their arguments on a causeless cause, a mere assertion, but she treats ordered and intelligible nature as a given, a causeless cause. Why is nature both well-ordered and deeply intelligible? Galt's miraculous motor is clumsy and inefficient when compared to the inner workings of the smallest, simplest living cell. If Rand allows human technological wonders to be tangible proofs of the human mind as cause, then the things of nature should likewise demonstrate the existence of a mind that made them.

She was blind to this possibility. She decided, when very young, that God could not exist, and refused to revisit that premise. Her mind was closed by her self-determined dogma against following out the logical conclusions of her legitimate insights.

2. SELFISHNESS IS NOT THE CURE FOR COLLECTIVISM OR MORAL RELATIVISM

Rand presents false dichotomies, either-or choices between two extremes: either collectivism or individualism, either living entirely for the state or living entirely for oneself, either complete self-sacrifice to the point of annihilation or complete selfishness to the point of narcissism. She flees the first extreme and embraces the second. Philosophically speaking, she tries to avoid Marx by embracing the radical individualism sown by Thomas Hobbes that comes to full fruition in Friedrich Nietzsche. In this, she resides within the same general intellectual liberal secular tradition that produced Marx.

She tried to make this radical individualism the foundation for capitalism. As we have seen in our previous chapters, the conservative affirmation of the primacy of local economic life against the interference by the state is rooted in the moral duty of families to provide for themselves, not in individual selfishness (which is a vice, not a virtue). That is why Aristotle considered the family the fundamental economic unit as well as the cradle of morality. Rand's selective use of Aristotle makes her appear more conservative than she actually is, and we may return to Aristotle to discover the error of Rand.

The oath taken by all the heroic members of Galt's Gulch in *Atlas Shrugged* was certainly taken by Rand herself: "I swear—by my life and my love of it—that I will never live for the sake of another man, nor ask another man to live for mine."[52] This is about as radical an individualism as one could hope to pronounce, and it provides the foundation of both her morality and her economics. It also runs dead against the obvious fact of human existence (pointed out by Aristotle) that human beings are social by nature, and moral and economic life begin in a family. We may use Rand's own argumentative strategy against her. Just as human beings had to understand nature to survive, long before there were skeptical philosophers, so too human beings were born into families long before Rand ever formulated her radical individualism. Families could not have survived if fathers and mothers had taken John Galt's oath and selfishly sought to provide only for themselves; naturally, fathers and mothers provide for their children. Furthermore, as we have seen with Aristotle, the natural moral contours of the family provide the actual origins of morality. The love of husband and wife, of father and mother, that brings them to work for the good of each other and their children—this familial love is at the foundation of moral obligation and provides the fundamental economic building block of society, not Rand's selfishness or pure individualism.

Not surprisingly, the family doesn't appear in *Atlas Shrugged.* We find only full-grown individuals divided socially and economically into radical individualists and pathetic moochers. There are no children, and the heroic industrialists only work for themselves. The family as the most natural of facts doesn't fit into Rand's moral scheme, and didn't fit into Rand's life. She disliked childhood. Having determined that she was going to be a writer by age nine, she decided as an early adolescent that children "would interfere with my career."[53] Her husband Frank wanted to have children, but he knew "it wouldn't fit with Ayn." Unsurprisingly,

Rand had an abortion in the early 1930s, and was a fervent, life-long supporter of what we now call "abortion rights."[54] "An embryo," she asserted, "*has no rights.*"[55] She would not sacrifice anything to anyone, as she made clear to her husband in denying him children. Presented with a hypothetical situation where she and a baby were trapped in a tower and only one could survive, Rand unhesitatingly affirmed that she would save her own life.[56]

On the deepest level, Rand's philosophical mistake was again due to her rejection of Christianity. Self-love is natural and good, which is why the Judeo-Christian command is to love one's neighbor *as oneself.* Selfishness as preached by Rand is a distortion of proper self-love. Rand arrived at selfishness as a reaction to collectivism and its war against the individual. But a well-founded individualism is to be found not in selfishness, but in the idea of unique, eternal, God-given souls that, as the founders had it, are endowed by their creator with certain unalienable rights. In contrast to some religions and philosophies, like Buddhism or classical stoicism, Christianity denies that the individual after death is absorbed into God or into the absolute or into the cosmos as a drop of water into an ocean. It also denies that the individual should be absorbed into a state like a cog in a machine in this life. The Judeo-Christian tradition, had Rand been willing to appreciate it, would have given some grounding to her philosophy which otherwise rests, again, only on her personal dogma.

We must also recognize that Rand's radical individualism, while it certainly made her quite rich, did not get her the joy she promised as the fruit of her philosophy. As the three biographies of Rand by Branden, Burns, and Heller make morbidly clear on page after distressing page, Rand was not, on the whole, a happy person, and became more miserable as she got older and more economically successful. Her intense selfishness was the cause of the misery in her marriage, the cause of her breaking with one friend after another, and the cause of her inflicting on her own disciples every kind of insult, degradation, and psychological damage. It also brought her to deny—quite hypocritically—that she had ever received any help, either intellectually, socially, economically, or emotionally. Perhaps most damning of all, her intense selfishness infected her reason, the very power that defined her and her philosophy.

3. Objectivism Becomes Subjectivism; Reason Becomes Rand

Rand championed the power of reason, and that is all right and good. But on a closer look at her philosophy and her life, it turns out to be, all too often, *her* reason that is exalted, not reason itself. We have already pointed to the morally depraved and absurd charade of Rand announcing that her "affair" with Nathan was entirely reasonable (and it was therefore irrational for her husband Frank and Nathan's wife Barbara to voice any objections). The underlying narcissism of Rand nicely surfaces in the copy of *Atlas Shrugged* she signed for Barbara, then her leading woman disciple in the Objectivist movement and the woman whose husband she was happily and regularly bedding: "To Barbara—for the sense of life which is mine and yours—for starting with the same values and accepting nothing less—to carry on my battle, my universe and *all* my values—Ayn."[57] My, my, my—that was Rand's anthem.

As her disciples grew more numerous, she tightened her intellectual hold. She demanded assent without murmur, or excommunication ensued. Objectivism became a cult-like movement, with Rand holding court over her loyal devotees. *Atlas Shrugged* was their Bible.[58] Philosopher John Hospers, who was originally attracted to Rand, wrote her a letter describing the deep irony he experienced sitting among the faithful at the feet of Rand and

Nathan in lectures at the Nathaniel Branden Institute, the official teaching organization of Objectivism.

> I felt as if I were in a strange church where I didn't belong, where all the other people were singing the chants they were expected to and only I did not conform, and where to deny a single thing was considered heresy.... And the attitude of the audience in the lecture hall shocked me even more. Rational? Good heavens— an Army of the Faithful, repeating the same incantations and asking questions only about details or applications, never questioning the tenets of the True Faith.[59]

The tight control extended far beyond the tenets of Objectivism as defined by Rand. As another recovering Randian noted, Rand's personal tastes became dogma as well.

> There was more than just a right kind of politics and right kind of moral code. There was also a right kind of music, a right kind of art, a right kind of interior design, a right kind of dancing. There were wrong books which we could not buy, and right ones which we should.... And on everything, absolutely everything, one was constantly being judged, just as one was expected to be judging everything around him.... It was a perfect breeding ground for insecurity, fear, and paranoia.[60]

As biographer Burns notes, "Striving to become good Objectivists, Rand's followers tried to conform to her every dictate, even those that were little more than personal preferences. Rand harbored a dislike of facial hair, and accordingly her followers were all clean shaven."[61]

The self-proclaimed champion of free rational inquiry had more in common with the dogmatic and querulous Marx, Lenin, and Stalin than should make any conservative comfortable. As Rand's popularity grew, and Ayn Rand and Objectivist societies began springing up on their own, she cracked down on all those not directly under her control through the Nathaniel Branden Institute (NBI). An Ayn Rand Society at the University of Virginia received a threat from Rand's lawyer, demanding the society remove a quote from John Galt from its stationery. A group at the University of Maryland was surprised when a local NBI representative burst into a classroom and announced that the teacher was not "approved" by the Institute, and Rand wrote a public repudiation of the erring professor.[62]

In her later life, when she deigned to allow a public interview, she demanded not only that all questions be submitted in advance for her approval, but that no critics of her work be quoted, and that in no way could any interview take the format of a debate.[63] Rand had had a bad experience debating with well-trained philosophers. Among her awed disciples who sat at her feet, she could hold forth without contradiction. But when she went to Harvard to present a paper at the 1962 American Aesthetics Association, she was astonished and mortified at the legitimate questioning of her arguments by those of equal mind and more thorough philosophic education.[64] Never again. Reason must mean what Rand said it meant; no one must be permitted to check *her* premises.

4. PHILOSOPHY OF SELFISHNESS OR PERSONALITY DISORDER?

Anyone who has had any significant contact with someone who has Narcissistic Personality Disorder, or who is at least familiar with the *Diagnostic and Statistical Manual of Mental Disorders*, cannot help but see Rand as manifesting in her life every clinical symptom of a narcissist to the highest degree.[65]

Narcissists entirely lack empathy for others. In an early, unfinished novella, *The Little Street* (1928), Rand describes her main character approvingly: "He doesn't understand, because thankfully *he has no organ for understanding*, the necessity, meaning, or importance of other people." As Heller rightly remarks, this "is practically a diagnostic description of narcissism, and also a description of Rand herself."[66]

Ayn had no recognition of the pain and inconvenience she caused others, whether she was ripping a wayward disciple to shreds publicly, keeping others up all night with her typing, entirely stripping her husband of any independent existence other than as a projected romantic ideal, or humiliating him by sending him off in the evening while she bedded a man half her age.

Narcissists are enflamed by a feeling of grandiose self-importance and demand to be considered above all others—Rand to a "T." As noted, she truly believed that she had constructed *the* only philosophy, entirely by her own efforts. The problem here is not her devotion to finding *the* truth; it was her laughable notion that no one else in the history of philosophy (save Aristotle) had said anything of any merit. In truth, she hadn't read that much philosophy. As entirely self-taught, she was (despite her pretensions) a comparative dilettante. She was certainly intelligent, but it was her narcissistic assumption that *she* knew the truth that made it seem entirely implausible to her that anyone else really had anything much to say.

Narcissists live in dream worlds of exceptional success, power, beauty, genius, or perfect love. Rand's "romantic realism" as portrayed in *Atlas Shrugged* and lived out in her life illustrate her confusion between fantasy and reality, and she and her followers came to conflate her fiction with fact as *Atlas Shrugged* became a kind of biblical proof text. As Rand herself oddly maintained about *Atlas Shrugged*, "I trust that no one will tell me that men such as I write about don't exist. That this book has been written—and published—is my proof that they do."[67] Rand really thought she was Dagny Taggart. She really thought that Nathaniel Branden was John Galt.

And the list goes on. Narcissists think that they are so far above the crowd that only a few select people can truly understand them (and the narcissist does the selecting); they demand excessive amounts of praise and adulation, and immediate compliance of others with their wishes; they exploit others without a second thought; they are prone to angry outbursts, and are supremely arrogant; they believe that everyone envies them because of their unparalleled excellence.

All dead on. If you were looking for a clinical exemplar of Narcissistic Personality Disorder, Ayn Rand would provide the clearest, most complete specimen. That is one more, very powerful reason that those enamored with Rand's *Atlas Shrugged* must read the above-listed biographies.

But that leads us to a very startling possibility. I have tried to demonstrate something that Rand herself maintained most fervently: that her philosophy and her life were one. Could it be that—whatever its merits, and they are considerable—her Objectivism is ultimately a projection of a personality disorder? That *Atlas Shrugged* is, even with all its insights, at bottom not about the truth, but about Ayn Rand? Or to put it another way, if you were a narcissist, wouldn't you find Rand's philosophy exceedingly attractive? What other philosophy would be a better match for a narcissist? What novel besides *Atlas Shrugged* would a narcissist more greedily devour (except perhaps *The Fountainhead*)?

If Ayn Rand's exaltation of selfishness as the most important, indeed the only virtue, is merely a projection of herself *as* a narcissist, then what do we make of *Atlas Shrugged*? Is her rejection of God merely a narcissistic rejection of a power greater than herself? However we might answer these questions, it should be clear that conservatism is not narcissism; it is not the worship of selfishness; and Objectivism, as Rand would tell you herself, is certainly not conservatism at all.

Conclusion

As I said right from the beginning, there are many more books that every conservative should read, and many more after that. There is no end of books, good and bad, although sometimes it seems the bad outnumber the good. So, I could very easily write *Ten More Books Every Conservative Must Read*, and even more easily, *Ten More Books that Screwed Up the World*.

But I hope readers will agree, now that they've reached the end, that the fourteen books I've chosen as must-reads are books that can deepen the conservative conversation and lift us from our twittering, texting, media-enervated age to see again the wisdom that is built on experience.

The ultimate text for conservatives is not actually a book; it is the lessons of nature and human nature, which are open to all. That is why you'll so often find more practical wisdom—and innate conservatism—among common folk, most especially rural folk immersed in the rhythm of the seasons, the tilling of the land, working with livestock, and the strong bonds of family and community, than among the city-dwelling intelligentsia who think themselves so uncommonly clever. Conservatives believe in local government run by local people precisely because they believe that the sources of practical wisdom are ordinary.

That having been said, the habit of gathering practical wisdom into a book is old and worthy. Such are the Proverbs of the Old Testament. The word "old" is important here too. The modern prejudice is that old is synonymous with outdated and foolish. This prejudice has severed us from the wisdom and experience that could guide us out of current troubles. Instead, we are like children, unaware of the lessons of the past that provide sage counsel for the present. Actually, it is worse than that, because while our disdain for the past breeds foolishness, our increasing technological skill makes us ever more powerful. Power in the hands of a fool is a self-evidently dangerous thing. For our own survival as human beings, the more technologically advanced we become, the more conservative we have to be—the more we must cling to the most ancient insights about human nature, especially about human pride, folly, and sin, and the necessity of providing curbs and reins to power.

Part of the reason conservatives fear big government is that big government draws all power to itself, and this enormous power is then wielded by a very small number of people over everyone else. The actual character of those few people—their pride, their follies, their sins—is then magnified by the power they've received. If human beings were always wise, prudent, and good, then no one would fear the concentration of political power.

There is another important thing to remember here, too. Conservatives take differences and particularities seriously. Liberals tend to brush them aside, because they believe that universal liberalism is the goal of history, the very point to which "progress" is leading us. "Progress" is synonymous with the production of a homogenized world culture. This is why, to the liberal, anti-federalist notions that break up power and give it to particular communities are unpalatable. Liberals love the United Nations precisely because they dislike actual nations.

It is also why liberalism has an inherent animosity to real religion, even while it remains friendly to vague spirituality. Vague spirituality, having no definable content, can be co-opted to liberalism and used for its purposes. Solid, sharply defined beliefs of particular peoples that have existed for centuries, even millennia, are obstacles to the advance of liberalism toward its goal of a homogenized, secular world culture. For several reasons, the greatest obstacle to the progress of liberalism is Christianity. Orthodox Christianity has the most sharply defined doctrinal edges. The doctrine of sin slashes at the liberal notion of human perfectibility; the doctrine of grace cuts through the cant about the state itself being our redeemer. Moreover, as Voegelin so cogently argues, in important respects modern liberalism is a kind of Christian heresy, that is, a quasi-religious movement defined against Christianity even while it borrows from it. The utopianism of liberalism is a secularized version of the Kingdom of God, except without the God part; it is heaven dragged down to earth. The universalist push of liberalism is a secularization of the Christian desire for the conversion of all peoples. The original, as presented by Christianity, stands as a witness against liberalism's tinny imitation, and disallows the state from becoming a religious idol.

This is why I chose the Bible as one of the books that every conservative must read. It is precisely the distinction between church and state, developed during the Middle Ages but rooted in the

Judeo-Christian distinction between the supernatural and natural, the City of God and the City of Man, that is meant to keep the powers of the state from being subsumed into a theocracy (as in Islam), or of the state becoming a religion in itself (as in pagan Rome, Soviet Russia, and Nazi Germany, the latter two responsible for incomparably more horror, bloodshed, and oppression over the course of a few decades than any and all wars or persecutions that a liberal can lay at the feet of Christianity over the course of 2,000 years).

Again, I am not identifying Christianity with conservatism. Conservatives naturally take the side of religion because religion is natural to man and lends itself naturally to reverence for the past, humility before wisdom gleaned from experience, and a justified fear in transgressing moral boundaries that can be summarized as "The fear of God is the beginning of wisdom."

Most of all, conservatives are realists (or believers in original sin). They do not believe that government can make men perfect. They are more likely to fear that government will become a destructive vehicle of our own short-sightedness, unruly passions, foolish schemes, and penchant for self-destruction. So, while conservatism is not to be identified with Christianity, conservatives can certainly see the divine fit of central Christian doctrines to what defines and what ails humanity.

Margaret Thatcher once said that the facts of life are conservative. So they are. They are the facts of our nature. That is why liberals want to change man's nature, acting as both creator and redeemer. Liberalism also reminds us, in what it attacks, of what we are meant to conserve.

Notes

INTRODUCTION

1. I realize that Hayek often claimed Hume as a major influence on his thinking, but the distance which separates them, both in time and temperament, allowed what Hayek took from Hume to be purified through other influences. Unlike Hume, Hayek was not an intimate with Enlightenment revolutionaries–or post-Enlightenment revolutionaries–and his agnosticism was tempered by a real appreciation of the necessity for religion to provide a foundation for moral, and hence economic, order.

CHAPTER 1

1. His admonition actually occurs in his *Nicomachean Ethics,* 1095a1–12.

2. Sometimes the best way to make headway in a heated argument is to let go of familiar hot philosophical or political partisan and party names, and begin with the obvious and undeniable.

3. Aristotle, *The Politics,* trans. Carnes Lord (Chicago, IL: the University of Chicago Press, 1984), 1252a25–31. (I am using the standard notation—the strange looking number/letter combination—that appears in every edition of Aristotle's texts. These are much like the standard biblical chapter/verse numbers that appear in every Bible.)

4. Aristotle, *The Politics,* 1252b10–1253a3. I am not altogether satisfied with Lord's translation, and will make free, in this popular presentation, to substitute what I take to be better renderings of the Greek. Interested readers may compare these to Lord's, but I will

not interrupt the flow of the narrative to point out any changes, track them in footnotes, or include the original Greek. My own renditions will generally come from my doctoral dissertation *The Interdependence of Ethics, Politics, Physics, and Metaphysics in Aristotle* (Vanderbilt, 1994)

5. See his later discussion, *Politics*, 1326a26–1326b25.

6. It is a common theme in both ancient sophistic thought and modern liberalism that society is made up of a multitude of individuals who get together and write up a set of artificial rules, a kind of social contract they all agree upon as suitable for getting what each individually wants and for avoiding harm. To see the ancient and modern versions, compare Plato, *Gorgias*, 482–483 (as with Aristotle, these are standard notation numbers for any translation of Plato's dialogues) and *Republic*, 336b–339a, with Thomas Hobbes, *Leviathan*, Part I, ch. 14.

7. On the connection between friendship and justice, see Aristotle's *Nicomachean Ethics* 1155a17–29, 1162a16–27, and *Eudemian Ethics*, 1242a21–28.

8. That is why the rule of a household is fundamentally distinct from rule of a city. Aristotle, *The Politics*, 1252a7–23.

9. Aristotle, *The Politics*, 1335b20–26.

10. Ibid., 1252a31–1252b5.

11. Interestingly, Aristotle remarks elsewhere that if objects like chisels, hammers, stoves, weaving shuttles, and musical instruments would, magically, act on command and do their work automatically, then "master craftsmen would no longer have a need for subordinates, or masters for slaves." The notion seems to be that extraordinary technology would make slavery dispensable. Ibid., 1253b34–1254a1.

12. Ibid., 1259a39–41. Emphasis added.

13. Aristotle, *Nicomachean Ethics*, 1161a10–26. Emphasis added.

14. Aristotle, *The Politics*, 1279a33–1279b10.

15. I say "more or less" because there are significant differences and historical developments that would need to be thoroughly understood, and that would add considerable complexity beyond the scope of our argument.

16. Aristotle, *The Politics*, 1278b37–1279a2.

17. Aristotle, *Nicomachean Ethics*, 1160b33–1161a2.

18. Aristotle, *The Politics*, 1284b25-34; 1325b10–13.

19. Ibid., 1280a9–10.

20. Ibid., 1290b16–20.

21. See the entire discussion, Ibid., 1295a25–1297a12.

22. Ibid., 1318b8–1319a37.

23. Ibid., 1296a18–19.

24. Ibid., 1303b26–30. For our purposes, I won't be distinguishing (as Aristotle does) between a democratic revolution from within a polity, and a democratic revolution in a democratic regime itself. The same goes for oligarchic tugs within a polity, and oligarchic revolutions in an oligarchy.

25. Ibid., 1303b14–16.

26. Ibid., 1304b20–1305a33.

27. Ibid., 1310a27–33. The last part occurs in the text as part of a quote from the poet Euripides.

28. Ibid., 1313b33–1314a29, 1319b29–30.

29. Ibid., 1319b5–11.

30. Ibid., 1297a10–12.

31. Ibid., 1292b5–6.

32. Ibid., 1298a38–39, 1303a14–18.

33. Ibid., 1305b27–33.

34. Ibid., 1305b40–41.

35. Ibid., 1253a30–37.

CHAPTER 2

1. G. K. Chesterton, *Orthodoxy* (New York: Doubleday, 1959), ch. V, p. 67.

2. Quoted in Michael Ffinch, *G. K. Chesterton* (New York: Harper, 1986), 37.

3. Ibid., 42–43.

4. Chesterton, *Orthodoxy*, Ch. II, p. 20.

5. Ibid., 23.

6. Ibid., 22.

7. Ibid., 24.

8. Ibid., ch. III, p. 33.

9. Ibid., 43.

10. Ibid., 33.

11. On these connections see (respectively) the fine study by John Mansley Robinson, *An Introduction to Early Greek Philosophy* (New York: Houghton Mifflin, 1968), chs. 10–12, and my *Moral Darwinism: How We Became Hedonists* (Downers Grove, IL: InterVarsity Press, 2002).

12. Chesterton, *Orthodoxy*, ch. IV, p. 58.

13. He thought in fact that modern science had misappropriated the word "law" to give its theories unjustifiable weight. It would take a very thick book to tease out and confirm just how profound Chesterton is on this point. For a very modest beginning in understanding it, see my *Meaningful World: How the Arts and Sciences Reveal the Genius of Nature*, co-authored with Jonathan Witt (Downers Grove, IL: InterVarsity Press, 2006).

14. Chesterton, *Orthodoxy*, ch. IV, pp. 56–57.

15. Ibid., 49.

16. The law of gravity, if we must speak of it as a law, is there to allow us to be able to walk where we will on the ground, rather than float helplessly in space. The laws of chemistry allow humans to go wither they will, for good or evil; a smoothly functioning mind and body are prerequisites for both benevolence and malevolence. The wonderful regularities of nature that we call "laws" are, properly understood, what make all human law possible. For human laws assume that we can break them.

17. Chesterton, *Orthodoxy*, ch. IV, p. 62.

18. Ibid., 61.

19. Ibid., 46.

20. Ibid., ch. VII, p. 115.

21. Ibid., ch. IV, pp. 46–47.

22. Ibid., ch. VII, p. 115.

23. Ibid., ch. III, p. 41.

24. Ibid., ch. IV, pp. 47–48

25. Ibid., ch. VIII, p. 125.

26. Ibid., 127.

27. Ibid., ch. II, p. 15.

28. Ibid., ch. VII, p. 118

29. Ibid., 119.

30. Ibid., 115.

31. Ibid., ch. V, pp. 70, 72.

32. Ibid., ch. IX, p. 153.

CHAPTER 3

1. He requested that the First Letter of John, 2:15–17 and the Gospel of John, 12: 24–25, be read at his funeral. For a good biographical overview, on which I've relied for the most part, see Ellis Sandoz, *The Voegelinian Revolution: A Biographical Introduction*, 2nd edition (Piscataway, NJ: Transaction Publishers, 2000), ch. 2.

2. Chesterton, *Orthodoxy*, ch. VI, p. 101.

3. Eric Voegelin, *The New Science of Politics: An Introduction* (Chicago: University of Chicago Press, 1952), Introduction, 5.

4. Ibid.

5. Ibid., 11.

6. Ibid., 19.

7. Ibid., ch. II, 67–68.

8. Devotees of Voegelin will forgive me for collapsing the densest chapters of *The New Science of Politics*, chapters I–II, into two mere paragraphs; for those new to Voegelin, it would probably be best to take this short overview as sufficient, and skip to chapters IV–VI.

9. Eric Voegelin, *The New Science of Politics*, ch. IV, 118.

10. Ibid., ch. III, 106.

11. Ibid., ch. IV, 107.

12. Ibid. I can be no more precise in this notation because the whole chapter needs to be read to understand Voegelin's points. Voegelin concentrates primarily on Hobbes, but I don't think he would object to my having included Spinoza as well, who was a follower of Hobbes but introduced a form of spiritualism, pantheism, that really gave to modern materialism the form of an immanentized Gnostic heresy.

CHAPTER 4

1. C. S. Lewis, *Surprised by Joy: The Shape of My Early Life* (New York, 1956), ch. I, p. 27.

2. This early-on training of Lewis's imagination is no small point. Arguments are a good thing, so good that they often make us forget the importance of the proper formation of the imagination. Imagination has a great transformative power—it is what unites head and heart in the adventurous quest for the great loves: the love of beauty, goodness, and truth. Lewis's well-watered and fertile imagination provided a seedbed for faith. His intellect took that faith and burst it into flower, creating such literary masterpieces as *The Chronicles of Narnia, The Space Trilogy (Out of the Silent Planet, Perelandra,* and *That Hideous Strength),* and *Till We Have Faces,* as well as renowned apologetic works such as *Mere Christianity, The Screwtape Letters, The Problem of Pain, Miracles,* and *The Abolition of Man.*

3. Lewis, *Surprised by Joy,* ch. I, pp. 21–23.

4. Ibid., ch. IV, pp. 74–75.

5. Ibid., ch. XV, pp. 223–24.

6. C. S. Lewis, *The Abolition of Man, or, Reflections on Education with Special Reference to the Teaching of English in the Upper Forms of Schools* (New York: MacMillan, 1955, 1947), ch. 1, p. 13.

7. Ibid., 14.

8. Ibid., ch. 2, p. 41, fn 1.

9. Ibid., 41, fn 1.

10. For more on Hobbes, the reader may wish to consult my *Ten Books That Screwed Up the World* (Washington, D.C.: Regnery Publishing, Inc., 2008); Leo Strauss, *Natural Right and History* (Chicago: University of Chicago, 1953); and of course, as we've already mentioned, Eric Voegelin, *The New Science of Politics.*

11. Lewis, *The Abolition of Man,* ch. 2, pp. 56–57. Lewis almost always refers to the Way as the *Tao,* from the classic Chinese philosophical-religious text written by Lao Tzu, the *Tao Te Ching,* the word "tao" meaning "way." I am not so certain, after going back and rereading the *Tao Te Ching,* that one can so easily identify it with the natural law, except insofar as both are derived from experience of, and deference toward, the order of nature, and both can be contrasted to the purposeful attempt to overcome any and all of nature's limits by technical power. But at least we may say that, in rough but important generalities, western natural law and eastern Taoism

understand moral goodness to consist in conforming one's mind, passions, and actions to nature, and each contends that to ignore these natural limits leads to self-destruction, and to be mindful of them leads to wisdom and moral goodness. That having been said, perhaps a better text to illustrate the universality of "traditional" morality would have been the *Analects* of Confucius, which runs a closer parallel to, say, Aristotle's *Nicomachean Ethics*, Cicero's *On Duties*, and the Proverbs of the Old Testament, than the *Tao Te Ching*. For this reason, I shall beg to differ a bit from Lewis, and call the Way the natural law, rather than the Tao.

12. Lewis, *The Abolition of Man*, ch. 2, pp. 56–57.

13. Robert Mackey, "Afghan Husbands Win Right to Starve Wives," *New York Times*, August 17, 2009; available at: http://thelede.blogs.nytimes.com/2009/08/17/afghan-husbands-win-right-to-starve-wives/.

14. For a fuller account of these not-God moralities see my *Ten Books that Screwed Up the World* (Washington, D.C.: Regnery, 2008).

15. Lewis, *The Abolition of Man*, ch. 2, p. 44.

16. Ibid., 44–51.

17. Ibid., ch. 3, p. 69.

18. Ibid., 72–73.

19. Mark Henderson, "DNA swap could cure inherited diseases," *Times*, August 27, 2009; available at: http://www.timesonline.co.uk/tol/news/uk/science/article6811080.ece.

20. See Alice Park, "Scientists Create Human Sperm Cells from Stem Cells," *Time*, July 8, 2009; available at: http://www.time.com/time/health/article/0,8599,1909164,00.html.

21. Russell Kirk, *The Conservative Mind, from Burke to Eliot*, 7th edition (Washington, D.C.: Regnery, 1986), 8.

CHAPTER 5

1. Quoted in Russell Kirk, *Edmund Burke: A Genius Reconsidered* (Wilmington, DE: ISI, 1997), 13.

2. Edmund Burke, *Reflections on the Revolution in France* (Indianapolis, IN: Bobbs-Merril, 1955). Unfortunately, Burke's original has no divisions of the text. I will follow the numbering of this edition edited by Thomas Mahoney, broken into Chapters and Sections. Hence, this quote comes from Part I, VI.2, p. 110.

3. Ibid., 112.

4. Ibid., Part I, IX. 4, p. 152.

5. See my *Ten Books that Screwed Up the World* and the masterful Jonathan Israel, *Radical Enlightenment: Philosophy and the Making of Modernity, 1650-1750* (Oxford: University of Oxford Press, 2001). Israel is especially good at rooting out the secular origins of modern thought, in particular, the vast influence of Spinoza. Peter Gay's *The Enlightenment: The Rise of Modern Paganism* (New York: Norton, 1966) is still well worth reading on the militant secular origins of modernity.

6. Edmund Burke, *Reflections on the Revolution in France*, Part I, IX.4, p. 154.

7. Ibid., Part I, X.1, p. 162.

8. Ibid., Part I, X.4, p. 176.

9. Burke's prophecies of someone like Napoleon as inevitable are astounding. See Part II, IV.3–4, pp. 247–66.

10. Ibid., Part I, VIII.1, p. 127.

11. Ibid., X.1, p. 161.

12. Ibid.

13. Ibid., VIII.3, pp. 143–44.

14. Ibid., Part II, I.2, p. 195.

15. Ibid., 2, p. 199.

16. Ibid., Part I, VIII.3, p. 139.

17. Ibid., 140.

18. Ibid., Part II, III.1, p. 223.

19. Ibid., 223–25.

20. Ibid., p. 226.

21. Ibid.

22. Ibid., 227.

23. Ibid., 229.

24. Ibid., III.2, p. 230.

25. Ibid., II.1, p. 202.

26. Ibid., 216.

27. Ibid., III.2, p. 231.

28. Ibid., V.1, p. 269.

CHAPTER 6

1. Alexis de Tocqueville, *Democracy in America*, translated and edited, with an introduction by Harvey Mansfield and Delba Winthrop (Chicago, IL: University of Chicago Press, 2000), Editors' Introduction, p. xvii.

2. Ibid., Volume I, "Introduction," p. 13.

3. Ibid., Part I, Chapter 2, p. 28.

4. Ibid., 30.

5. Ibid.

6. Ibid., 32.

7. Ibid., 32–44

8. Ibid., 39–40.

9. Ibid., Chapter 5, pp. 56–57.

10. Ibid., 65.

11. Ibid., Chapter 2, p. 40.

12. Ibid., 42.

13. Ibid., 43.

14. Ibid., 43–44.

15. Ibid., Chapter 3, p. 52.

16. Ibid., Part II, Chapter 7.

17. Ibid., Volume II, Part II, Chapter 1, p. 482.

18. Ibid., Chapter 7, p. 426.

19. Ibid., Part II, Chapter 9, pp. 505–6.

20. Ibid., Chapter 15, p. 519.

21. Ibid., Volume I, Part II, Chapter 6, p. 232.

22. Ibid., Volume II, Part II, Chapter 13, p. 511.

23. Ibid., Chapter 10, p. 506.

24. Ibid., Chapter 11, p. 509.

25. Ibid., Chapter 13, p. 514.

26. Ibid., 511–12.

27. Ibid., 512. Emphasis added.

28. Ibid., Volume I, Part II, Chapter 5, p. 189.

29. Ibid., 200–1.

CHAPTER 7

1. Alexander Hamilton, Federalist XXXIII, in Alexander Hamilton, James Madison, and John Jay, *The Federalist* (Washington, D.C.: Regnery, 1998), 255–56.

2. Hamilton, Federalist XXX, 239; see also Madison, Federalist XLIV, 354.

3. Ibid., 237.

4. Hamilton, Federalist XXXIII, 255.

5. Hamilton, Federalist I, 49.

6. Hamilton, Federalist XXX, 239.

7. Hamilton, Federalist XV, 139–40.

8. Hamilton, Federalist XXX, 239.

9. Hamilton, Federalist XXXI, 245. Emphasis added.

10. Ibid., 243.

11. Ibid., 245.

12. Hamilton, Federalist XXX, 240–41.

13. Hamilton, Federalist XXXIV and Madison, Federalist XLI.

14. Hamilton, Federalist XXXI, 246–48 and Madison, Federalist XLV, 363.

15. Hamilton, Federalist XXXVII, 284.

16. Hamilton, Federalist XXXIII, 256.

17. Madison, Federalist XLVI, 369.

18. Hamilton, Federalist XVII, 154–55; see also Madison, Federalist XLVI, 367.

19. Hamilton, Federalist XVI, 150.

20. Hamilton, Federalist XXIII, 197.

21. Hamilton, Federalist XXVII, 222.

22. Tocqueville, *Democracy in America*, Volume II, Part IV, Chapter 6, p. 662.

23. Ibid., 663.

24. See Hamilton, Federalist XLVII.

25. Hamilton, Federalist LI, 398–99.

26. Ibid., 399.

27. Madison, Federalist XLIII, 341 and Madison, Federalist XXXIX, 304.

28. Hamilton, Federalist XXII, 187.

29. Madison, Federalist XIV, 134.

30. Ibid., 136, 132.

31. Madison, Federalist X, all.

CHAPTER 8

1. Aristotle, *Politics,* 1313a40–1313b6.

2. See especially Hannah Arendt, *The Origins of Totalitarianism* (Orlando, FL: Harcourt, 1976), Part III.

3. Tocqueville, *Democracy in America.*

4. See, for example, Old Whig, Letter II.

5. Cato, Letter II, in Bruce Frohnen, ed., *The Anti-Federalist: Selected Writings and Speeches* (Washington, D.C.: Regnery, 1999), 7.

6. Centinel, Letter I, 41.

7. Cato, Letter III, 13.

8. See Anti-Federalist Luther Martin, as quoted in Centinel, Letter XIV, 120.

9. The Federal Farmer, Letter VI, 190.

10. Centinel, Letter II, 56–57. See also the Federal Farmer, Letter VI, 188–89 (esp. his list at 194–95) and Federal Farmer, Letter XVI; Old Whig, Essay IV, 336–38, and Essay V, 339–43; Brutus, Essay II, 387–91.

11. Centinel, Letter IV, 70–71. See also Federal Farmer, Letter XVII, 294–95.

12. Centinel, Letter V, 78–80. Emphasis added. See also Federal Farmer, Letter III, 163–68 and Old Whig, Letter II, 324–26; Brutus, Essay I, 376.

13. Luther Martin as quoted in Centinel, Letter XIV, 117. See also Brutus, Essay V, 408–13.

14. Luther Martin, Ibid., 118. See also Federal Farmer, Letter XVII, 291–94, and Old Whig, Essay VI, 348–51.

15. Brutus, Essay VI, 418.

16. Federal Farmer, Letter III, 164.

17. Ibid., Letter XVII, 299.

18. Ibid., Letter XIII, 250.

19. Ibid., Letter VI, 192–93, and Letter VIII, 211.

20. Ibid., Letter X, 227.

21. Ibid., Letter IX, 219.

22. Constitution, Article I, Section 8, emphasis added.

23. Constitution, Article VI, emphasis added.

24. Brutus, Essay VI, 415.

25. Ibid., Essay I, 375.

26. Speeches of Patrick Henry before the Virginia Ratifying Convention, 5 June 1788, p. 688.

27. Ibid., Essay VI, 419–20.

28. Ibid., Essay I, 378.

29. Ibid., Essay XII, 455.

30. Ibid., Essay XV, 480.

31. Ibid., Essay XII, 456.

32. Ibid., 462. Emphasis added.

33. Ibid., Essay XV, 478.

34. Ibid., Essay I, 380–81.

35. Old Whig, Essay IV, 335.

36. Federal Farmer, Letter XVII, 290–91.

37. Old Whig, Essay IV, 335.

38. Federal Farmer, Letter XVII, 296.

39. Ibid., 295.

40. Ibid., 290–91.

PART III INTRODUCTION

1. Aristotle, *History of Animals*, 622a3–9.

2. Aristotle, *Politics*, 1253a2–5; *Nicomachean Ethics*, 1097b7–12, 1162a16–18, 1169b17–22; *History of Animals*, 487b35–488a13.

CHAPTER 9

1.   Alexis de Tocqueville, *Democracy in America*, Volume Two, Part Two, Chapter 10, p. 506.

2.   There is some dispute whether Aristotle wrote the entire treatise, or whether it consists of a compilation of ideas by his early followers. I do not need to settle that dispute, but we can certainly agree that Book I is consonant with what Aristotle says in the *Politics*.

3.   Hilaire Belloc, *The Servile State* (Indianapolis, IN: Liberty Fund, 1977, following the 1913 edition), 45. Emphasis added.

4.   Ibid.

5.   Ibid., 46.

6.   Ibid., 47. Emphasis added.

7.   Ibid., 50.

8.   Ibid., Section Three.

9.   Ibid., 50.

10. Ibid., 49.

11. Ibid., Section Four.

12. Ibid., 140–41.

13. Ibid., 142.

14. Ibid., 140.

15. Ibid., 145.

CHAPTER 10

1.   Tocqueville, *Democracy in America*, Volume II, Part IV, Chapter 6, p. 663. Hayek quotes from the Henry Reeve translation, for which I have substituted the one we've used so as not to confuse the reader. See his "Preface to the 1956 American Paperback Edition" in F. A. Hayek, *The Road to Serfdom: Text and Documents, the Definitive Edition*, ed. Bruce Caldwell (Chicago: University of Chicago Press, 2007), 49. The original text was published in 1944. This edition is Volume II of *The Collected Works of F. A. Hayek*.

2.   F. A. Hayek, *The Road to Serfdom*, Chapter 7, p. 124.

3.   F. A. Hayek, "Foreword to the 1956 American Paperback Edition," in *The Road to Serfdom*, 48.

4.   Hayek, *The Road to Serfdom*, Chapter 6, p. 115.

5. From a University of Chicago Roundtable radio broadcast on *The Road to Serfdom*, NBC, April 22, 1945. Quoted in Alan Ebenstein, *Friedrich Hayek: A Biography* (New York: Palgrave, 2001), Chapter 16, p. 126. Emphasis added.

6. University of Chicago Roundtable radio broadcast, quoted in Ebenstein, *Friedrich Hayek*, 126.

7. Hayek, *The Road to Serfdom*, Chapter 1, p. 71. See also Chapter VI, p. 118.

8. Ibid., Chapter 3, p. 86.

9. Ibid., 88.

10. Ibid., Chapter 9, p. 148.

11. Appended to Hayek's *Constitution of Liberty* (Chicago: University of Chicago Press, 1960).

12. Hayek, "Preface to the 1976 Edition" in F. A. Hayek, *The Road to Serfdom: Text and Documents, the Definitive Edition*, 54–55.

13. Ebenstein, *Friedrich Hayek*, 13.

14. See Edward Feser, ed., *The Cambridge Companion to Hayek* (Cambridge: Cambridge University Press, 2006), 6.

15. Ebenstein, *Friedrich Hayek*, 23.

16. Ibid., 37.

17. Ibid., Chapter 17.

18. Hayek, *The Road to Serfdom*, Chapter 6, p. 114.

19. Ibid.

20. Ibid., Chapter 14, p. 216.

21. Ibid., 217.

22. Ibid.

23. Ibid., Chapter 10, p. 165.

24. Ibid., 165–66.

25. Ibid., Chapter 6, pp. 114–16.

26. Ibid., Chapter 5, p. 109.

27. Ibid., Chapter 4, pp. 91–94.

28. Ibid., Chapter 3, pp. 86–87.

29. Ibid., Chapter 15, p. 234.

30. Ibid., Chapters 10–13.

31. Ibid., Chapter 14, p. 212. See also Hayek's Nobel speech against scientism, available at: http://nobelprize.org/nobel_prizes/ economics/laureates/1974/hayek-lecture.html.

32. Ibid., Chapter 4, p. 97.

CHAPTER 11

1. William Shakespeare, *The Tempest*, Act I, Scene 2, lines 147–48, in David Bevington, ed., *The Complete Works of Shakespeare*, 3rd edition (New York: HarperCollins, 1980).

2. I.2, 73–74.

3. II.1, 149–69.

4. II.1, 198–298.

5. II.2 and III.2.

6. I.2, 348–52.

7. II.2, 182–85.

8. I.2, 11–12.

9. V.1, 183–86.

10. V.1, 50–57.

CHAPTER 12

1. Elizabeth Kantor, *The Politically Incorrect Guide™ to English and American Literature* (Washington, D.C.: Regnery, 2006), 138.

2. Jane Austen, *Sense and Sensibility* (New York: Dover, 1996), Volume I, Chapter 1, pp. 3–4.

3. Ibid., I.12, p. 38.

4. Ibid., I.13, pp. 42–43.

5. Ibid., II.9, p. 141.

6. Ibid., III.8, p. 221.

7. Ibid., III.1, pp. 179–80.

8. Ibid., III.7, p. 209.

9. Ibid., III.10, pp. 236–37.

10. Elizabeth Kantor, *The Politically Incorrect Guide™ to English and American Literature*, 137–38.

CHAPTER **13**

1. My guide in setting out the main outlines for Tolkien's life has been Humphrey Carpenter, *Tolkien: A Biography* (New York: Ballantine Books, 1978).

2. Humphrey Carpenter, *Tolkien*, Part II, Chapter 6, pp. 71–72. See also Tolkien's *Letters*, 297.

3. J. R. R. Tolkien, *The Lord of the Rings: The Fellowship of the Ring* (New York: Houghton Mifflin, 1994), Chapter XI, pp. 189–90.

4. J. R. R. Tolkien, *The Lord of the Rings: the Return of the King*, Chapter V, p. 951.

5. Quoted in Humphrey Carpenter, *Tolkien*, Part V, Chapter 1, p. 197.

6. Ibid., Chapter 2, p. 214.

7. From the Introductory Note of "On Fairy Stories," as contained in J. R. R. Tolkien, *Poems and Stories* (Boston: Houghton Mifflin, 1994), 115. The essay runs from pp. 116–88.

8. This is not from the essay, but quoted in Humphrey Carpenter, *Tolkien*, Part III, Chapter 1, p. 105.

9. J. R. R. Tolkien, "On Fairy Stories," in *Poems and Stories*, 142.

10. Ibid., 167.

11. Ibid., 165.

12. J. R. R. Tolkien, *The Lord of the Rings*, Prologue, 3, p. 9.

13. Ibid., 1, p. 3.

14. Quoted in Humphrey Carpenter, *Tolkien*, Part II, Chapter 8, p. 91. A "batman" for the Brits is a soldier-valet assigned to a commissioned officer to look after him and his things.

15. J. R. R. Tolkien, *The Lord of the Rings: the Two Towers*, Chapter VIII, p. 696.

16. J. R. R. Tolkien, *The Lord of the Rings: the Return of the King*, Chapter IX, p. 861.

17. J. R. R. Tolkien, *The Lord of the Rings: the Two Towers*, Chapter II, p. 423.

18. J. R. R. Tolkien, *The Lord of the Rings: the Return of the King*, Chapter V, p. 947.

19. Ibid., Chapter VIII, p. 852.

CHAPTER 14

1. I use the American spelling of carcasses, rather than the British carcases, so as not to confuse the readers.

2. J. R. R. Tolkien, "On Fairy Stories," in *Poems and Stories*, 149.

3. I know some skeptics will be inclined to doubt this, but it is simply a fact. Read, for example, K. A. Kitchen, *On the Reliability of the Old Testament* (Grand Rapids, MI: Eerdmans, 2003), and Richard Bauckham, *Jesus and the Eyewitnesses: The Gospels as Eyewitness Testimony* (Grand Rapids, MI: Eerdmans, 2006).

4. J. R. R. Tolkien, "On Fairy Stories," in *Poems and Stories*, 179–80.

5. This is not to deny the obvious—that murder and war are in the Bible and in Christian and Jewish history—but it is to underscore that while sin cannot be abolished, and while some wars can be justified, the standard set by the Bible is to honor and preserve human life as God's creation.

CHAPTER 15

1. Quoted in Jennifer Burns, *Goddess of the Market: Ayn Rand and the American Right* (Oxford: Oxford University Press, 2009), 195.

2. Ibid., 275.

3. Ibid., 104.

4. Ibid., 175–76.

5. Ibid., 258.

6. See Stephen Moore, "'Atlas Shrugged': From Fiction to Fact in 52 Years," *Wall Street Journal*, January 9, 2009; available at: http://online.wsj.com/article/SB123146363567166677.html.

7. Ayn Rand Center for Individual Rights, "Sales of 'Atlas Shrugged' Soar in the Face of Economic Crisis"; available at: http://www.aynrand.org/site/News2?page=NewsArticle&id=22647; and Ayn Rand Institute, "Atlas Shrugged Sets a New Record," January 21, 2010; available at: http://atlasshrugged.com/book/press-release-2010-01-21.html.

8. Barbara Branden, *The Passion of Ayn Rand* (New York: Doubleday, 1987); Jennifer Burns, *Goddess of the Market*; Anne Heller, *Ayn Rand and the World She Made* (New York: Nan A. Talese, 2009).

9. Ayn Rand, *Atlas Shrugged*, with an Introduction by Leonard Peikoff (New York: Plume, 1999), "About the Author," appearing after the end of the novel, 1170–171.

10. Anne Heller, *Ayn Rand and the World She Made*, 11.

11. Jennifer Burns, *Goddess of the Market*, 11; Barbara Branden, *The Passion of Ayn Rand*, 9.

12. Quoted in Barbara Branden, *The Passion of Ayn Rand*, 5.

13. Ibid., 33–34.

14. Ibid., 10.

15. Ibid., 7–8. Other favorite "tiddlywink music" (as she called it) included "Get Out and Get Under," the tango "El Choclo," "Destiny Waltz," "Canadian Capers," and other similar popular ditties. To hear a collection of Rand's tiddlywinks music go to http://www.dismuke.org/ aynrand/selections.html.

16. Barbara Branden, *The Passion of Ayn Rand*, 386.

17. Ibid., 386–87.

18. Ibid., 13.

19. "About the Author," in Rand, *Atlas Shrugged*, 1170–171.

20. This actually occurred while she was attending the University of Petrograd. Barbara Branden, *The Passion of Ayn Rand*, 44.

21. Barbara Branden, *The Passion of Ayn Rand*, 43–44.

22. Anne Heller, *Ayn Rand and the World She Made*, 17.

23. Ibid., 16, 20.

24. Barbara Branden, *The Passion of Ayn Rand*, 35–36.

25. She seems to have read Aristotle before, but her first in-depth encounter was at university.

26. "About the Author," in Rand, *Atlas Shrugged*, 1171.

27. Anne Heller, *Ayn Rand and the World She Made*, 54–57.

28. Ibid., 55–56.

29. Ibid., 12, 14.

30. Barbara Branden, *The Passion of Ayn Rand*, 258.

31. Ibid., 277.

32. Anne Heller, *Ayn Rand and the World She Made*, 345.

33. Ibid., 353.

34. Ayn Rand, *Atlas Shrugged*, Part III, Chapter III, 852.

35. Ibid., 861.

36. Ibid., 857–60.

37. Ibid., Chapter VII, 1002.

38. Ibid., 1009–69.

39. Ibid., 1012.

40. Ibid., 1017.

41. Ibid., Part I, Chapter VI, 131.

42. Ibid., 132–33.

43. Ibid., 133.

44. Ibid., Part III, Chapter VII, 1049.

45. Ibid., 1051.

46. See Galt's discussion of the virtues, Ibid., 1017–23.

47. Ibid., Part II, Chapter II, 410–15.

48. I thank Monsignor Stuart Swetland for providing this insight.

49. Ibid., Part III, Chapter I, 730–31.

50. Ibid., Chapter V, 951.

51. Ibid., Chapter VII, 1016.

52. This occurs several times throughout *Atlas Shrugged*, including the ending flourish of Galt's speech, Part III, Chapter VII, 1069.

53. Barbara Branden, *The Passion of Ayn Rand*, 33.

54. Anne Heller, *Ayn Rand and the World She Made*, 128.

55. Jennifer Burns, *Goddess of the Market*, 263.

56. Anne Heller, *Ayn Rand and the World She Made*, 136–37. Rand did eventually come up with a justifying reason—the baby couldn't survive without her—but that she could so quickly and easily decide against the kind of self-sacrificial love natural to a mother reveals all too much about her radical individualism and her own character.

57. Barbara Branden, *The Passion of Ayn Rand*, 295.

58. Ibid., 327–30, 361–63, 386–89; Jennifer Burns, *Goddess of the Market*, 154–55, 182–85, 221–22, 232–39.

59. Quoted in Jennifer Burns, *Goddess of the Market*, 233.

60. Ibid., 236.

61. Ibid.

62. Ibid., 221.

63. Barbara Branden, *The Passion of Ayn Rand,* 367–68.

64. Jennifer Burns, *Goddess of the Market,* 187–88.

65. The information in the *Diagnostic and Statistical Manual of Mental Disorders* is available all over the web, and the literature on narcissism is vast and growing.

66. Anne Heller, *Ayn Rand and the World She Made,* 70.

67. "About the Author," in Rand, *Atlas Shrugged,* 1171.

Index

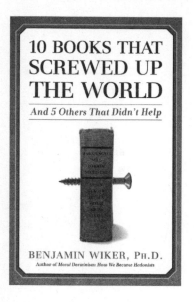